R. Gupta's®

POPULAR MASTER GUIDE

Delhi District Courts
Junior Judicial Assistant
& Data Entry Operator

TIER-I

Recruitment Exam

- Specialised Study & Practice Material
- Numerous Solved Multiple Choice Questions
- Solved Question Paper

by
RPH Editorial Board

2020
EDITION

RAMESH PUBLISHING HOUSE, NEW DELHI

Published by
O.P. Gupta *for* Ramesh Publishing House

Admin. Office
12-H, New Daryaganj Road, Opp. Officers' Mess,
New Delhi-110002 ☎ 23261567, 23275224, 23275124

E-mail: info@rameshpublishinghouse.com
Website: www.rameshpublishinghouse.com

Showroom
● Balaji Market, Nai Sarak, Delhi-6 ☎ 23253720; 23282525
● 4457, Nai Sarak, Delhi-6, ☎ 23918938

Book Code: R-1946

ISBN: 978-93-86845-96-2

HSN Code: 49011010

SCHEME OF EXAM

TIER-I

The Objective Test for the post of **Junior Judicial Assistant & Data Entry Operator** shall contain Questions on General English & Comprehension, General Knowledge (Including Current Affairs) and General Intelligence.

Part	Exam Type	Subjects	Questions	Marks	Duration of Exam.
Part-I		General English & Comprehension	60	60	
Part-II	Objective Type	General Knowledge (Including Current Affairs)	30	30	**120 Minutes**
Part-III		General Intelligence	30	30	
		Total	**120**	**120**	

NOTE:
- Each question will carry 01 (one) mark. There shall be 01 (one) mark for each correct answer. There shall be negative marking of 0.25 marks for each wrong answer.
- Paper will consist of Objective Type— Multiple choice questions only. The questions will be in English language only.
- It will be online examination and, therefore, applicant is expected to know about the basic keys and input commands of keyboard and mouse.

TIER-II

Skill Test (Typing Test) for the posts of Junior Judicial Assistant & Data Entry Operator: The candidates who scored 50% marks for General Category i.e. 60 Marks (50% of 120 Marks) and 45% marks for Reserved Category candidates i.e. 54 Marks (45% of 120 Marks) in the Preliminary MCQ Test or 25 times of the total vacancies (which ever will be minimum numbers) will be called for the skill test i.e. **typing test @ 40 w.p.m. This skill test will be of qualifying in nature.**

TIER-III

Descriptive Test for the posts of Junior Judicial Assistant & Data Entry Operator: The candidates who qualify the Skill Test will be called for a "Descriptive Test" of English language (Total 100 Marks). It would consist of Essay (300 words = 50 Marks), Grammar (30 Marks) and Translation (25 words = 20 Marks). Minimum passing marks for General Category candidates will be 50% (i.e., 50 Marks out of 100 Marks) and for Reserved Category candidates will be 45% (i.e., 45 Marks out of 100 Marks). **Duration of the test will be of 120 Minutes.**

TIER-IV

Interview of 30 Marks (for Maximum of ten times of the total vacancies) will be conducted for the post of **Junior Judicial Assistant.** The minimum passing marks for General Category candidates will be 12 marks (40% of 30 marks) and for Reserved Category (including PWD) candidates will be 10 Marks (round off) (35% of 30 marks).

Whereas, Interview of 35 Marks (for Maximum of ten times of the total vacancies) will be conducted for the post of **Data Entry Operator.** The minimum passing marks for General Category candidates will be 14 marks (40% of 35 marks) and for Reserved Category (including PWD) candidates will be 12 Marks (round off) (35% of 35 marks).

CONTENTS

———————

Delhi District Courts—Junior Judicial Assistant
Recruitment Exam, 2018*

GENERAL AWARENESS

1. Which of the following living birds lays the world's largest egg?
A. Vulture   B. American Robin
C. Black Tern   D. Ostrich

2. On which of the following river banks is the city of Agra located?
A. Ganga   B. Yamuna
C. Sabarmati   D. Tapti

3. Which award is also known as Academy awards?
A. Golden Globe
B. The Oscars
C. BAFTA
D. Screen Actors Guild

4. Where is the headquarters of Food and Agriculture Organization of the United Nations situated?
A. Italy   B. Germany
C. Greece   D. Poland

5. Where is the Melkote Temple Wildlife Sanctuary located?
A. Chhattisgarh   B. Kerala
C. Odisha   D. Karnataka

6. Which state election department has entered the 'Limca Book of Records' for formation of biggest human logo in October 2017?
A. Meghalaya   B. Himachal Pradesh
C. Mizoram   D. Assam

7. The Great Sphinx of Giza is one of the famous landmarks of:
A. Russia   B. France
C. Italy   D. Egypt

8. The Jaisalmer Fort, one of the largest fully preserved fortified cities in the world, is situated in the Indian state of:
A. Rajasthan   B. Tamil Nadu
C. Punjab   D. Uttar Pradesh

9. Which of the following books has NOT been authored by Charles Dickens?
A. Oliver Twist
B. A Tale of Two Cities
C. Christmas Day in the Morning
D. David Copperfield

10. "La Tomatina" is a food fight festival held in:
A. Portugal   B. Spain
C. France   D. Morocco

11. On which of the following days does the festival of Easter fall?
A. Thursday   B. Friday
C. Saturday   D. Sunday

12. Which of the following countries are connected by the Palk Strait?
A. Pakistan and China
B. India and China
C. India and Sri Lanka
D. Bhutan and Bangladesh

13. Where was the first ASEAN-India Music Festival held in October 2017?
A. Visakhapatnam   B. New Delhi
C. Surat   D. Ahmedabad

14. Who propounded the three laws of planetary motion?
A. Newton   B. Copernicus
C. Kepler   D. Galileo

15. Chandigarh is the capital of:
   A. Punjab
   B. Haryana
   C. Himachal Pradesh
   D. Both (A) and (B)

16. Which of the following planets is also known as the "Red Planet"?
   A. Mars   B. Saturn
   C. Uranus   D. Venus

17. Piyush Goyal is the present .... Minister of India.
   A. Railway
   B. Science and Technology
   C. Tribal Affairs
   D. None of these

18. The splitting of white light into its component colours is known as:
   A. Reflection   B. Refraction
   C. Dispersion   D. Transmission

19. The percentage of deposits which commercial banks are required to keep as cash with the RBI is known as:
   A. Fixed reserve ratio
   B. Minimum reserve ratio
   C. Cash reserve ratio
   D. Statutory liquidity ratio

20. In which of the following cities will the Olympic Games be hosted in 2020?
   A. Tokyo   B. Rio de Janeiro
   C. Istanbul   D. Beijing

21. Which of the following instruments is used to view distant objects in space?
   A. Microscope   B. Stereoscope
   C. Periscope   D. Telescope

22. The Right to Free and Compulsory Education Act is an Act of the Parliament of India for children of age group from ....
   A. 5 to 11   B. 5 to 15
   C. 6 to 12   D. 6 to 14

23. When is the "World Polio Day" observed?
   A. 30th October   B. 28th October
   C. 25th October   D. 24th October

24. .... has been listed among India's Intangible Cultural Heritage of Humanity.
   A. Koodiyattam   B. Ramman
   C. Chhau dance   D. All of these

25. With which of the following discoveries is Alexander Graham Bell associated?
   A. Electricity   B. Computer
   C. LASER   D. Telephone

26. Which of the following airports will introduce a helicopter-taxi (heli-taxi) service to ease commuting process during extreme traffic?
   A. Chhatrapati Shivaji International Airport
   B. Kempegowda International Airport
   C. Chennai International Airport
   D. Indira Gandhi International Airport

27. Which of the following Indian states presently has women as its Chief Minister?
   A. Goa
   B. Jammu and Kashmir
   C. Kerala
   D. None of these

28. Shubha Mudgal is associated with:
   A. Sports
   B. Classical dance
   C. Hindustani classical music
   D. Mural painting

29. The Chutak Hydroelectric Plant in Kargil district is built on the .... river.
   A. Jhelum   B. Kunar
   C. Suru   D. Ravi

30. Which of the following is India's first mission to study the Sun?
   A. Aditya-L1   B. GSAT-11
   C. Chandrayaan-2   D. Mangalyaan-2

31. When is the "World Population Day" observed?
   A. 8th July   B. 10th July
   C. 11th July   D. 19th July

32. Who among the following is the first Indian fellow of the Royal Society of London?
   A. Srinivasa Ramanujan
   B. Jagadish Chandra Bose
   C. Ardaseer Cursetjee
   D. C. V. Raman

33. Which of the following is NOT a routine session of the Indian Parliament?
A. Budget session   B. Monsoon session
C. Summer session   D. Winter session

34. What is the expansion of VGA?
A. Video Graphics Array
B. Video Geometric Array
C. Video Graphics Arrangement
D. Video Geographic Array

35. Dynamite, which is an explosive, was invented by:
A. Albert Hofmann   B. Alfred Nobel
C. Eugen Goldstein   D. Charles Parson

36. Who was the first woman to fly in Space?
A. Valentina Tereshkova
B. Kathryn Sullivan
C. Susan Helms
D. Roberta Bondar

37. "The Peacock Throne", which was a famous jewelled throne, was built for:
A. Humayun   B. Shah Jahan
C. Babur   D. Akbar

38. A file that has not been altered, compressed, or manipulated in anyway by the computer is known as:
A. Raw file   B. Temp file
C. Permanent file   D. Extension file

39. Bridgetown is the capital of:
A. Barbados   B. Belarus
C. Belize   D. Bahamas

40. The world's largest combustion research centre was started in:
A. IISER, Mohali   B. IIT, Madras
C. IISc, Bangalore   D. IIT, Bombay

41. Who won the China Open Tennis tournament held in October 2017?
A. Nick Kyrgios   B. Novak Djokovic
C. Rafael Nadal   D. Roger Federer

42. In "IPv6" internet protocol, IP address have a length of:
A. 32 bits   B. 64 bits
C. 128 bits   D. 256 bits

43. Which of the following is a circular colonnaded building built in the Imperial Style?
A. Parliament House
B. Lotus Temple
C. Rashtrapati Bhavan
D. Birla Mandir

44. What is the expansion of CBI?
A. Central Board of Investigation
B. Central Board of Invigilation
C. Central Bureau of Investigation
D. Central Bureau of Invigilation

45. Who among the following won the Indira Gandhi Prize for Peace, Disarmament and Development-2017?
A. Atal Bihari Vajpayee
B. Mamata Banerjee
C. Raghuram Rajan
D. Manmohan Singh

46. "Maximum City : Bombay Lost and Found" is a book authored by:
A. Suketu Mehta
B. Upamanyu Chatterjee
C. Tarjun Tejpal
D. Jerry Pinto

47. Which of the following flowers is a state symbol of Andhra Pradesh?
A. Orchid   B. Palash
C. Marigold   D. Water lily

48. Darwin's Finch is a distinguished group of .... species.
A. Snake   B. Bird
C. Butterfly   D. Lizard

49. Which of the following metals was/were used in the Harappan civilization?
A. Copper   B. Gold
C. Brass   D. All of these

50. Which commercial bank in India will launch the first integrated lifestyle and banking digital service platform named "YONO"?
A. Axis Bank
B. State Bank of India
C. Indian Overseas Bank
D. Punjab National Bank

GENERAL INTELLIGENCE AND REASONING ABILITY

51. Complete the series.

4, 11, 30, 67, 128, (...)
A. 219
B. 228
C. 231
D. 237

52. Choose from the alternatives the number that can replace the questions mark(?) in the given figure.

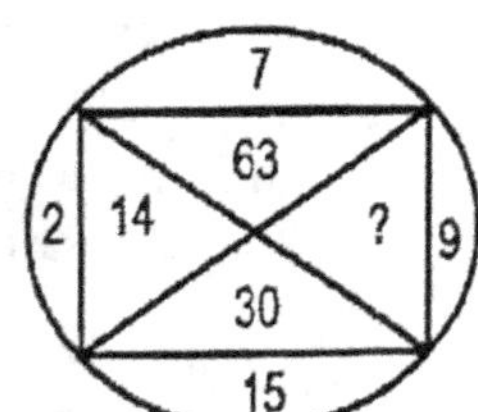

A. 18
B. 33
C. 135
D. 145

53. Choose the alternative that best resembles the unfolded form of the given cube.

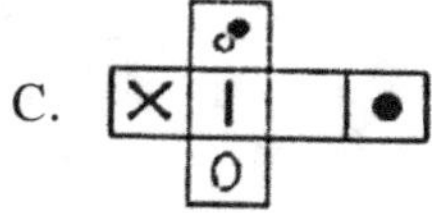 A.

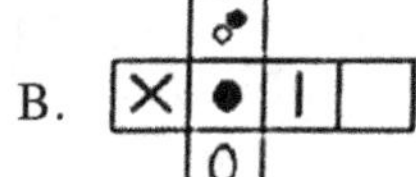 B.

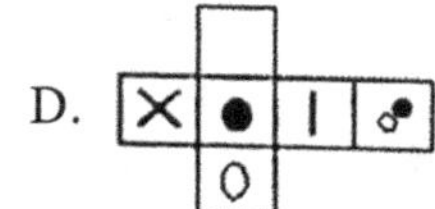 C.

D.

54. If in a certain code 'OLISPAH' is coded as 28, where O, L, I is coded as 1, 2, 3 respectively and so on, then how will 'SOAP' be coded in that code?
A. 16
B. 18
C. 61
D. 81

55. If in a certain code 'ALTERED' is written as 'ZOGVIVW', then how will 'RELATED' be written in that code?
A. IVOGZVW
B. IVOZGWV
C. IVOZGVW
D. VIOZGVW

56. In this question, three statements are given followed by four conclusions. Choose the conclusions which best fit logically.

Statements:
1. Mangoes are oranges.
2. No orange is a banana.
3. Some bananas are apples.

Conclusions:
   I. No banana is an apple.
   II. Some mangoes are bananas.
   III. No banana is an orange.
   IV. No orange is an apple.
A. Only conclusions I and II follow
B. Only conclusion II follows
C. Only conclusions II and IV follow
D. Only conclusion III follows

57. Choose the alternative that contains a given figure as a part of it.

 A.

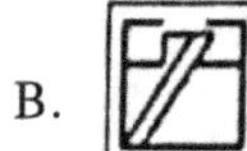 B.

C.

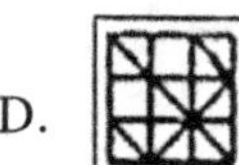 D.

58. A piece of paper is folded and a cut is made on it as shown in figures (X), (Y) and (Z). Choose the alternative that closely resembles the unfolded form of figure (Z).

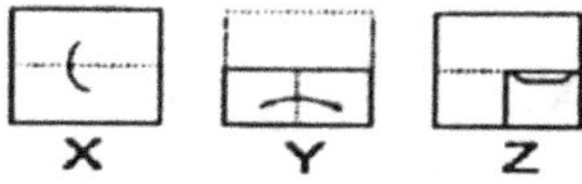

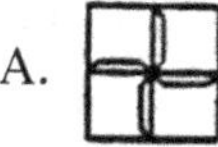 A.

B.

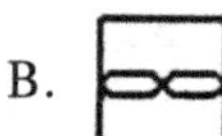 C.

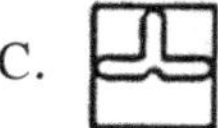 D.

59. Choose the alternative that best completes the pattern given below.

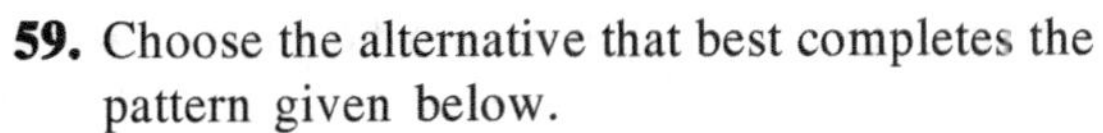

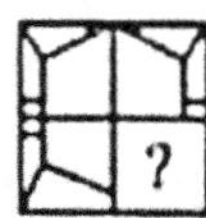

A.    B. 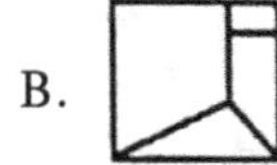

C. 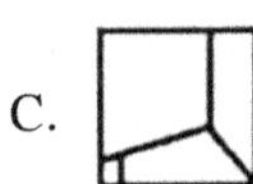   D. 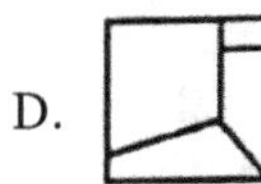

60. A man said to a lady, "Your mother's husband's sister is my aunt". How is the lady related to the man?
A. Daughter
B. Granddaughter
C. Mother
D. Sister

61. Five students—Pooja, Sonu, Kavin, Balu and Vino participated in a scholarship examination. Sonu scored higher than Pooja. Kavin scored lower than Balu but higher than Sonu. Vino scored between Pooja and Sonu. Who scored the lowest in the examination?
A. Kavin   B. Pooja
C. Vino   D. Sonu

62. Which word will best complete the relationship given below?

Lung : Man :: Gill : ?
A. Cow   B. Hen
C. Fish   D. Snake

63. Choose the alternative that best replaces the question mark(?) in the given figure.

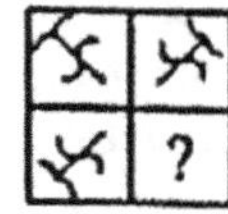

A. 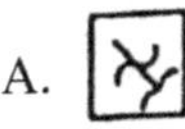   B. 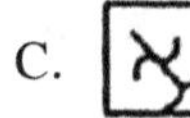

C.   D.

64. If in a certain code 'CORNER' is written as 'GSVRIV', then how will 'CENTRAL' be written in that code?
A. DFOUSBM   B. GIRXVEP
C. GJRYVEP   D. GNFJKER

65. Vinod is brother of Santhosh and Manik is father of Vinod. Jegan is brother of Priya and Priya is daughter of Santhosh. Who is the uncle of Jegan?
A. Vinod   B. Santhosh
C. Manik   D. None of these

66. The letters L, M, N, O, P, Q, R, S and T are substituted by nine integers from 1 to 9 but not in the same order and 4 is assigned to P. The difference between integers assigned to P and T is 5. The difference between integers assigned to N and T is 3. What integer is assigned to N?
A. 4   B. 5
C. 6   D. 7

67. Choose the figure that best represents the relationship among the classes given below.
Boys, Students, Athletes

A.    B.

C.   D.

68. Find the ODD one out.
A. Chord   B. Diagonal
C. Tangent   D. Diameter

69. Which number will best complete the relationship given below?

35 : 6 :: 120 : ?
A. 12   B. 11
C. 10   D. 9

70. Choose the group in which the words show the same relationship as in the given group.

Mountain : Height : Climber
A. River : Length : Water
B. Land : Farmer : Crop
C. College : Building : Student
D. Sea : Depth : Diver

71. Ram started walking down a road facing the sun in the early morning. After walking for sometime, he turns left and then turns right after walking sometime. Then he turns to his right once again. Which direction is he facing now?
A. East
B. West
C. North
D. South

72. Kumar walks 20 m north, and he turns right and walks 30 m, then he turns right and walks 35 m, then he turns left and walks 15 m, then he turns left and walks 15 m. He again turns left and walks 15 m. Which direction is Kumar facing now?
A. East
B. West
C. North
D. South

73. Select the alternative which represents the given figures which when fitted into each other would form a complete hexagon.

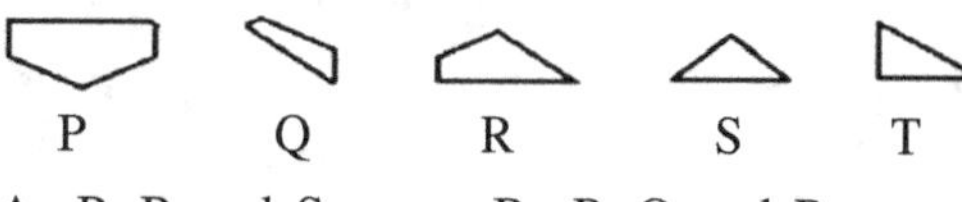

P   Q   R   S   T

A. P, R and S
B. P, Q and R
C. R, S and T
D. Q, R and S

74. In this question, a statement is given followed by two conclusions. Choose the conclusion which best fits logically.

Statement: Now-a-days parents are ready to pay huge amounts for proper education for their children.

Conclusions:
I. With the growth of economy, all parents these days have amassed huge money.
II. Parents now have become more obsessed with the desire for a proper development of their children through good schooling.
A. Only conclusion I follows
B. Only conclusion II follows
C. Neither conclusion I nor II follows
D. Both conclusions I and II follow

75. Anish is taller than Meera; Charu is taller than Anish, Deepan is taller than Charu, Sunil is the tallest of all. If they are made to stand according to their heights, who will be at the centre?
A. Anish
B. Deepan
C. Meera
D. Charu

76. Pointing to a girl, Avinash said, "She is daughter of the only child of my father". How is Avinash's wife related to that girl?
A. Daughter
B. Mother
C. Niece
D. Sister

77. Choose the figure from the given options that most closely resembles the mirror image of the given figure.

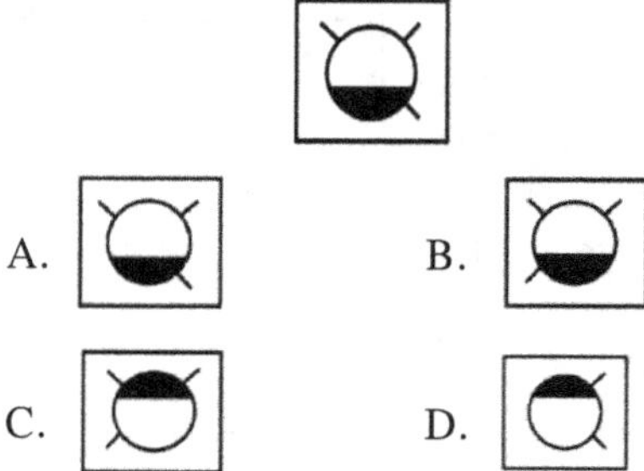

78. Find the wrong number in the series.
7, 28, 63, 124, 215, 342, 511
A. 7
B. 28
C. 124
D. 342

79. Find the number of squares in the given figure.

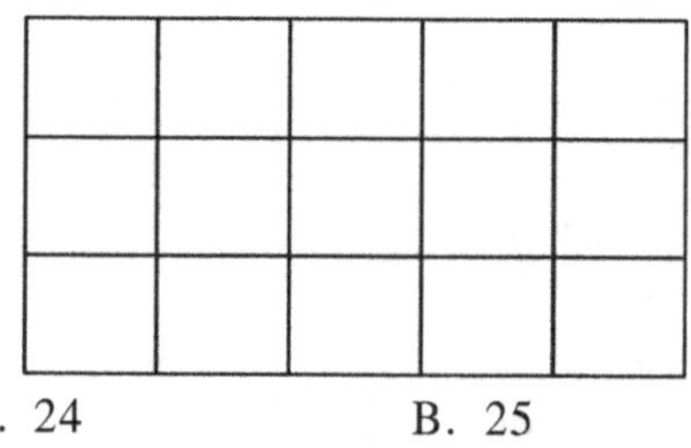

A. 24
B. 25
C. 26
D. 27

80. In this question, three statements are given where the third statement is the conclusion drawn from the first two statements. If the first two statements are definitely true, identify whether the conclusion drawn is TRUE or FALSE.
1. Sushil is the son of the teacher.
2. Mohan is a teacher, and he has a son and a daughter.

3. Mohan is the father of Sushil.
A. Definitely true   B. Probably true
C. Definitely false   D. Irrelevant

81. Find the ODD one out.

A. 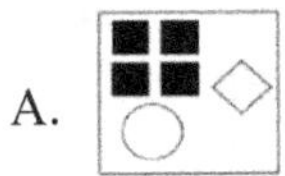   B. 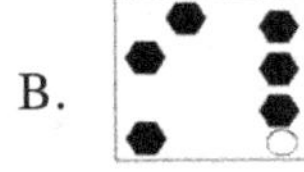

C. 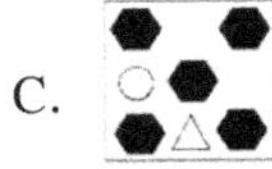   D. 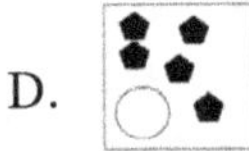

Directions (Q. No. 82-84): *In the following questions, the criteria for selection of candidates are given followed by the details of the candidates. Read the criteria carefully and based on the given criteria choose the decisions given in options that should be taken for the given candidates.*

Following are the criteria for admitting a student in engineering courses:

The student must:

(*i*) have passed XII examination with mathematics and have secured at atleast 60%.

(*ii*) be of 18 years of age as on 1st September 2016.

(*iii*) have obtained 75% marks in the entrance test.

(*iv*) be able to pay ₹ 20000 at the time of admission.

In case of a candidate who satisfies all the other criteria except (*iii*) above, but has obtained 85% marks in the XII examination, should be referred to the principal.

82. Mahesh has passed XII examination with mathematics and secured 90% marks. His date of birth is 15th July 1996. He has obtained 55% marks in the entrance test. and he can pay ₹ 20000 at the time of admission.
A. The student is to be admitted
B. The student is not to be admitted
C. The student is to be referred to the principal
D. None of these

83. Anju was born on 5th April 1995. She has secured 75% marks in XII examination with mathematics and has secured 90% marks in the entrance test, and he can pay ₹ 20000 at the time of admission.
A. The student is to be admitted
B. The student is not to be admitted
C. The student is to be referred to the principal
D. None of these

84. Karan was 17 years old as on 11th September 2015. He has secured 80% marks in the XII examination with mathematics. He has secured 80% marks in the entrance test.
A. The student is to be admitted
B. The student is not to be admitted
C. The student is to be referred to the principal
D. None of these

Directions (Q. No. 85-88): *Read the following information carefully and answer the questions given below.*

In a survey regarding a proposed measure to be introduced, 2878 persons took part of which 1652 were male. 1226 persons voted against the proposal of which 796 were male. 1425 persons voted for the proposal. 196 females were undecided.

85. How many females were NOT in favour of the proposal?
A. 430   B. 496
C. 586   D. 1226

86. How many persons were undecided?
A. 31   B. 196
C. 227   D. 426

87. How many females voted for the proposal?
A. 430   B. 600
C. 620   D. 640

88. How many males were undecided?
A. 31   B. 227
C. 426   D. 581

Directions (Q. No. 89-92): *Read the following information carefully and answer the questions given below.*

Some friends are sitting on a bench. Sekar is sitting next to Priya, and Madhan is sitting next to Vino. Vino is not sitting with Sudhir. Sudhir is on the left end of the bench, and Madhan is on second position from right hand side. Sekar is on the right side of Priya. Sekar and Madhan are sitting together.

89. Sudhir is sitting on the:
A. Third place from right
B. Second place from left
C. Extreme left
D. Extreme right

90. Sekar is sitting between:
A. Priya and Vino
B. Sudhir and Vino
C. Priya and Madhan
D. Madhan and Sudhir

91. How many places away from Vino is Priya sitting?
A. 1   B. 2
C. 4   D. 5

92. Who is sitting in the middle?
A. Sudhir   B. Sekar
C. Vino   D. Madhan

Directions (Q. No. 93-96): *Read the following information carefully and answer the questions given below.*

Seven types of paints—P1, P2, P3, P4, P5, P6 and P7 of different colours—red, green, yellow, black, blue, white and orange are filled in different tins—T1, T2, T3, T4, T5, T6 and T7. The order of the types of paints, colours and the tins are not necessarily in the same order. Paint P2 is not kept in tins T2 or T3 and is white in colour. Paints P4 is kept in the tin T7 and is not blue or red. P6 is kept in tin T1 and is green in colour. Paints P3 and P5 are kept in tins T5 and T6, and are black and yellow in colour respectively. P7 is not blue in colour. Red paint is not kept in tin T2.

93. Which tin contains blue paint?
A. T1   B. T3
C. T4   D. None of these

94. Paint P2 is kept in which tin?
A. T3   B. T4
C. T2   D. Either (B) or (C)

95. Which of the following combination of paint-tin-colours is correct?
A. P1-T2-red
B. P1-T3-blue
C. P6-T1-black
D. P7-T3-red

96. Which of the following paints is orange in colour?
A. P1   B. P3
C. P4   D. P7

Directions (Q. No. 97-100): *Read the following information carefully and answer the questions given below.*

Madhu and Shoba are good in dramatics and computer science. Anjali and Madhu are good in computer science and physics. Anjali, Poonam and Nisha are good in physics and history. Nisha and Anjali are good in physics and mathematics. Poonam and Shoba are good in history and dramatics.

97. Who is good in physics, history and dramatics?
A. Anjali   B. Poonam
C. Madhu   D. Shoba

98. Who is good in physics, history and mathematics but not in computer science?
A. Anjali   B. Madhu
C. Nisha   D. Poonam

99. Who is good in history, physics, computer science and mathematics?
A. Nisha   B. Poonam
C. Madhu   D. Anjali

100. Who is good in computer science, history and dramatics?
A. Anjali   B. Madhu
C. Shoba   D. Nisha

ARITHMETICAL AND NUMERICAL ABILITY

101. A cone of height 9 cm with a base diameter 18 cm is carved out from a wooden solid sphere of radius 9 cm. Find the percentage of the wood wasted.
A. 25%
B. 40%
C. 55%
D. 75%

102. The ratio of number of managers to management trainees is 3 : 5. When 21 new management trainees are recruited, the ratio becomes 3 : 8. How many managers will be there in the group?
A. 21
B. 24
C. 27
D. None of these

103. The difference between a positive fraction and its reciprocal is $\dfrac{9}{20}$. Find the sum of that fraction and its reciprocal.
A. $\dfrac{9}{20}$
B. $\dfrac{11}{20}$
C. $\dfrac{17}{20}$
D. $\dfrac{41}{20}$

104. The ratio of the sum to the LCM of two natural numbers is 7 : 12. If their HCF is 4, then find the smaller number.
A. 8
B. 12
C. 16
D. 20

105. A sum of ₹ 1550 is lent out into two parts, one at 8% and another one at 6% at Simple Interest respectively. If the total annual income is ₹ 106, find the money lent at each rate.
A. ₹ 600 and ₹ 950
B. ₹ 650 and ₹ 900
C. ₹ 700 and ₹ 850
D. ₹ 500 and ₹ 1100

106. The sum of two numbers is 2490. If 6.5% of one number is equal to 8.5% of the other, find the numbers.
A. 989, 1501
B. 1011, 1479
C. 1401, 1089
D. 1411, 1079

107. A motor car does a journey in 10 hours; the first half at 21 km/hr, and the rest at 24 km/hr. Find the distance.
A. 220 km
B. 224 km
C. 228 km
D. 232 km

108. In a mixture of 255 litres, the ratio of milk to water is 9 : 6. If 17 litres of water is added to the mixture, find the ratio of milk to water in the new mixture.
A. 3 : 4
B. 6 : 7
C. 9 : 7
D. 13 : 17

109. Suresh and Ramesh can do a work in 45 days and 40 days respectively. They began the work together, but Suresh left after some time, and Ramesh finished the remaining work in 23 days. After how many days did Suresh leave?
A. 9
B. 15
C. 18
D. 24

110. A reduction of 20% in the price of wheat enables a person to buy 3.5 kg more wheat for ₹ 385. Find the original price of wheat.
A. ₹ 20 per kg
B. ₹ 22.50 per kg
C. ₹ 25 per kg
D. ₹ 27.50 per kg

111. Rahul's earning is 10% more than that of Ram. Sathish's earning is 15% more than that of Ram. What percent is Rahul's earning of Sathish's?
A. 94.25%
B. 95.65%
C. 96.5%
D. 98%

112. Six bells start ringing together and then ring at intervals of 4, 8, 10, 12, 15 and 20 seconds respectively. How many times will they ring together in 90 minutes?
A. 31
B. 46
C. 55
D. 61

113. Find the value of
$$1\frac{7}{9}+3\frac{5}{8}-2\frac{1}{18}+4\frac{7}{16}-9\frac{5}{18}+1\frac{71}{144}.$$
A. 0
B. 1
C. 2
D. 3

114. The product of two numbers is 4056 and their HCF is 26. How many such pairs will conform to the above mentioned criteria?
A. 1
B. 2
C. 3
D. 4

115. Find the least number which should be added to 28523 so that the sum is exactly divisible by 3, 5, 7 and 8.
A. 17
B. 27
C. 37
D. 47

116. A trader sells rice at a profit of 5% and uses a weight which is 25% less. Find the total percentage gain.
A. 20%
B. 30%
C. 40%
D. 50%

117. Simplify: $0.5 \times 2(75) - 6.7 + 8.33$
A. 67.27
B. 76.63
C. 78.82
D. 80.36

118. A sum of ₹ 12500 amounts to ₹ 15500 in 4 years at the rate of Simple Interest. What is the rate of interest?
A. 3%
B. 4%
C. 5%
D. 6%

119. The marked price of an article is ₹ 400. The tradesman allows a discount of 25% and still makes a profit of 50%. Had he not allowed the discount, what would have been his profit?
A. 50%
B. 100%
C. 150%
D. 200%

120. The average age of 5 members in a family is 21 years. If the age of the youngest member is 5 years, find the average age of the family at the birth of the youngest member.
A. 15 years
B. 18 years
C. 20 years
D. 25 years

121. Find the value of $\dfrac{3.6 \times 0.48 \times 2.50 \times 9.9}{0.12 \times 0.09 \times 0.5 \times 5.5}$.
A. 800
B. 1200
C. 1440
D. 1600

122. A hall is 15 m long and 12 m broad. If the sum of the areas of the floor and the ceiling is equal to the sum of areas of the four walls, find the volume of the hall.
A. 720 m³
B. 900 m³
C. 1200 m³
D. 1800 m³

123. Simplify: $6.4 \times 15.2 + 115\left(\dfrac{2}{5}\right)$
A. 130.52
B. 135.62
C. 143.28
D. 165.68

124. A car is running at a speed of 108 km/hr. What distance will it cover in 15 seconds?
A. 45 m
B. 55 m
C. 450 m
D. 550 m

125. For what value of 'p' will the expression $(12.86 \times 12.86 + 12.86 \times p + 0.14 \times 0.14)$ be a perfect square?
A. 0.14
B. 0.26
C. 0.28
D. 1

126. The radii of two cones are in the ratio of 2 : 1 and their volumes are equal. Find the ratio of their heights.
A. 1 : 8
B. 1 : 4
C. 2 : 1
D. 4 : 1

127. Find the largest number of five digits which when divided by 16, 24, 30, and 36 leaves the same remainder 10 in each case.
A. 99269
B. 99279
C. 99350
D. 99370

128. At what rate of Compound Interest per annum will a sum of ₹ 1500 become ₹ 1749.60 in 2 years?
A. 5%
B. 8%
C. 12%
D. 15%

129. Simplify: $\dfrac{2+\sqrt{3}}{2-\sqrt{3}} + \dfrac{2-\sqrt{3}}{2+\sqrt{3}} + \dfrac{\sqrt{3}-1}{\sqrt{3}+1}$
A. $2-\sqrt{3}$
B. $2+\sqrt{3}$
C. $40-\sqrt{3}$
D. $16-\sqrt{3}$

130. Simplify: $10.74 \times 5 - 0.17 + 25$
A. 71.05
B. 78.53
C. 86.2
D. 91.25

131. Reduce $\dfrac{4329}{4662}$ to its lowest term.
A. $\dfrac{7}{12}$
B. $\dfrac{7}{13}$
C. $\dfrac{13}{14}$
D. $\dfrac{13}{17}$

132. If a number when divided by the sum of 555 and 445 gives two times their difference as quotient and 30 as remainder, then find the number.
A. 1220
B. 1250
C. 22030
D. 220030

133. Ravi covers first 20% of the distance at 10 km/hr, 50% at 5 km/hr and the remaining distance at 15 km/hr. Find his average speed.
A. 6.15 km/hr
B. 7.14 km/hr
C. 8.45 km/hr
D. 9.84 km/hr

134. If 6 men and 8 boys can do a piece of work in 10 days while 26 men and 48 boys can do the same in 2 days, find the time taken by 15 men and 20 boys in doing the same type of work.
A. 2 days
B. 4 days
C. 6 days
D. 7 days

135. A pair of article was bought for ₹ 37.40 at a discount of 15%. What must be the marked price of each of the articles?
A. 11
B. 22
C. 33
D. 44

136. In how many years will ₹ 150 produce the same interest at 8% Simple Interest as ₹ 800 produce in 3 years at 5%?
A. 6
B. 8
C. 10
D. 12

137. Find the value of 'y', if $\dfrac{17 \times 32 \div y + 12}{6^2 \div 9 \times 4 - 8} = 10$
A. 4
B. 6
C. 8
D. 12

138. If 12 men and 16 women can do a piece of work in 5 days, 13 men and 24 women can do it in 4 days, then find the ratio of the daily work done by a man to that of a woman.
A. 2 : 1
B. 3 : 1
C. 3 : 2
D. 5 : 4

139. It takes 8 hours for a 600 km journey if 120 km is done by train and the rest by car. It takes 20 minutes more if 200 km is done by train and the rest by car. Find the ratio of the speed of the train to that of the car.
A. 2 : 3
B. 3 : 2
C. 3 : 4
D. 4 : 3

140. What is the least multiple of 7 which leaves a remainder of 4 when divided by 6, 9, 15 and 18?
A. 343
B. 364
C. 371
D. 385

141. Karthik loses 10% when he sells his radio for ₹ 450. For how much should he sell it in order to gain 5%?
A. ₹ 500
B. ₹ 510
C. ₹ 525
D. ₹ 540

142. Seats for maths, physics and biology are in the ratio of 5 : 7 : 8 respectively. There is a proposal to increase these seats by 40%, 50% and 75% respectively. What will be the respective ratio of increased seats?
A. 2 : 3 : 4
B. 6 : 7 : 8
C. 6 : 8 : 9
D. 7 : 4 : 3

143. What will be the difference between Simple and Compound Interest at 10% per annum on the sum of ₹ 1000 after 4 years?
A. ₹ 32
B. ₹ 32.1
C. ₹ 40.4
D. ₹ 64.1

144. In how many years will a sum of ₹ 1600 at 10% per annum Compound Interest, compounded half yearly become ₹ 1944.81?
A. 2
B. 3
C. 4
D. 5

Directions (Q. No. 145-147): *Study the following table and answer the questions given below.*

Distribution of marks obtained by 100 students in two papers (I and II) in mathematics.

Paper	Marks out of 50				
	40 and above	30 and above	20 and above	10 and above	0 and above
I	5	22	67	82	100
II	8	31	79	91	100
Aggregate (Average)	6	27	71	88	100

145. What should be the pass marks if minimum 80 students are required to be qualified with compulsory passing only in Paper I?
A. Below 20
B. Above 20
C. Below 40
D. None of these

146. What is the approximate percentage of students who obtained 60% and more marks in Paper II over the number of students who obtained 40% and more marks in aggregate?
A. 40%
B. 44%
C. 48%
D. 52%

147. What will be the difference between the number of students passed with 30 as cut-off marks in Paper II and the number of students passed with same cut-off marks in aggregate?
A. 2
B. 3
C. 4
D. 8

Directions (Q. No. 148-150): *Study the given pie charts carefully and answer the questions that follow.*

The given pie charts show the percentage of workers of different categories of a factory for two different years. The total number of workers in 2015 and 2016 are 2000 and 2400 respectively.

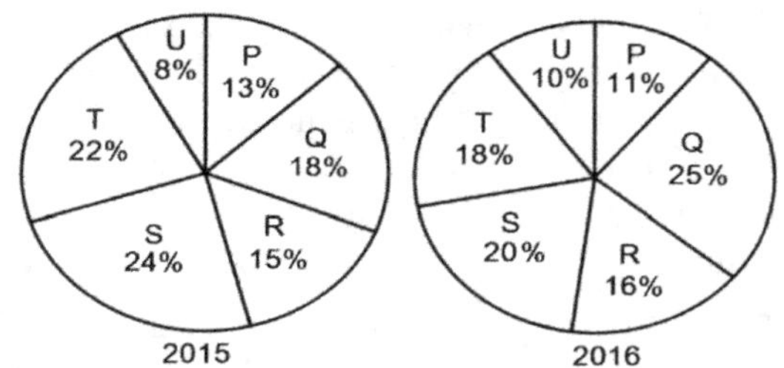

148. What is the total number of increased workers for the categories in which the number of workers has increased?
A. 382
B. 404
C. 408
D. None of these

149. Which category has shown decrease in the number of workers from 2015-2016?
A. P
B. R
C. S
D. T

150. Find the percentage increase in the number of workers in category U in 2016.
A. 25%
B. 50%
C. 65%
D. 80%

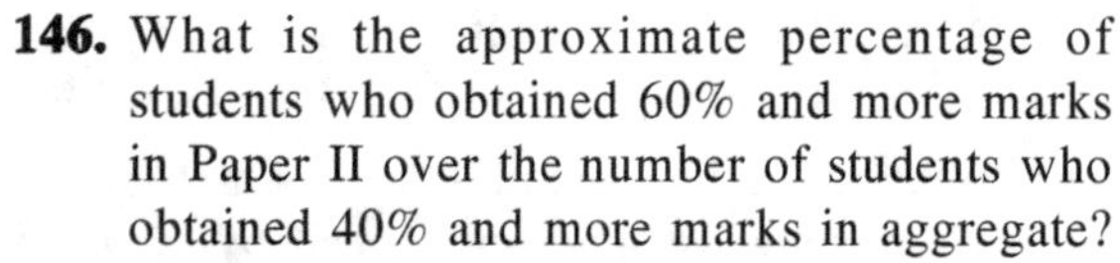

151. विलोम शब्द लिखिए :
दाता
A. दानी
B. याचक
C. पाचक
D. दायक

152. मुहावरे का अर्थ लिखिए :
अपनी खिचड़ी अलग पकाना।
A. खाना पकाना
B. सब के लिए खाना पकाना
C. मिलकर न रहना
D. एक साथ मिलकर काम करना

153. वाक्यांश को पढ़कर त्रुटि पहचानिए :
खेल शुरू होने के एक घंटा पहले (अ) / खिलाड़ी मैदान में जाकर (ब) / कुछ कसरत कर लेते हैं। (स) / कोई त्रुटि नहीं (द)
A. (अ)
B. (ब)
C. (स)
D. (द)

154. निर्देशानुसार वाक्य को पूरा कीजिए :
90% से अधिक अंक पाकर तुमने तो कमाल कर दिया। (विस्मयादिबोधक)
A. अरे वाह!
B. हाय-हाय
C. छिः छिः
D. आ हा!

155. सर्वनाम के उचित रूप से रिक्त स्थान की पूर्ति कीजिए :
.... चाबी खो गई। (मैं)
A. अपना
B. अपनी
C. मेरी
D. मेरा

156. एक शब्द लिखिए :
जनता द्वारा चलाया जाने वाला राज्य।
A. जनतातंत्र
B. जनतंत्र
C. मानवतंत्र
D. राजतंत्र

157. पर्यायवाची शब्द लिखिए :

मौत

A. निधन   B. निदान

C. निर्धन   D. निर्धनता

158. पर्यायवाची शब्द लिखिए :

सेना

A. दल   B. दाल

C. डाल   D. ढाल

159. पर्यायवाची शब्द लिखिए :

नौकर

A. सेवा   B. सेवक

C. सहचर   D. सहचरी

160. निर्देशानुसार वाक्य को पूरा कीजिए :

काशी शहर गंगा नदी .... पर बसा है।

(संबंध बोधक)

A. के पास   B. के बीच

C. के तट   D. के सामने

161. वाक्य को क्रम से लिखिए :

  I. शेर की नींद टूट गई।

  II. चूहा शेर के ऊपर चढ़ गया।

  III. शेर गहरी नींद सो रहा था।

  IV. गुस्से से शेर ने चूहे को पकड़ लिया।

A. II, IV, III, I   B. I, IV, II, III

C. III, II, I, IV   D. IV, II, III, I

162. सर्वनाम के उचित रूप से रिक्त स्थान की पूर्ति कीजिए :

.... बड़ी बहन कहाँ रहती है? (आप)

A. आपका   B. आपको

C. आपकी   D. आपने

163. एक शब्द लिखिए:

आकाश को छूनेवाला।

A. गगनधारी   B. गगनभेदी

C. गगनचुम्बी   D. गगनछेदी

164. मुहावरे का अर्थ लिखिए :

कठपुतली बनना।

A. नाचना

B. किसी को बाँधना

C. दूसरों के संकेत पर चलना

D. किसी को बुलाना

165. वाक्य को सुधारिए :

बाढ़ पीड़ित लोगों को धन की आवश्यकता है। (धन)

A. रोटी, कपड़ा और मकान

B. भोजन

C. घर

D. वस्त्र

166. एक शब्द लिखिए :

जिसमें शक्ति न हो

A. नशक्त   B. आशक्त

C. अशक्त   D. नाशक्त

167. वाक्य को क्रम में लिखिए :

  I. किनारे खड़ा पाँचवां लड़का पानी में गिर पड़ा।

  II. पाँच लड़के नदी के किनारे घूमने गए।

  III. उसे तैरना नहीं आता था।

  IV. चारों लड़के बातें करने में इतने व्यस्त थे कि उन्होंने डूबते हुए अपने मित्र को देखा तक नहीं।

A. I, IV, III, II   B. II, I, III, IV

C. II, III, I, IV   D. IV, III, I, II

168. वाक्यांश को पढ़कर त्रुटि पहचानिए :

जो मेहमान दिल्ली से आए थे (अ) / उन सबको (ब) / माँ ने चाय पिलाया (स) / कोई त्रुटि नहीं (द)

A. (अ)   B. (ब)

C. (स)   D. (द)

169. निर्देशानुसार वाक्य को पूरा कीजिए :

जोकर को देखकर सभी बच्चे .... हँस पड़े।

(क्रिया-विशेषण)

A. खिलखिलाकर   B. शोकपूर्ण होकर

C. सिर हिलाकर   D. शांतिपूर्वक

170. विलोम शब्द लिखिए :

कठिनाई

A. सरलता   B. सरसता

C. नीरसता   D. सरल

निर्देश (प्र. 171-175): *अवतरण को पढ़कर दिए गए प्रश्नों के उत्तर विकल्पों से चुनकर दीजिए :*

सच्चा मित्र वही है जो मित्र के दुःख में काम आता है। वह मित्र के कण जैसे दुःख को भी मेरू के समान भारी मानकर उसकी सहायता करता है। मित्र सुख-दुःख का साथी है। वह केवल दुःख में ही नहीं सुख में भी साथ देता है। मित्र के होने पर हमारे सुख के क्षण रंगीन हो उठते हैं। कोई भी खुशी, पार्टी या महफिल मित्रों के बिना नहीं जमती। सच्चा मित्र हमारे लिए प्रेरक, सहायक, और मार्ग-दर्शक का काम करता है। जब भी हम निराश होते हैं, मित्र हमारी हिम्मत बढ़ाता है। जब हम परास्त होते हैं, वह उत्साह देता है। जब हम शिथिल होते हैं, वह प्रेरणा देता है। जब हम रास्ता भूलते हैं, वह मार्ग-दर्शन करता है। सच्चा मित्र हमारे लिए शक्तिवर्धक औषधि बनकर सामने आता है। सच्चा मित्र हमें पथ-भ्रष्ट होने से बचाता है और सन्मार्ग पर भी अग्रसर कराता है। सच्ची मित्रता वस्तुतः एक वरदान है।

171. इस अवतरण का एक उचित शीर्षक दीजिए :
A. मित्रता और शत्रुता
B. पथ प्रदर्शक
C. सच्ची मित्रता एक वरदान
D. मित्रता से नुकसान

172. सच्चा मित्र कौन होता है?
A. जो सुख में अपने मित्र के साथ रहता है।
B. जो दुःख में अपने मित्र के साथ रहता है।
C. जो सुख-दुःख और सभी अवस्थाओं में मित्र का साथ देता है।
D. जो पार्टी में मित्र का साथ देता है।

173. निराश होने पर मित्र क्या करता है?
A. हमारी हिम्मत बढ़ाता है।
B. हमें उपदेश देता है।
C. हमारी सहायता करता है।
D. हमें धन देता है।

174. भटकने पर मित्र क्या करता है?
A. हमें अपने घर ले जाता है।
B. हमें घर के भीतर बंद रखता है।
C. हमारा मार्ग-दर्शन कर हमें सन्मार्ग पर लाता है।
D. हमें कुमार्ग से नहीं बचाता है।

175. सच्चा मित्र अपने मित्र के दुःख को कैसे समझता है?
A. मित्र के छोटे से दुःख को पर्वत की तरह बड़ा समझता है।
B. मित्र के दुःख को छोटा समझाता है।
C. मित्र के दुःख को बहुत बड़ा समझता है।
D. इनमें से कोई नहीं

GENERAL ENGLISH & COMPREHENSION

176. Choose the option which best expresses the meaning of the idiom/phrase given below.

"A piece of the pie"
A. Something outstanding
B. A slice of cake
C. An unbelievable tale
D. A share of something such as money, profits

177. Choose the correct antonym of the given word from the options given below.

LOQUACIOUS
A. Taciturn   B. Garrulous
C. Verbose   D. Profuse

178. Choose the correct antonym of the given word from the options given below.

PRIMORDIAL
A. Antique   B. Primal
C. Modern   D. Pristine

179. Choose the most appropriate verb to complete the sentence given below.

When I _______ the station the train had started. (reach)
A. Has reached   B. Reaches
C. Reached   D. Reaching

180. Fill in the blank with the most appropriate word which will suit the context of the sentence.

The charity _______ most of its money through private donations.
A. Receives
B. Borrows
C. Uses
D. Catches

181. The following sentence is divided into four parts (P, Q, R and S). Rearrange it in the proper sequence in order to make a meaningful sentence.
P. The top of Everest since 1953. In fact
Q. Nepal and China have turned the prospect
R. Hundreds of climbers have reached
S. Of climbing Mount Everest into a significant industry
A. QSRP
B. RPQS
C. RSQP
D. QPSR

182. Choose the CORRECTLY spelt word.
A. Arguement
B. Buisness
C. Chauffeur
D. Dilemna

183. The following sentence is divided into four parts (P, Q, R and S). Rearrange it in the proper sequence in order to make a meaningful sentence.
P. What will strike you is an amazing
Q. In management of a nation's mindset
R. If you read up some of Gandhi's famous quotes
S. And unnatural depth in leadership styles
A. RQSP
B. QPSR
C. RPSQ
D. PQRS

184. Choose from the four options, the word that best substitutes the given phrase.

"An occasion when the people of a country vote on an important issue"
A. Referendum
B. Appointment
C. Determination
D. Assignation

185. Choose the MISSPELT word.
A. Bizarre
B. Beginning
C. Appearance
D. Apparantly

186. In the following question, the given sentence has four parts marked P, Q, R and S. Choose the part of sentence with the error and mark as your answer. If there is no error, mark 'No error (S)' as your answer.

My best friend and advisor (P)/ has made (Q)/ this suggestion. (R)/ No error (S)
A. P
B. Q
C. R
D. S

187. Choose the option which best expresses the meaning of the idiom/phrase given below.

"Water under the bridge"
A. Events that are past and no longer important
B. The water flowing under the bridge
C. To have caught severe cold
D. To build a bridge above water

188. Choose the correct synonym of the given word from the options given below.

EPILOGUE
A. Prolog
B. Preface
C. Commencement
D. Postscript

189. Choose from the four options, the word that best substitutes the given phrase.

"Something that becomes outdated"
A. Contemporary
B. Obsolete
C. Current
D. Handy

190. Choose the CORRECTLY spelt word.
A. Coleague
B. Disastrous
C. Equiepment
D. Facinating

191. Choose the correct tense form of the underlined verb in the sentence given below.

I suppose it <u>will be raining</u> when we start.
A. Present tense
B. Future continuous tense
C. Present perfect continuous tense
D. Future perfect tense

192. In the following question, the given sentence has four parts marked P, Q, R and S. Choose the part of sentence with the error and mark as your answer. If there is no error, mark 'No error (S)' as your answer.

The Chief Minister reiterated (P)/ that he want farmers (Q)/to come and talk to him at his office. (R)/ No error (S)

A. P   B. Q
C. R   D. S

193. Choose the correct synonym of the given word from the options given below.

INDIGENOUS
A. Expatriate   B. External
C. Homegrown   D. Unfamiliar

194. Choose the MISSPELT word.
A. Embarass   B. Dilemma
C. Caribbean   D. Assassination

195. Fill in the blank with the most appropriate word which will suit the context of the sentence.

The young, thin boy surprised his wrestling opponent with his _______ strength.
A. Fraudulent   B. Wiry
C. Frolicsome   D. Pretentious

Directions (Q. No. 196-200): *Read the following passage carefully and answer the questions given below.*

Most terrestrial areas of Earth experience some form of drought on occasion. Whether the drought is permanent, as in deserts and other drylands, or more temporary, as in other environments during unusual stagnant dry periods, drought can take a toll on the plants, animals, and other living things in the affected area. "Drought" is the name for an extended period of rainless weather that throws off the balance in the water table, which then leads to social, environmental, and economic problems in the affected area. Some of the visible signs that a drought is occurring include crop damage, reductions in the flow of rivers and streams, and lowered lake levels. Below ground, droughts are often characterized by steep reductions in soil moisture and drawdowns of aquifers.

Drought occurs when evaporation and transpiration outpace the rate of precipitation over a long period of time. Unlike other weather phenomena such as tornadoes and tropical cyclones, the signs of drought are slow to develop. They can take as little as several weeks to set in, and they can last for several years before relief in the form of increased precipitation arrives. According to the National Integrated Drought Information System (NIDIS), by the end of April 2016, some of the year's most significant drought-affected areas were southern Europe along the shores of the Mediterranean, western North America, eastern Brazil and Venezuela, and south-eastern India.

196. Identify the FALSE statement, based on the information provided in the passage.
A. Drought affects plants, animals and other living things
B. Drought will vanish within a week from the day it began
C. During the drought there is decrease in the yield from crops
D. During the drought water level in the lakes decrease

197. Which of the following can be inferred from the passage?
A. Drought occurs only in deserts
B. In 2016, south-eastern India was affected by drought
C. There are a few rivers where the flow of water does not reduce during drought
D. During drought there is increased moisture in soil

198. What is the main idea of the passage?
A. Droughts, its consequences and signs
B. Usual time taken to recover from drought
C. Consequences of tornadoes
D. Damaged crops

199. What is the meaning of the underlined word "precipitation"?
A. Rain   B. Drought
C. Dearth   D. Desiccation

200. Which of the following problems are caused by drought?
A. Social problems
B. Environmental problems
C. Economic problems
D. All of these

ANSWERS

1	2	3	4	5	6	7	8	9	10
D	B	B	A	D	A	D	A	C	B

11	12	13	14	15	16	17	18	19	20
D	C	B	C	D	A	A	C	C	A

21	22	23	24	25	26	27	28	29	30
D	D	D	D	D	B	D	C	C	A

31	32	33	34	35	36	37	38	39	40
C	C	C	A	B	A	B	A	A	B

41	42	43	44	45	46	47	48	49	50
C	C	A	C	D	A	D	B	D	B

51	52	53	54	55	56	57	58	59	60
A	C	B	A	C	D	A	B	D	D

61	62	63	64	65	66	67	68	69	70
B	C	D	B	A	C	D	B	B	D

71	72	73	74	75	76	77	78	79	80
D	B	B	B	D	B	B	B	C	B

81	82	83	84	85	86	87	88	89	90
C	C	A	B	A	C	B	A	C	C

91	92	93	94	95	96	97	98	99	100
B	B	D	B	D	C	B	C	D	C

101	102	103	104	105	106	107	108	109	110
D	A	D	B	B	D	B	C	A	D

111	112	113	114	115	116	117	118	119	120
B	B	A	B	C	C	B	D	B	C

121	122	123	124	125	126	127	128	129	130
C	C	C	C	C	B	D	B	D	B

131	132	133	134	135	136	137	138	139	140
C	D	B	B	B	C	C	A	C	B

141	142	143	144	145	146	147	148	149	150
C	A	D	A	D	B	C	C	D	B

151	152	153	154	155	156	157	158	159	160
B	C	D	A	C	B	A	A	B	C

161	162	163	164	165	166	167	168	169	170
C	C	C	C	A	C	B	C	A	A

171	172	173	174	175	176	177	178	179	180
C	C	A	C	A	D	A	C	C	A

181	182	183	184	185	186	187	188	189	190
B	C	C	A	D	D	A	D	B	B

191	192	193	194	195	196	197	198	199	200
B	B	C	A	D	B	B	A	A	D

EXPLANATORY ANSWERS

51.

4	11	30	67	128	219
↓	↓	↓	↓	↓	↓
$1^3 + 3$	$2^3 + 3$	$3^3 + 3$	$4^3 + 3$	$5^3 + 3$	$6^3 + 3$

54. Given,

O L I S P A H
↓ ↓ ↓ ↓ ↓ ↓ ↓
$1 + 2 + 3 + 4 + 5 + 6 + 7 = 28$

Similarly

S O A P
↓ ↓ ↓ ↓
$4 + 1 + 6 + 5 = 16$

55. Given,

A L T E R E D
↓ ↓ ↓ ↓ ↓ ↓ ↓
Z O G V I V W

Reverse order in English alphabets.

Similarly

R E L A T E D
↓ ↓ ↓ ↓ ↓ ↓ ↓
I V O Z G V W

Reverse order in English alphabets.

60.

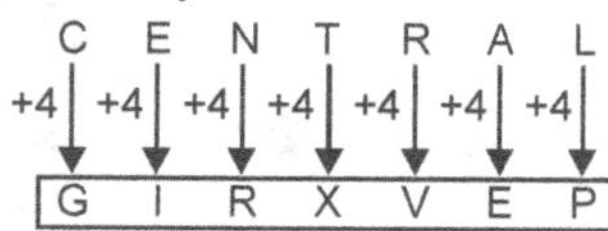

So the lady is the sister of the man.

61. Balu > Kavin > Sonu > Vino > Pooja
↑
Score lowest

62. Lungs is the respiratory organ of man, similarly Gills is the respiratory organ of fish.

64. Given,

C O R N E R
+4 +4 +4 +4 +4 +4
G S V R I V

Similarly,

C E N T R A L
+4 +4 +4 +4 +4 +4 +4
G I R X V E P

65.

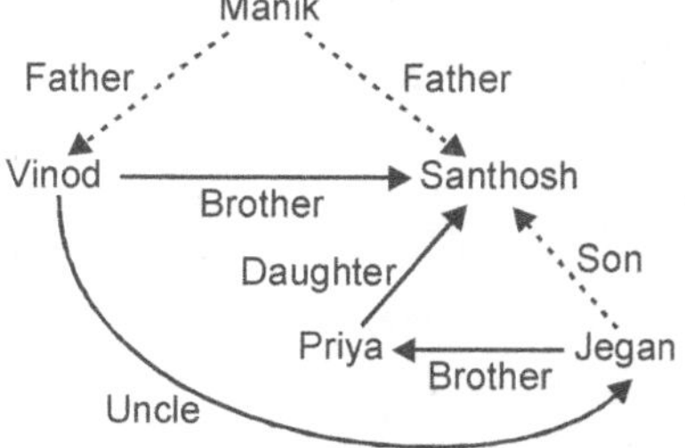

So, Vinod is the uncle of Jegan.

66.

L	M	N	O	P	Q	R	S	T
		↓		↓				↓
		6		4				9

$(\because T - N = 3)$ $(\because T - P = 5)$

So, integer '6' is assigned to N.

67.

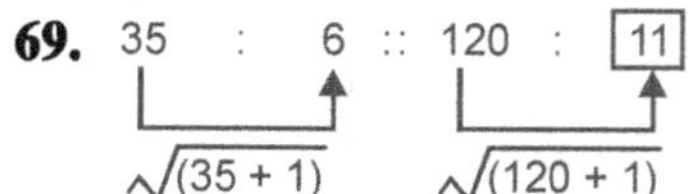

68. Except option (B), all others are the part of a circle.

69.

35 : 6 :: 120 : 11
$\sqrt{(35 + 1)}$ $\sqrt{(120 + 1)}$

71.

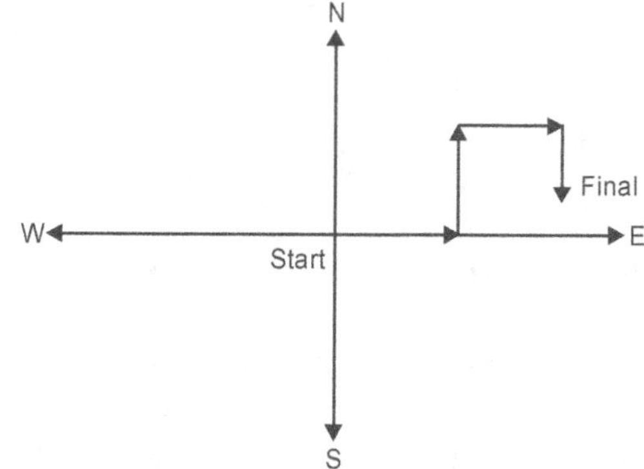

Ram is facing towards south direction now.

72.

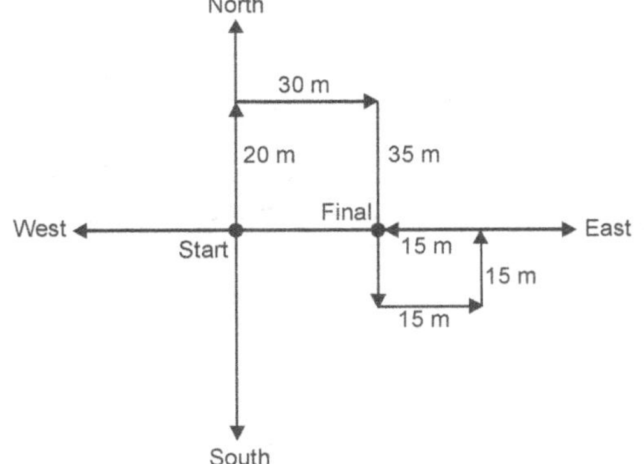

Kumar is facing towards West direction.

75. Sunil > Deepan > Charu > Anish > Meera

↑

Centre

76.

Father

Only Child

Avinash ⟶ Wife

Father

Mother

Girl (Daughter)

So, Avinash's wife is the mother of that girl.

78.

$$7 \quad 26 \quad 63 \quad 124 \quad 215 \quad 342 \quad 512$$
$$\downarrow \quad \downarrow \quad \downarrow \quad \downarrow \quad \downarrow \quad \downarrow \quad \downarrow$$
$$2^3 - 1 \quad 3^3 - 1 \quad 4^3 - 1 \quad 5^3 - 1 \quad 6^3 - 1 \quad 7^3 - 1 \quad 8^3 - 1$$

Hence, 28 is the wrong term in the series.

82. Criteria (*i*) follow

15th July 1996 to 1st September 2016

Age → 18 years

Criteria (*ii*) follow

Criteria (*iii*) not follow

Criteria (*iv*) follow

∵ Criteria (*iii*) is not follow but he obtained 90% marks in the XII examination.

The student is to be referred to the principal.

83. Criteria (*i*) follow

Criteria (*ii*) follow (age > 18 years)

Criteria (*iii*) follow

(marks in the entrance exam > 75%)

Criteria (*iv*) follow

So, the student is to be admitted.

84. Criteria (*i*) follow

Criteria (*ii*) follow (age > 18 years)

Criteria (*iii*) follow

Criteria (*iv*) not follow

So, the student is not to be followed.

For Q. No. 85 to 88

Total person = 2878

Male = 1652

Female = 2878 − 1652 = 1226

No. of person who voted against the proposal = 1226

No. of male who voted against the proposal = 796

No. of female who voted against the proposal = 1226 − 796 = 430

No. of person who voted for the proposal = 1425

Number of undecided female = 196

85. Required no. of females who were voted for the proposal

= 1226 − 796

= 430.

86. No. of persons who were undecided

= 31 + 196

= 227.

87. No. of females who voted for the proposal

= 1226 − (430 + 196)

= 1226 − 626

= 600

88. No. of male who voted in favour of the proposal

= 1425 − 600 = 825

No. of males who were undecided

$= 1652 - (796 + 825)$

$= 1652 - 1621$

$= 31$

For Q. No. 89-92

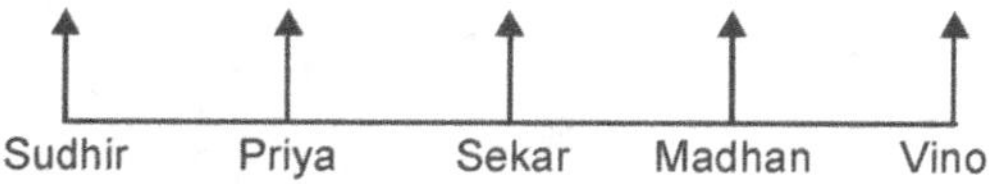

For Q. No. 93-96

Colours	Paints	Tins
Red	P7	T3
Green	P6	T1
Yellow	P5	T6
Black	P3	T5
Blue	P1	T2
White	P2	T4
Orange	P4	T7

For Q.No. 97-100

	Dramatics	Computer Science	Physics	History	Mathematics
Madhu	✓	✓	✓	✗	✗
Shoba	✓	✓	✗	✓	✗
Anjali	✗	✓	✓	✓	✓
Poonam	✓	✗	✓	✓	✓
Nisha	✗	✗	✓	✓	✓

101. Volume of cone $= \dfrac{1}{3}\pi r^2 h$

$$= \frac{1}{3} \times \pi \times \left(\frac{18}{2}\right)^2 \times 9$$

$$= \frac{1}{3} \times \pi \times 9 \times 9 \times 9$$

$$= 243\ \pi\ \text{cm}^3$$

Volume of sphere $= \dfrac{4}{3}\pi r^3$

$$= \frac{4}{3}\pi(9)^3$$

$$= 972\ \pi\ \text{cm}^3$$

Required percentage of the wasted wood

$$= \frac{972\pi - 243\pi}{972\pi} \times 100$$

$$= \frac{729}{972} \times 100$$

$$= 75\%.$$

102. Let the number of manager, and management trainee is $3x$ and $5x$ respectively

According to the question,

$$\frac{3x}{5x+21} = \frac{3}{8}$$

$$24x = 15x + 63$$

$$9x = 63$$

$$x = 7$$

No. of managers in the group $= 3x$

$$= 3 \times 7$$

$$= 21.$$

103. Let the fraction $= \dfrac{x}{y}$

According to the question,

$$\frac{x}{y} - \frac{y}{x} = \frac{9}{20}$$

After taking square of both side, we get,

$$\frac{x^2}{y^2} + \frac{y^2}{x^2} - 2 \times \frac{x}{y} \times \frac{y}{x} = \frac{81}{400}$$

$$\frac{x^2}{y^2} + \frac{y^2}{x^2} - 2 = \frac{81}{400}$$

Adding '4' in both sides:

$$\frac{x^2}{y^2} + \frac{y^2}{x^2} - 2 + 4 = \frac{81}{400} + 4$$

$$\frac{x^2}{y^2} + \frac{y^2}{x^2} + 2 = \frac{81}{400} + 4$$

$$\left(\frac{x}{y} + \frac{y}{x}\right)^2 = \frac{1681}{400}$$

$$\frac{x}{y} + \frac{y}{x} = \sqrt{\frac{1681}{400}}$$

$$= \frac{41}{20}$$

21

$$\frac{x}{y}+\frac{1}{\left(\dfrac{x}{y}\right)}=\frac{41}{20}$$

Required sum $=\dfrac{41}{20}$.

104. Let the numbers are $4x$ and $4y$

According to the question,

$$\frac{4x+4y}{\text{LCM}(4x,\ 4y)}=\frac{7}{12}$$

$$\frac{4(x+y)}{4xy}=\frac{7}{12}$$

$$\frac{x+y}{xy}=\frac{7}{12}$$

$$\frac{x+y}{xy}=\frac{4+3}{4\times3}$$

After comparing $x=4$, $y=3$

$\therefore$ The numbers are $4x=4\times4=16$

$$4y=4\times3=12$$

Hence, smaller number $=12$.

105. Let the money lent at $8\%=$ ₹ x

Then the money lent at $6\%=$ ₹ $1550-x$

$\because\qquad \text{SI}=\dfrac{p\times r\times t}{100}$

According to the question,

$$\frac{x\times8\times1}{100}+\frac{(1550-x)\times6\times1}{100}=106$$

$$8x+9300-6x=10600$$

$$2x=1300$$

$$x=650$$

$\therefore$ Money lent at $8\%=$ ₹ 650

Money lent at $6\%=1550-650=$ ₹ 900.

106. Let the numbers are x and y

According to the question,

$$x+y=₹\ 2490 \qquad\qquad ...(i)$$

$$x\times6.5\%=y\times8.5\%$$

$$\frac{x}{y}=\frac{8.5}{6.5}$$

$$\frac{x}{y}=\frac{17}{13}$$

$$x=\frac{17}{13}y$$

From equation (i) we get,

$$\frac{17}{13}y+y=2490$$

$$30y=2490\times13$$

$$y=\frac{2490\times13}{30}$$

$$y=1079\ (\text{Second number})$$

First Number $=x=\dfrac{17}{13}\times1079$

$$=1411.$$

107. Let distance $=x$ km

$\because\qquad \text{Time}=\dfrac{\text{Distance}}{\text{Speed}}$

According to the question,

$$\frac{\dfrac{x}{2}}{21}+\frac{\dfrac{x}{2}}{24}=10$$

$$\frac{x}{42}+\frac{x}{48}=10$$

$$\frac{8x+7x}{336}=10$$

$$15x=3360$$

$$x=\frac{3360}{15}$$

$$=224$$

Hence, the required distance is 224 km.

108. Milk in the mixture $=255\times\dfrac{9}{9+6}$

$$=255\times\frac{9}{15}$$

$$=153\ \text{litre}$$

Water in the mixture $=255-153$

$$=102\ \text{litre}$$

Water in the new mixture

$$=102+17=119\ \text{litre}$$

Required ratio of milk to water in the new mixture

$$=\frac{153}{119}=\frac{9}{7}.$$

109. Ram can do work in one day $= \dfrac{1}{45}$

Ramesh can do work in one day $= \dfrac{1}{40}$

Ramesh can do work in 23 days $= \dfrac{23}{40}$

Remaining works $= 1 - \dfrac{23}{40} = \dfrac{17}{40}$

$\dfrac{17}{40}$ unit works completed by Ram and Ramesh

Ram and Ramesh together can do work in one day

$$= \dfrac{1}{45} + \dfrac{1}{40}$$

$$= \dfrac{8+9}{360}$$

$$= \dfrac{17}{360} \text{ unit}$$

$\dfrac{17}{360}$ unit work is completed by Ram and Ramesh = 1 day

$\dfrac{17}{40}$ unit work is completed by Ram and Ramesh

$$= \dfrac{360}{17} \times \dfrac{17}{40}$$

$$= 9 \text{ days.}$$

Hence, Suresh leave after 9 days.

110. Let the original price of wheat

$= ₹\, x$ per kg

New price $= 80\% x$

$$= ₹\dfrac{4}{5} x \text{ per kg}$$

According to the question,

$$\dfrac{385}{\dfrac{4}{5}x} - \dfrac{385}{x} = 3.5$$

$$\dfrac{1925}{4x} - \dfrac{385}{x} = 3.5$$

$\therefore$

$$x = \dfrac{1925}{4 \times 3.5} - \dfrac{385}{3.5}$$

$$= 137.5 - 110$$

$$= ₹\, 27.5 \text{ per kg.}$$

111. $\dfrac{\text{Rahul's earning}}{\text{Ram's earning}} = \dfrac{11}{10} = \dfrac{22}{20}$

$\dfrac{\text{Satish's earning}}{\text{Ram's earning}} = \dfrac{23}{20}$

$\dfrac{\text{Rahul's earning}}{\text{Satish's earning}} = \dfrac{22}{23}$

Required percentage $= \dfrac{22}{23} \times 100$

$$= 95.65\%$$

112. Bell's rings together after time

$= \text{LCM } (4, 8, 10, 12, 15, 20)$

$= 120 \text{ second}$

All Bells ring together after 120 second.

Required time $= \dfrac{90 \times 60}{120} + 1$

$$= 45 + 1$$

$$= 46.$$

113. We have,

$$1\dfrac{7}{9} + 3\dfrac{5}{8} - 2\dfrac{1}{18} + 4\dfrac{7}{16} - 9\dfrac{5}{18} + 1\dfrac{71}{144}$$

We can written this as

$$= 1 + \dfrac{7}{9} + 3 + \dfrac{5}{8} - 2 - \dfrac{1}{18} + 4 + \dfrac{7}{16} - 9 - \dfrac{5}{18} + 1 + \dfrac{71}{144}$$

$$= (1 + 3 - 2 + 4 - 9 + 1)$$

$$+ \left(\dfrac{7}{9} + \dfrac{5}{8} - \dfrac{1}{18} + \dfrac{7}{16} - \dfrac{5}{18} + \dfrac{71}{144} \right)$$

$$= -2 + \left(\dfrac{112 + 90 - 8 + 63 - 40 + 71}{144} \right)$$

$$= -2 + \dfrac{288}{144}$$

$$= -2 + 2$$

$$= 0.$$

114. Let the numbers is $26x$ and $26y$

According to the question,

$$26x \times 26y = 4056$$
$$676xy = 4056$$
$$xy = 6$$

Required pairs (1, 6) (2, 3) or (3, 2) (6, 1)

Total pairs = 2.

115. LCM (3, 5, 7, 8) = 840

$$\therefore \qquad 840\,\overline{)\,28523\,}\,(\,33$$
$$\underline{2520}$$
$$3323$$
$$\underline{2520}$$
$$803$$

Required least number = 840 – 803 = 37.

116. Let the weight of 1 kg rice = ₹ 1

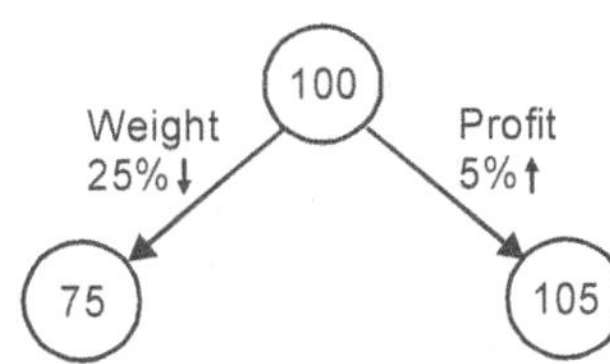

$$\therefore \quad \text{Net profit} = \frac{105 - 75}{75} \times 100$$

$$= \frac{30}{75} \times 100$$

$$= 40\%.$$

117. $0.5 \times 2(75) - 6.7 + 8.33$

$$= 75 - 6.7 + 8.33$$

$$= 83.33 - 6.7$$

$$= 76.63.$$

118. We have, sum (p) = ₹ 12500

$$\text{SI} = ₹ 15500 - ₹ 12500$$

$$= ₹ 3000$$

Time (t) = 4 years

$$\because \qquad \text{SI} = \frac{p \times r \times t}{100}$$

$$3000 = \frac{12500 \times r \times 4}{100}$$

$$r = \frac{3000}{500}$$

$$r = 6\%.$$

119. We have $\quad$ MP $\quad \rightarrow \quad$ ₹ 400
$$\downarrow -25\%$$
$$\text{SP} \quad \rightarrow \quad ₹\,300$$
$$\uparrow \text{Profit } 50\%$$
$$\text{CP} \quad \rightarrow \quad ₹\,200$$

If the discount is not given then

$$\text{SP} = ₹\,400$$

$$\% \text{ profit} = \frac{\text{SP} - \text{CP}}{\text{CP}} \times 100$$

$$= \frac{400 - 200}{200} \times 100$$

$$= \frac{200}{200} \times 100$$

$$= 100\%.$$

120. Sum of age of 5 members

$$= 5 \times 21$$
$$= 105 \text{ years}$$

Required average at the birth of the youngest member

$$= \frac{105 - 5 \times 5}{4}$$

$$= \frac{105 - 25}{4}$$

$$= \frac{80}{4}$$

$$= 20 \text{ years.}$$

121. $\dfrac{3.6 \times 0.48 \times 2.5 \times 9.9}{0.12 \times 0.09 \times 0.5 \times 5.5} = \dfrac{42.768}{0.0297} = 1440$

122. We have

$$l = 15 \text{ m}$$
$$b = 12 \text{ m}$$

According to the question,

$$l \times b + l \times b = 2(l + b) \times h$$
$$2\,lb = 2(l + b) \times h$$
$$h = \frac{lb}{l + b}$$

$$= \frac{15 \times 12}{15 + 12}$$

$$= \frac{180}{27}$$

$$= \frac{20}{3}$$

Volume of the hall $= l \times b \times h$

$$= 15 \times 12 \times \frac{20}{3}$$

$$= 1200 \text{ m}^3.$$

123. $6.4 \times 15.2 + 115\left(\frac{2}{5}\right)$

$$= 97.28 + 46$$

$$= 143.28$$

124. Speed of car $= 108$ km/hr

$$= 108 \times \frac{5}{18}$$

$$= 30 \text{ m/s}$$

$\therefore$ Distance $=$ speed $\times$ time

$$= 30 \times 15$$

$$= 450 \text{ m}$$

125. We have,

$12.85 \times 12.86 + 12.86 \times p + 0.14 \times 0.14$

Let $\qquad a = 12.85$

$$b = 0.14$$

$$= a \times a + a \times p + b \times b$$

$$= a^2 + a \times p + b^2$$

$\therefore \qquad (a + b)^2 = a^2 + 2ab + b^2$

After comparing, we get

$\therefore \qquad p = 2b$

$$= 2 \times 0.14$$

$$= 0.28.$$

126. $\dfrac{r_1}{r_2} = \dfrac{2}{1}$

$$V_1 = V_2$$

Volume of cone $= \dfrac{1}{3}\pi r^2 h$

$$\frac{1}{3}\pi r_1^2 h_1 = \frac{1}{3}\pi r_2^2 h_2$$

$$\frac{h_1}{h_2} = \left(\frac{r_2}{r_1}\right)^2 = \left(\frac{1}{2}\right)^2 = \frac{1}{4}.$$

128. $\because$ A $= P\left(1 + \dfrac{r}{100}\right)^t$

$$1749.60 = 1500\left(1 + \frac{r}{100}\right)^2$$

$$\frac{174960}{1500} = \left(\frac{100 + r}{100}\right)^2$$

$$\frac{100 + r}{100} = \sqrt{\frac{1749.60}{1500}}$$

$$\frac{100 + r}{100} = \sqrt{1.1664}$$

$$\frac{100 + r}{100} = 1.08$$

$$100 + r = 108$$

$$r = 108 - 100$$

$$= 8\%.$$

129. $\dfrac{2 + \sqrt{3}}{2 - \sqrt{3}} + \dfrac{2 - \sqrt{3}}{2 + \sqrt{3}} + \dfrac{\sqrt{3} - 1}{\sqrt{3} + 1}$

$$= \frac{\left(2 + \sqrt{3}\right)^2 + \left(2 - \sqrt{3}\right)^2}{\left(2 - \sqrt{3}\right)\left(2 + \sqrt{3}\right)} + \frac{\sqrt{3} - 1}{\sqrt{3} + 1}$$

$$= \frac{2\left(2^2 + \left(\sqrt{3}\right)^2\right)}{(2)^2 - \left(\sqrt{3}\right)^2} + \frac{\sqrt{3} - 1}{\sqrt{3} + 1}$$

$$= \frac{2(4 + 3)}{4 - 3} + \frac{\sqrt{3} - 1}{\sqrt{3} + 1}$$

$$= 14 + \frac{\sqrt{3} - 1}{\sqrt{3} + 1}$$

$$= \frac{14\sqrt{3} + 14 + \sqrt{3} - 1}{\sqrt{3} + 1}$$

$$= \frac{15\sqrt{3} + 13}{\sqrt{3} + 1}$$

After rationalization,

$$= \frac{15\sqrt{3}+13}{\sqrt{3}+1} \times \frac{\sqrt{3}-1}{\sqrt{3}-1}$$

$$= \frac{\left(15\sqrt{3}+13\right)\left(\sqrt{3}-1\right)}{\left(\left(\sqrt{3}\right)^2 - (1)^2\right)}$$

$$= \frac{1}{2}\left(45 - 15\sqrt{3} + 13\sqrt{3} - 13\right)$$

$$= \frac{1}{2}\left(32 - 2\sqrt{3}\right)$$

$$= 16 - \sqrt{3}.$$

130. $10.74 \times 5 - 0.17 + 25$

$= 53.7 - 0.17 + 25 = 78.7 - 0.17 = 78.53.$

132. Let the number $= x$

Divisor $= 555 + 445 = 1000$

Quotient $= 2(555 - 445) = 2 \times 110 = 220$

Remainder $= 30$

Number $=$ Divisor $\times$ Quotient $+$ Remainder

$= 1000 \times 220 + 30$

$= 220000 + 30$

$= 220030$

133. Let distance $= x$ km

Average speed

$$= \frac{\text{Total distance}}{\text{Time taken to cover distance}}$$

$$= \frac{x}{\dfrac{x \times 20\%}{10} + \dfrac{x \times 50\%}{5} + \dfrac{x \times 30\%}{15}}$$

$$= \frac{1}{\dfrac{1}{50} + \dfrac{1}{10} + \dfrac{1}{50}}$$

$$= \frac{50}{1 + 5 + 1}$$

$$= \frac{50}{7}$$

$$= 7.14 \text{ km/h.}$$

134. $M_1 D_1 = M_2 \times D_2$

$(6M + 8B) \times 10 = (26M + 48B) \times 2$

$60M + 80B = 52M + 96B$

$8M = 16B$

$M = 2B$

$(6M + 8B) \times 10 = (15M + 20B) \times D$

$(6 \times 2B + 8B) \times 10 = (15 \times 2B + 20B) \times D$

$20B \times 10 = 50B \times D$

$$D = \frac{200B}{50B}$$

$$= 4 \text{ days.}$$

135. $$SP = MP\left(1 - \frac{d\%}{100}\right)$$

$$MP = \frac{SP}{1 - \dfrac{d\%}{100}}$$

$$= \frac{37.5}{1 - \dfrac{15}{100}}$$

$$= \frac{37.5 \times 100}{85}$$

$$= \frac{3750}{85} \approx ₹\ 44$$

Marked price of each article

$$= \frac{44}{2} = ₹\ 22.$$

136. $\because SI = \dfrac{p \times r \times t}{100}$

$$\frac{150 \times 8 \times t}{100} = \frac{800 \times 3 \times 5}{100}$$

$$t = \frac{800 \times 3 \times 5}{150 \times 8}$$

$$= \frac{12000}{1200} = 10$$

Hence, required time $= 10$ years.

137. We have

$$\frac{17 \times 32 \div y + 12}{6^2 \div 9 \times 4 - 8} = 10$$

$$\frac{\dfrac{17 \times 32}{y} + 12}{4 \times 4 - 8} = 10$$

$$\frac{17 \times 32}{y} + 12 = 80$$

$$\frac{17 \times 32}{y} = 68$$

$$y = \frac{17 \times 32}{68}$$

$$= \frac{32}{4} = 8.$$

138.
$$M_1 D_1 = M_2 D_2$$
$$5(12M + 16W) = 4(13M + 24W)$$
$$60M + 80W = 52M + 96W$$
$$8M = 16W$$
$$\frac{M}{W} = \frac{16}{8} = \frac{2}{1}.$$

139. Let the speed of train $= x$ km/hr

and speed of car $= y$ km/hr

Case I: Distance travelled by car
$$= 600 - 120$$
$$= 480 \text{ km}$$

According to the question,

$$\because \quad \text{Time} = \frac{\text{Distance}}{\text{Speed}}$$

$$\therefore \quad \frac{120}{x} + \frac{480}{y} = 8$$

$$\frac{15}{x} + \frac{60}{y} = 1 \qquad \qquad ...(i)$$

Case II: Distance travelled by car
$$= 600 - 200$$
$$= 400 \text{ km}$$

$$\because \quad \text{Time} = \frac{\text{Distance}}{\text{Speed}}$$

According to the question,

$$\frac{200}{x} + \frac{400}{y} = 8 + \frac{20}{60}$$

$$\frac{200}{x} + \frac{400}{y} = 8 + \frac{1}{3}$$

$$\frac{200}{x} + \frac{400}{y} = \frac{25}{3}$$

$$\frac{8}{x} + \frac{16}{y} = \frac{1}{3}$$

$$\frac{1}{x} + \frac{2}{y} = \frac{1}{24} \qquad \qquad ...(ii)$$

Eq. (i) $- 15 \times$ eq. (ii)

$$\frac{60}{y} - \frac{30}{y} = 1 - \frac{15}{24}$$

$$\frac{30}{y} = \frac{9}{24}$$

$$y = \frac{24 \times 30}{9}$$

$$= 80 \text{ km/h}$$

From eq. (i)

$$\frac{15}{x} + \frac{60}{80} = 1$$

$$\frac{15}{x} = 1 - \frac{6}{8}$$

$$\frac{15}{x} = \frac{2}{8}$$

$$\therefore \quad x = 60 \text{ km/h}$$

Required ratio of the speed of train and car

$$= 60 : 80$$

$$= 3 : 4.$$

140. No. which is divided by 6, 9, 15 and 18

$= \text{LCM}(6, 9, 15, 18)$

$= 90$

$\therefore$ Required number is of the form $= 90K + 4$

Least value of K, so that $90K + 4$ is divisible by 7,

$K = 1, 90 \times 1 + 4 = 90 + 4 = 94$ (✗)

$K = 2, 90 \times 2 + 4 = 180 + 4 = 184$ (✗)

$K = 3, 90 \times 3 + 4 = 270 + 4 = 274$ (✗)

$K = 4, 90 \times 4 + 4 = 360 + 4 = 364$ (✓)

Hence, required no. $= 364$.

141. Cost price of the radio

$= \left(\dfrac{100}{100 - \text{Loss Per cent}} \right) \times \text{SP}$

$= \left(\dfrac{100}{100 - 10} \right) \times 450$

$= \dfrac{100}{90} \times 450$

$= ₹ \, 500$

Selling price to gain 5%

$= \left(\dfrac{100 + \text{Profit per cent}}{100} \right) \times \text{CP}$

$= \left(\dfrac{100 + 5}{100} \right) \times 500$

$= \dfrac{105}{100} \times 500$

$= ₹ \, 525.$

142. Let the seats for maths, physics and biology are $5x$, $7x$ and $8x$ respectively.

Respective ratio of increased seats

$= 5x \times 140\% : 7x \times 150\% : 8x \times 175\%$

$= 700x : 1050x : 1400x$

$= 2 : 3 : 4.$

143. $\because \text{SI} = \dfrac{p \times r \times t}{100}$

$\therefore$ SI after 4 years $= \dfrac{1000 \times 4 \times 10}{100} = ₹ \, 400$

$\because \text{CI} = P\left[\left(1 + \dfrac{r}{100} \right)^t - 1 \right]$

$\therefore$ CI after 4 years $= 1000\left[\left(1 + \dfrac{10}{100} \right)^4 - 1 \right]$

$= 1000\left[\left(\dfrac{11}{10} \right)^4 - 1 \right]$

$= 1000\left[\dfrac{14641}{10000} - 1 \right]$

$= 1000\left[\dfrac{4641}{10000} \right]$

$= ₹ \, 464.1$

Required difference $= 464.1 - 400 = ₹ \, 64.1.$

144. $\because$ Interest is compounded half yearly

$$r = \dfrac{10}{2} = 5\%$$

$\because$
$$A = P\left(1 + \dfrac{r}{100} \right)^t$$

$$1944.81 = 1600\left(1 + \dfrac{5}{100} \right)^t$$

$$\dfrac{1944.81}{1600} = \left(\dfrac{21}{20} \right)^t$$

$$\left(\dfrac{21}{20} \right)^t = \dfrac{194481}{160000}$$

$$\left(\dfrac{21}{20} \right)^t = \left(\dfrac{21}{20} \right)^4$$

$\therefore t = 4$ years

Interest compounded half yearly

Required time $= \dfrac{t}{2} = 2$ years.

146. 60% marks = 50 × 60% = 30

Number of students who obtained 60% marks and above in paper II

= 40% marks = 50 × 40% = 20

Number of students who obtained aggregate 40% and more marks = 71

Required percentage = $\dfrac{31}{71} \times 100$

$= 43.66\% \simeq 44\%$.

147. Number of students who passed with 30 as cut-off marks in paper II = 31

Number of students who passed with 30 as cut-off marks in aggregate = 27

Required difference = 31 – 27 = 4.

148. Number of increased worker in factory P

$= 2400 \times 11\% - 2000 \times 13\%$

$= 264 - 260$

$= 4$.

Number of increased worker in factory U

$= 2400 \times 10\% - 2000 \times 8\%$

$= 240 - 160$

$= 80$

Number of increased worker in factory Q

$= 2400 \times 25\% - 2000 \times 18\%$

$= 600 - 360$

$= 240$

Number of increased worker in factory R

$= 2400 \times 16\% - 2000 \times 15\%$

$= 384 - 300$

$= 84$

∴ Required sum = 80 + 240 + 84 + 4 = 408.

149. Number of workers work in factory P in 2015

$= 2000 \times 13\%$

$= 260$

Number of workers work in factory P in 2016

$= 2400 \times 11\%$

$= 264$

Number of workers work in factory R in 2015

$= 2000 \times 15\%$

$= 300$

Number of workers work in factory R in 2016

$= 2400 \times 16\%$

$= 384$

Number of workers work in factory S in 2015

$= 2000 \times 24\%$

$= 480$

Number of workers work in factory S in 2016

$= 2400 \times 20\%$

$= 480$

Number of workers work in factory T in 2015

$= 2000 \times 22\%$

$= 440$

Number of workers work in factory T in 2016

$= 2400 \times 18\%$

$= 432$

Hence, factory T workers decrease from 2015 to 2016.

150. Required percentage increase in the number of workers in category U in 2016

$= \dfrac{2400 \times 10\% - 2000 \times 8\%}{2000 \times 8\%} \times 100$

$= \dfrac{240 - 160}{160} \times 100$

$= \dfrac{80}{160} \times 100$

$= 50\%$.

GENERAL AWARENESS

NATIONAL SYMBOLS

NATIONAL EMBLEM

State emblem of India is an adaptation from the Sarnath Lion Capital of Ashoka. It was adopted by the Government of India on January 26, 1950. In the adapted form, only three lions are visible, the fourth being hidden from the view. The wheel (Dharma Chakra) appears in relief in the centre of the abacus with a bull on the right and a horse on the left.

The bell-shaped lotus has been omitted. The words "Satyameva Jayate" meaning "Truth alone triumphs" are inscribed below the Emblem in Devanagari script.

NATIONAL FLAG

The National Flag of India is a horizontal tricolour of deep saffron (Kesari), white and dark green in equal proportion. In the centre of the white band there is a wheel in navy blue colour. It has 24 spokes. The ratio of the length and the breadth of the flag is 3 : 2. Its design was adopted by the Constituent Assembly of India on July 22, 1947.

NATIONAL ANTHEM

Rabindranath Tagore's song 'Jana-gana-mana' was adopted by the Constituent Assembly as the National Anthem of India on January 24, 1950.

Jana-gan-mana-adhinayaka jaya he, Bharata-bhagya-vidhata
Punjab-Sindh-Gujarat-Maratha-Dravida-Utkala-Banga
Vindhya-Himachala-Yamuna-Ganga Uchhala-jaladhi-taranga.
Tava subha name jage, Tava subha asisa mange, Gahe tava jaya gatha,
Jana-gana-mangala-dayak, jaya he Bharata bhagya vidhata,
Jaya he, jaya he, jaya he, Jaya jaya jaya, jaya he.

NATIONAL SONG

Bankim Chandra Chatterji's 'Vande Mataram' which was a source of inspiration to the people in their struggle for freedom, has been adopted as National Song. It has an equal status with the National Anthem.

Vande Mataram
Sujalam, suphalam, malcyaja-shitalam,
Shasya shyamalam, Mataram
Shubhrajyotsna,pulkita yaminim,
Phulla kusumita drumadalashobhinim,
Subhasinim sumadhura—bhashinim,
Sukhadam, Varadam, Mataram.

National Bird and Animal of India: Peacock and Tiger; **National Aquatic Animal:** Dolphin; **National Flower:** Lotus; **National Game:** Hockey; **National Calendar:** It was adopted on March 22, 1957. It has 365 days in the year and the first month of the year is Chaitra.

NATIONAL CALENDAR

It is based on the Saka era with Chaitra as its first month and a normal year of 365 days. It was adopted from March 22, 1957. Dates of the national calendar have a permanent correspondence with dates of Gregorian calendar as Chaitra I falls on March 22 in a normal year and March 21 in a leap year. In official communications, both Saka and Gregorian calendar dates are written. Months of the national calendar are Chaitra, Vaishakha, Jaishtha, Ashada, Shravan, Bhadra, Ashvina, Kartika, Margashirsha, Pausha, Magha and Phalguna.

NATIONAL ANIMAL

The magnificent tiger — Panthera tigris (Linnaeus) is the national animal of India. Tiger is found in several parts of the country and is known for its grace, strength, agility and enormous power. 'Project Tiger' was launched in 1973 to check their dwindling population in India.

NATIONAL BIRD

The Indian Peacock — Pavo Christatus (Linnaeus) is the national bird of India. It is a colourful, swan-sized bird with a fan-shaped crest of feathers on its head and a long-slander neck. The male species is more colourful with blue breast and a spectacular bronze-green train of around 200 elongated feathers.

National Flower—Lotus

National Tree—Banyan

National Fruit—Mango

National Currency—Rupee '₹'

(One Rupee = 100 Paise)

National Aquatic Animal—Dolphin

BOOKS AND AUTHORS

Name of Book	Author	Name of Book	Author
Ain-e-Akbari	Abul Fazal	Mother (Maa)	Maxim Gorky
Anand Math	Bankim Chandra Chatterjee	Mother India	Katherine Mayo
An Unknown Indian	Nirad C. Chaudhuri	My Experiments with Truth	Mahatma Gandhi
Arthshastra	Kautilya	My Presidential Years	R. Venkataraman
Coolie	Mulk Raj Anand	Neeti Shatak	Bhartrihari
Das Kapital	Karl Marx	Nehru and His Vision	Dr. K.R. Narayanan
Discovery of India	Jawaharlal Nehru	Old Man and the Sea	Ernest Hemingway
Eternal India	Mrs. Indira Gandhi	One World	Wendell Wilkie
Godan	Prem Chand	Panchtantra	Vishnu Sharma
Gitanjali	Rabindranath Tagore	Paradise Lost	John Milton
Gora	Rabindranath Tagore	Ramayana	Valmiki (in Sanskrit)
Geet Govinda	Jayadeva	Raghuvansham	Kalidas
Harsha Charit	Bana Bhatta	Rajtarangini	Kalhan
Hindu View of Life	Dr. S. Radhakrishnan	Ram Charit Manas	Tulsi Das
India Wins Freedom	Maulana Abul Kalam Azad	Abhijnan Shakuntalam	Kalidas
Jobs of Millions	V.V. Giri	Satanic Verses	Salman Rushdie
Jungle Book	Rudyard Kipling	Saket	Maithili Sharan Gupta
Kamayani	Jai Shankar Prasad	Speed Post	Shobha De
Kadambari	Bana Bhatta	The God of Small Things	Arundhati Roy
Life Divine	Sri Aurobindo	Treasure Island	R.L. Stevenson
Last days of Netaji	G.D. Khosla	Twelfth Night	William Shakespeare
Les Miserables	Victor Hugo	Train to Pakistan	Khuswant Singh
Mahabharat	Veda Vyas	Uttara Ram Charitra	Bhava Bhuti
Macbeth	William Shakespeare	Vanity Fair	W.M. Thackeray
Mein Kempf	Hitler	War and Peace	Leo Tolstoy
Meghduta	Kalidas	Wealth of Nations	Adam Smith
		Wake up India	Annie Besant

INVENTIONS AND DISCOVERIES

Geographical Discoveries

Discovery	Discoverer
America	Columbus
Brazil	Cabral
North Pole	Robert Peary
Everest (Conquered)	Tabie Junko
Planetary Motion	Kepler
Hawaiian Islands	Captain Cook
South Pole	Amundsen
Solar System	Copernicus

Chemistry and Physics

Discovery	Discoverer
Atom Bomb	Otto Hahn
Atomic Theory	Dalton
Atomic Numbers	Moseley
Cosmic Rays	R.S. Millikan
Dynamite	Alfred Nobel
Electrons Theory	Bohr
Electricity (current)	Volta
Electric Telegraphy (Code)	S. Morse

Discovery	Discoverer
Gravitation	Newton
Gas Light	Murdock
Oxygen	J. Priestly
Photography	L. Daguerre
Printing for the blind	Louis Braille
Radium	Madame Curie
Telegraph	Samuel Morse
Television	J.L. Baird
Telephone	Graham Bell
Wireless	G. Marconi
X-rays	W.K. Roentgen

Mechanical

Discovery	Discoverer
Aeroplane	Wright Brothers
Bicycle	Macmillan
Computer	Charles Babbage
Dynamo	Michal Faraday
Diesel Engine	Rudolf Diesel
Engine (Railway)	Stephenson
Fountain Pen	Waterman
Gramophone	Edison
Locomotive Power of Steam	James Watt
Helicopter	Brequet
Life Boat	Henry Greathead

Discovery	Discoverer
Microscope	Z. Jansen
Printing Press	Gutenberg
Revolver	Colt
Sewing Machine	Elias Howe
Thermometer	Fahrenheit
Transistor	W. Shockley
Typewriter	Sholes
Telescope	Hans Lippershey
Tank (Military)	Swinton

Medical

Discovery	Discoverer
Antiseptic Surgery	Lord Joseph Lister
Bacteria	Leeuwenhock
Circulation of Blood	William Harvey
Homoeopathy (Discovered)	Hahnemann
Insulin	F. Banting
Penicillin	Alexander Flemming
Malaria Parasite	Dr. Ronald Ross
Stethoscope	Laennec
Vitamins	Funk
Anti-Rabies Treatment	Pasteur

General

Discovery	Discoverer
Nylon	Carouthers
Science of Geometry	Euclids

WORLD'S GEOGRAPHICAL SURNAMES

● City of Sky-scrapers—New York ● City of Seven Hills—Rome ● City of Dreaming Spires—Oxford ● City of Golden Gate—San Francisco ● City of Magnificent Buildings—Washington D.C. ● City of Eternal Springs—Quito (S. America) ● China's Sorrow—Hwang Ho ● Cockpit of Europe—Belgium ● Dark Continent—Africa ● Emerald Isle—Ireland ● Eternal City—Rome ● Empire City—New York ● Forbidden City—Lhasa (Tibet) ● Garden City—Chicago ● Gate of Tears—Strait of Bab-el-Mandeb ● Gift of the Nile—Egypt ● Granite City—Aberdeen (Scotland) ● Hermit Kingdom—Korea ● Herring Pond—Atlantic Ocean ● Holy Land—Jerusalem ● Island Continent—Australia ● Islands of Cloves—Zanzibar ● Isle of Pearls—Bahrein (Persian Gulf) ● Key to the Mediterranean—Gibralter ● Land of Cakes—Scotland ● Land of Golden Fleece—Australia ● Land of Maple Leaf—Canada ● Land of Morning Calm—Korea ● Land of Midnight Sun—Norway ● Land of the Thousand Lakes—Finland ● Land of the Thunderbolt—Bhutan ● Land of White Elephant—Thailand ● Land of Thousand Elephants—Laos ● Land of Rising Sun—Japan ● Loneliest Island—Tristan De Gunha (Mid-Atlantic) ● Manchester of Japan—Osaka ● Pillars of Hercules—Strait of Gibraltar ● Pearl of the Antilles—Cuba ● Playground of Europe—Switzerland ● Quaker City—Philadelphia ● Queen of the Adriatic—Venice ● Roof of the World—The Pamirs, Central Asia ● Sugar bowl of the world—Cuba ● Venice of the North—Stockholm ● Windy City—Chicago ● Whiteman's grave—Guinea Coast of Africa ● Yellow River—Huang Ho (China) ● Sickman of Europe—Turkey

CAPITALS AND CURRENCIES OF COUNTRIES

Country	Capital	Currency	Country	Capital	Currency
Afghanistan	Kabul	Afghani	Indonesia	Jakarta	Rupiah
Algeria	Algiers	Dinar	Iran	Teheran	Rial
Angola	Luanda	New Kwanza	Iraq	Baghdad	Dinar
Argentina	Buenos Aires	Peso	Ireland	Dublin	Euro
Armenia	Yeravan	Dram	Israel	Jerusalem	Shekel
Australia	Canberra	Dollar	Italy	Rome	Euro
Austria	Vienna	Euro	Jamaica	Kingston	Dollar
Azerbaijan	Baku	Monat	Japan	Tokyo	Yen
Bahrain	Manama	Dinar	Jordan	Amman	Dinar
Bangladesh	Dhaka	Taka	Kazakhstan	Akmola	Tenge
Barbados	Bridgetown	Dollar	Kenya	Nairobi	Shilling
Belgium	Brussels	Euro	Korea (S)	Seoul	Won
Bhutan	Thimphu	Ngultrum*	Korea (N)	Pyongyang	Won
Bolivia	La paz	Boliviano	Kyrgyzstan	Bishkek	Som
Brazil	Brasilia	Cruzeiro	Kuwait	Kuwait City	Dinar
Bulgaria	Sofia	Lev	Laos	Vientiane	Kip
Byelorussia	Minsk	Zaichik	Latvia	Riga	Lat
Cambodia	Phnom-Penh	Riel	Lebanon	Beirut	Pound
Canada	Ottawa	Dollar	Libya	Tripoli	Dinar
Chile	Santiago	Peso	Lithuania	Vilnius	Litas
China	Beijing	Yuan	Malaysia	Kuala Lumpur	Ringgit
Colombia	Bogota	Peso	Maldives	Male	Rufiyya
Congo	Brazzaville	Franc	Mauritius	Port Louis	Rupee
Croatia	Zagreb	Kuna	Moldavia	Chisinau	Leu
Cuba	Havana	Peso	Mexico	Mexico City	Peso
Cyprus	Nicosia	Euro	Morocco	Rabat	Dirham
Czech Republic	Prague	Crown	Mozambique	Maputo	Metical
Denmark	Copenhagen	Krone	Myanmar	Yangon	Kyat
Egypt	Cairo	Pound	(Burma)	(Rangoon)	
Estonia	Tallinn	Kroon	Nepal	Kathmandu	Rupee
Ethiopia	Addis Ababa	Birr	Netherlands	Amsterdam	Euro
Fiji	Suva	Dollar	New Zealand	Wellington	Dollar
Finland	Helsinki	Euro	Nigeria	Abuja	Naira
France	Paris	Euro	Norway	Oslo	Krone
Georgia	Tbilisi	Lari	Oman	Muscat	Rial
Germany	Berlin	Euro	Pakistan	Islamabad	Rupee
Ghana	Accra	Cedi	Philippines	Manila	Peso
Greece	Athens	Euro	Poland	Warsaw	Zloty
Guatemala	Guatemala City	Quetzal	Portugal	Lisbon	Euro
Hong Kong	Victoria	Dollar	Qatar	Doha	Riyal
Hungary	Budapest	Forints	Romania	Bucharest	Leu
Iceland	Reykjavik	Krona	Russia	Moscow	Ruble
India	New Delhi	Rupee	Saudi Arabia	Riyadh	Rial

Country	Capital	Currency	Country	Capital	Currency
Slovakia	Bratislava	Euro	Turkey	Ankara	Lira
Spain	Madrid	Euro	Turkmania	Ashikabad	Manat
Sri Lanka	Colombo	Rupee	Uganda	Kampala	Shilling
Sudan	Khartoum	Dinar	Ukraine	Kiev	Hyrvna
Sweden	Stockholm	Krona	United Arab	Abu Dhabi	Dirham
Switzerland	Berne	Swiss Francs	Emirates		
Syria	Damascus	Pound	U.K.	London	Pound
South Africa	Capetown	Rand			Sterling
	(Legislative)		U.S.A.	Washington	Dollar
	Pretoria		Uzbekistan	Tashkent	Som
	(Administrative)		Vietnam	Hanoi	Dong
Tajikistan	Dushanbe	Somoni	Yemen	Sana'a	Rial/Dinar
Taiwan	Taipei	Dollar	Zimbabwe	Harare	Dollar
Tanzania	Dodoma	Shilling	Congo (Zaire)	Kinshasa	Zaire
Thailand	Bangkok	Baht	Zambia	Lusaka	Kwacha

INDIAN CITIES AND THEIR RIVERS

City	State	River	City	State	River
Agra	U.P.	Yamuna	Kanpur	Uttar Pradesh	Ganga
Ahmedabad	Gujarat	Sabarmati	Ludhiana	Punjab	Sutlej
Allahabad	U.P.	Confluence of the Ganga, Yamuna, and invisible Saraswati	Lucknow	Uttar Pradesh	Gomati
			Nasik	Maharashtra	Godavari
			Patna	Bihar	Ganga
			Srinagar	J & K	Jhelum
Alwaye	Kerala	Periyar	Surat	Gujarat	Tapti
Kolkata	West Bengal	Hooghly	Tiruchirapally	Tamil Nadu	Kaveri
Cuttack	Odisha	Mahanadi	Ujjain	Madhya Pradesh	Shipra
Delhi	Delhi	Yamuna	Vijayawada	Andhra Pradesh	Krishna
Haridwar	Uttarakhand	Ganga	Varanasi	Uttar Pradesh	Ganga

WONDERS OF THE WORLD

Seven Wonders of the Ancient World: (1) the Pyramids of Egypt, built in approximately 2700 BC; (2) the Hanging Gardens at Babylon; (3) the temple of Artemis at Emphesus; (4) the statue of Zeus at Olympia; (5) the tomb of Mausolus at Halicarnassus, built in nearly 350 BC; (6) the Colossus of Rhodes, built in nearly 280 BC; (7) the Pharos Lighthouse at Alexandria.

Seven Wonders of the Medieval World: (1) the Colosseum of Rome; (2) the Great Wall of China; (3) the Porcelain Tower of Nanking; (4) the Mosque at St. Sophia (Constantinople); (5) Stonehenge; (6) the Catacombs of Rome; (7) the Leaning Tower of Pisa.

Seven New Wonders of the World: (1) Taj Mahal of Agra (India); (2) Pyramid at Chichen Itza (Mexico); (3) Machu Picchu (Peru); (4) Statue of Christ The Redeemer (Brazil); (5) Great Wall of China; (6) Roman Colosseum, Italy; (7) Ruins of Petra, Jordan.

STATES OF INDIA (CAPITALS, PRINCIPAL LANGUAGES)

States / Principal Languages	Capitals	States / Principal Languages	Capitals
■ Andhra Pradesh *Telgu and Urdu*	Hyderabad	■ Meghalaya *Khashi, Jayantia and Garo*	Shillong
■ Arunachal Pradesh *Monpa, Adi, Nissi etc.*	Itanagar	■ Manipur *Manipuri*	Imphal
■ Assam *Assamese and Bengali*	Dispur	■ Mizoram *Mizo and English*	Aizawl
■ Bihar *Hindi and Maithili*	Patna	■ Nagaland *Naga, Assamese and English*	Kohima
■ Chattishgarh *Hindi*	Raipur	■ Odisha *Odiya*	Bhubaneshwar
■ Goa *Konkani*	Panaji	■ Punjab *Punjabi*	Chandigarh
■ Gujarat *Gujarati*	GandhiNagar	■ Rajasthan *Hindi, Rajasthani*	Jaipur
■ Haryana *Hindi*	Chandigarh	■ Sikkim *Sikkimese and Gorkhali*	Gangtok
■ Himachal Pradesh *Hindi and Pahari*	Shimla	■ Tamil Nadu *Tamil*	Chennai
■ Jammu & Kashmir *Kashmiri, Dongri, Urdu,* *Ladakhi, Dardi and Pahari*	Srinagar	■ Tripura *Bengali, Tripuri* *and Manipuri*	Agartala
■ Jharkhand *Hindi*	Ranchi	■ Uttar Pradesh *Hindi*	Lucknow
■ Kerala *Malyalam*	Thiruvananthpuram	■ Uttarakhand *Hindi*	Dehradun
■ Karnataka *Kannada*	Bengluru	■ West Bengal *Bengali*	Kolkata
■ Madhya Pradesh *Hindi*	Bhopal	■ Telangana *Telgu and Urdu*	Hyderabad
■ Maharashtra *Marathi*	Mumbai		

Union Territories / Principal Languages	Capitals	Union Territories / Principal Languages	Capitals
■ Andaman and Nicobar Islands *Hindi, Nicobarese, Bengali,* *Malayalam, Tamil, Telugu*	Port Blair	■ Daman and Diu *Gujarati*	Daman
■ Chandigarh *Hindi, Punjabi, English*	Chandigarh	■ Delhi *(Hindi, Punjabi)*	Delhi
■ Dadar and Nagar Haveli *Gujarati, Hindi*	Silvasa	■ Lakshadweep *Malayalam*	Kavaratti
		■ Puducherry *Tamil, Telugu, Malayalam,* *English and French*	Puducherry

HIGH COURTS IN INDIA

Name	Year	Territorial Jurisdiction	Seat
Allahabad	1866	Uttar Pradesh	Allahabad (Bench at Lucknow)
Andhra Pradesh#	2019	Andhra Pradesh	Amaravati
Mumbai	1862	Maharashtra, Goa, Dadar and Nagar Haveli and Daman and Diu	Mumbai (Benches at Nagpur, Panaji and Aurangabad)
Kolkata	1862	West Bengal and Andaman & Nicobar	Kolkata (Circuit Bench at Port Blair)
Chhattisgarh	2000	Chhattisgarh	Bilaspur
Delhi	1966	Delhi	Delhi
Guwahati	1948	Assam, Nagaland, Mizoram and Arunachal Pradesh	Guwahati (Benches at Kohima, Aizawl and Itanagar)
Gujarat	1960	Gujarat	Ahmedabad
Himachal Pradesh	1971	Himachal Pradesh	Shimla
Jammu & Kashmir	1928	Jammu & Kashmir	Srinagar and Jammu
Jharkhand	2000	Jharkhand	Ranchi
Karnataka	1884	Karnataka	Bengaluru (Circuit Benches at Dharwar and Gulbarga)
Kerala	1958	Kerala & Lakshadweep	Ernakulam
Madhya Pradesh	1956	Madhya Pradesh	Jabalpur (Benches at Gwalior and Indore)
Madras	1862	Tamil Nadu & Puducherry	Chennai (Bench at Madurai)
Odisha	1948	Odisha	Cuttack
Patna	1916	Bihar	Patna
Punjab and Haryana	1966	Punjab, Haryana and Chandigarh	Chandigarh
Rajasthan	1949	Rajasthan	Jodhpur (Bench at Jaipur)
Sikkim	1975	Sikkim	Gangtok
Uttarakhand	2000	Uttarakhand	Nainital
Tripura	2013	Tripura	Agartala
Meghalaya	2013	Meghalaya	Shillong
Manipur	2013	Manipur	Imphal
Telangana*	2019	Telangana	Hyderabad

\# High court of Andhra Pradesh to function at Amaravati from January 1, 2019.

* Originally known as Andhra Pradesh High Court and it was established on 5 November 1956 but it was renamed as High Court of Judicature at Hyderabad in 2014, renamed again as Telangana High Court on 1 January 2019.

HILL STATION

Station	State
1. Almora, Mussoorie Nainital	: Uttarakhand
2. Cherrapunji (Shillong), Khasi Hills (Shillong)	: Meghalaya
3. Ooty, Kodaikanal Yereaud	: Tamil Nadu
4. Dalhousie, Kassauli	: Himachal Pradesh
5. Darjeeling	: West Bengal
6. Gulmarg, Srinagar	: Kashmir
7. Mahabaleshwar	: Maharashtra
8. Mt. Abu	: Rajasthan
9. Panchmarhi	: Madhya Pradesh

NATIONAL PARKS

1. Corbett National Park	: Nainital, Uttarakhand
2. Dudhwa National Park	: Lakhimpur Kheri, Uttar Pradesh
3. Kaziranga National Park	: Jorhat, Assam
4. Kanha National Park	: Jabalpur, Bhedaghat
5. Gir National Park	: Rajkot, Junagarh, Gujarat
6. Guindy National Park	: Guindy, Chennai, Tamil Nadu
7. Nagairhole National Park	: Coorg, Karnataka
8. Bandipur National Park	: Mysore, Karnataka

NATIONAL WILDLIFE SANCTUARIES

1. Dachigam Wildlife Sanctuary	: Srinagar, Jammu and Kashmir	4. Tiger Project	: Sawai Madhopur, Rajasthan
2. Sariska	: Alwar, Rajasthan	5. Mudhumali Wildlife Sanctuary	: Mudhumalia, Nilgiri, Tamil Nadu
3. Hazaribagh Wildlife Sanctuary	: Hazaribagh, Jharkhand	6. Periyar Wildlife Sanctuary	: Idukki, Kottayam, Kerala

HOLY PLACES IN INDIA

1.	Amarnath	Kashmir
2.	Ayodhya	Uttar Pradesh
3.	Badrinath	Uttarakhand
4.	Dwarka	Gujarat
5.	Haridwar	Uttarakhand
6.	Kancheepuram	Tamil Nadu
7.	Kedarnath	Uttarakhand
8.	Mathura	Uttar Pradesh
9.	Puri	Odisha
10.	Rameswaram	Tamil Nadu
11.	Tirupati	Andhra Pradesh
12.	Ujjain	Madhya Pradesh
13.	Varanasi	Uttar Pradesh
14.	Bodh Gaya	Bihar

SPORTS

Terms Associated With Sports :

Cricket : Ashes, Bye, Bodyline, Bowling, Break, Cover-point, Creases, Chinaman, Chucker, Drive, Duck, Follow on, Googly, Hit-Wicket, Hat-trick, Leg-before-wicket, Leg break, Leg-bye, Maiden over, No ball, Night-watchman, Runner, Run-out, Stumped, Silly-point, Slip.

Football : Handball, Corner kick, Dribble, Free Kick, Hat-trick, Off-side, Penalty Kick, Try, Throw in, Wembley.

Hockey : Bully, Carry, Corner kick, Corner, Penalty stroke, Off-side, Penalty, Roll in scoop, Sticks, Sudden death, Striking circle, Short Corner, Scoop, Tie-breaker, Under-cutting, Hat-trick.

Tennis : Backhand drive, Deuce, Fault, Half-volley, Net, Let, Volley, Smash, Service.

Billiards : Break, Cannons, Cue, Pot, Jigger, Scratch, In Bauk, In, Off.

Bridge : Dummy, Finesse, Grand-slam, Little Slam, Revoke, Ruff slam, Trump, Tricks, Vulnerable.

Volley Ball : Booster, Love, Service, Volley, Smasher.

Badminton : Smash, Drop, Let.

Chess : Check, Checkmate, Gambit, State-mate.

Golf : Bogy, Caddie, Hole, Links, Stymie, Tee, Put.

Polo : Chukker, Mallet, Bunder.

Baseball : Bunting, Diamond, Pitcher, Put-out, Strike, Home.

Boxing : Knockout, Punch, Upper-cut, Jab, Hook.

FAMOUS TROPHIES

Agha Khan Cup	Hockey
Beighton Cup	Hockey
Corbillion Cup	World Table Tennis (Women)
Davis Cup	Lawn Tennis
Duleep Trophy	Cricket
Durand Cup	Football
Ezra Cup	Polo
I.F.A. Shield	Football
Irani Cup	Cricket (India)
Jayalaxmi Cup	Table Tennis (Women)
Lady Rattan Tata Trophy	Hockey (Women)
Nehru Cup	Hockey (India)
Obaidullah Cup	Hockey
Ranji Trophy	Cricket (India)
Rangaswamy Cup	Hockey (India)
Rovers Cup	Football (India)
Santosh Trophy	Football (India)
Subroto Cup	Football
Thomas Cup	Badminton
Uber Cup	Badminton (Women)
Wellington Trophy	Rowing (India)

BIGGEST, LARGEST, TALLEST OF THE WORLD

Airport, *Largest*—King Fahd International Airport, Dammon (Saudi Arabia)

Animal, *Tallest*—Giraffe (Average height 6.09 m); *Largest and Heaviest*—Blue Whale (190 tonnes)

Longest recorded Animal—Boot lace Worm (55 m); *Fastest*—Cheetah (Approximately 100 km/hr)

Bay, *With max. shore line*—Hudson Bay (Canada: 12268 km); *With maximum area*—Bay of Bengal (India: 217 million hc)

Bridge, *Highest*—Sidu River Bridge (China 1627 ft); *Railway (longest)*—Danyang—Kunshan Grand Bridge (China)

Continent, *biggest*—Asia ($31{,}845{,}872$ km^2); *Smallest*—Australia Mainland (Area $76{,}17{,}930$ km^2)

Dam, *Largest (concrete)*—Grand Coulee Dam (1272 m on Columbia River (Washington State, USA); *Highest*—Jinping-I (305 m)

Desert, *Largest*—Sahara (N. Africa; maximum length 5,150 km EW; maximum width 3,200 km NS)

Dome, *Largest*—Singapore National Stadium (310 m)

Fish, *Largest fresh water*—Plabeuk (China, Laos and Thailand); *Most abundant*—Bristle mouth; *Most venomous*—Stone Fish (Indo-Pacific Waters)

Fountain, *Tallest*—King Fahd's Fountain (Jeddah, Saudi Arabia)

Gulf, *Largest*—Gulf of Mexico (1,544,000 sq. km)

Island, *Biggest*—Greenland (now known as Kalaatdlit Nunaat---2,175,000 sq km)

Lake, *Largest*—Caspian Sea (Azerbaijan, Russia, Iran border: 37.18 lakh km^2); *Deepest*—Baikal (Siberia); *Largest (fresh water)*—Superior Lake (USA---Canada border: 82,350 km^2)

Mountain, *Highest peak*—Mt. Everest (8848 m; Nepal); *Highest range*—Himalayas, Asia (upto 4200 m); *Greatest mountain range*—Himalaya-Karakoram (96 out of 109 peaks over 7315 m are here)

Museum, *Largest*—American Museum of Natural History, New York

Ocean, *Largest and Deepest*—The Pacific (Area: 166,240,000 km^2; Depth: 10,924 m)

Platform, *Longest (rail)*—Gorakhpur (Uttar Pradesh; India, 1355.4 m. long)

Port, *Largest*—Port of New York and New Jersey (USA); *Busiest*—Rotterdam (Netherlands)

Railway Station, *Largest*—Grand Central Terminal (New York City; 19 hc); *Highest*—Condor (Bolivia; 4786 m)

Rivers, *Longest*—(i) Nile (6650 km) (ii) Amazon (6437 km)

Sea, *Largest*—South China Sea (2,974,600 sq. km); *Largest (inland)*—Mediterranean

Star, *Brightest*—Sirius A (also called Dog Star)

Telescope, *Largest (radio)*—Five Hundred meter Apertune Spherical Telescope (FAST), China.; *Largest (solar)*—Kitt Peak National Observatory, (Arizona; USA); *Largest refractor*—At Yerkes observatory (Wisconsin; USA; 18.9 m)

Temple, *Largest*—Angkor Vat (Cambodia: 402 acres)

Train, *Fastest*—Japan's magnetically levitated (magler) train (Speed over 500 km/hr)

Tunnel, *Longest (railway)*—Gotthard Base Rail Tunnel (Switzerland; 57.1 km); *Largest (road)*—Laerdal, Norway (24.51 km)

Volcano, *Greatest concentration in*—Indonesia; *Highest (extinct)*—Cerro Aconcagua (6960 m; Andes);

Zoo, *Largest*—Etosha Reserve (Namibia; area 10 million hc approx.).

FIRST IN INDIA

Governor General of Independent India — Lord Mountbatten

Commander-in-chief of free India — General Roy Bucher

Cosmonaut — Sq. Ldr. Rakesh Sharma

Field Marshal — S.H.F.J. Manekshaw

Indian Governor General of Indian Union — C. Rajagopalachari

Indian I.C.S. Officer — Satyendra Nath Tagore

Indian to swim across English Channel — Mihir Sen

Indian Women to swim across English Channel — Miss Arti Saha

Man to climb Mount Everest — Tenzing Norgay

Man to climb Mount Everest without Oxygen — Phu Dorjee

Man to climb Mount Everest twice — Nwang Gombu

Nobel Prize Winner — Rabindra Nath Tagore

President of Indian National Congress — W.C. Banerjee

President of Indian Republic — Dr. Rajendra Prasad

Talkie Film — Alam Ara (1931)

Test Tube Baby (Documented) — Indira

Viceroy of India — Lord Canning

Woman Minister of Indian Union — Rajkumari Amrit Kaur

Woman Governor — Mrs. Sarojini Naidu

Woman President of Indian National Congress — Dr. Annie Besant

Woman Prime Minister — Mrs. Indira Gandhi

Woman Speaker of a State Assembly — Mrs. Shanno Devi

Prime Minister of India — Pt. Jawaharlal Nehru

Muslim President of Indian Union — Dr. Zakir Hussain

Speaker of Lok Sabha — G.V. Mavlankar

Women to Climb Mount Everest — Bachhendri Pal

Woman Judge in Supreme Court — Mrs. Meera Sahib Fatima Biwi

Women Chief Justice of a High Court — Smt. Leela Seth

The First Indian Weightlifter to Win bronze medal in Olympics — Karnam Malleshwari (Sydney, in 2000)

World Chess Champion — Vishwanathan Anand

India's First Woman Merchant Navy Officer
— Sonali Banerjee

The First Woman Air Vice-Marshal
— P. Bandopadhyaya

The First Indian to be appointed as
United Nations Civilian Police Advisor
— Ms. Kiran Bedi

The First Women to be appointed Deputy
Governor of Reserve Bank of India — K.J. Udeshi

The First Indian Lady to win a medal in
World Athletic Championship
— Anju Bobby George

The First Sikh Prime Minister of India
— Dr. Manmohan Singh

IMPORTANT DAYS

15th January	—	Army Day
26th January	—	Republic Day
30th January	—	Leprosy Eradication Day/ Martyr's Day
28th February	—	National Science Day
8th march	—	International Women's Day
15th March	—	World Consumer's Day
21st March	—	World Disabled Day
5th April	—	National Marine Day
7th April	—	World Health Day
18th April	—	World Heritage Day
22nd April	—	International Earth Day
Ist May	—	Worker's Day
3rd May	—	International Sun Day
21st May	—	Anti-Terrorism Day
24th May	—	Commonwealth Day
31st May	—	World No Tobacco Day
5th June	—	World Environment Day
21st June	—	World Yoga Day
26th June	—	International Day against Drug Abuse
11th July	—	World Population Day
15th August	—	Independence Day
24th August	—	Sanskrit Day
5th September	—	Teacher's Day
8th September	—	World Literacy Day
27th September	—	World Tourism Day

1st October	—	World Elder's Day
4th October	—	World Animal Day
8th October	—	Air Force Day
10th October	—	National Solidarity Day
16th October	—	World Food Day
24th October	—	U.N. Day
14th November	—	World Diabetes Day
14th November	—	Children's Day
19th November	—	National Integration Day
26th November	—	Law Day
1st December	—	World AIDS Day
4th December	—	Navy Day
7th December	—	Flag Day
10th December	—	Human Rights Day

PARLIAMENTS OF IMPORTANT COUNTRIES

Afghanistan	—	Shora
Britain	—	Parliament House of Commons, House of Lords
Denmark	—	Folketing
The Netherlands	—	States General
India	—	Sansad
Israel	—	Knesset
Iran	—	Majlis
Ireland	—	Airetann
Iceland	—	Althing
Japan	—	Diet
Norway	—	Storting
Russia	—	Supreme Soviet
Spain	—	Cortes
Sweden	—	Riksdag
U.S.A.	—	Congress Senate
Germany	—	Bundestag

MINERAL RESOURCES OF THE WORLD

Mineral	Largest Producers
Iron Ore	China, Japan, Russia
Tin	China, Indonesia, Peru
Lead	China, Australia, U.S.A.
Zinc	China, Australia, Peru
Manganese	South Africa, Brazil, Australia
Aluminium	China, Russia, Canada
Petroleum	Saudi Arabia, Russia, USA
Silver	Peru, Mexico, China
Coal	China, USA, India

WORLD'S LARGEST PRODUCERS

Articles	Producers	Articles	Producers
Carpets	Iran	Cheese	USA
Cocoa	Cote d'Ivoire	Coffee	Brazil
Copper	Chile	Cotton	China
Diamonds	Russia	Jute	India
Rice	China	Rubber	Thailand
Silk	China	Steel	China
Sugar	Brazil	Tea	China
Tin	China	Wheat	China
Wool	Australia		

TEN LARGEST COUNTRIES BY AREAS

Rank by Area	Country	Area (sq. km.)
1.	Russia	17,075,400
2.	Canada	9,976,139
3.	China	9,561,000
4.	U.S.A.	9,363,123
5.	Brazil	8,511,965
6.	Australia	7,686,848
7.	India	3,287,263
8.	Argentina	2,776,889
9.	Kazakhstan	2,724,900
10.	Algeria	2,381,741

PRESIDENT OF INDIA

He is the constitutional head of the Republic but not the real executive.

Qualifications: (1) Indian citizen; (2) age not less than 35 years; (3) should have qualifications for election to Lok Sabha; (4) should not hold any office of profit; (5) should not be a Member of Parliament or State Legislature.

Election: He is elected by the elected Members of Parliament and State Legislative Assemblies in accordance with the system of proportional representation by means of single transferable vote.

Powers: He makes appointment to all the Constitutional posts. He can address either House of Parliament and send message to them. He can summon and prorogue either House of Parliament and dissolve Lok Sabha. All Bills passed by Parliament must receive his assent to become an Act. He issues Ordinance when Parliament is not in session. No money Bill can be introduced in Lok Sabha without his recommendation. He can grant pardon, reprieve or remit punishment and he can commute death sentences. He can declare national emergency, state emergency and financial emergency.

VICE-PRESIDENT OF INDIA

The Vice-President acts as the ex-officio Chairman of Rajya Sabha and acts as the President when the latter is unable to discharge his functions due to illness, absence or any other reason, or till the election of a new President when a vacancy is caused by the death, resignation or removal of the President.

The Vice-President is elected by an electoral college consisting of the members of both Houses of Parliament in accordance with the system of proportional representation by means of the single transferable vote. He must be a citizen of India, not less than 35 years of age, and should be eligible for election as a member of the Council of States.

PRIME MINISTER OF INDIA

The Prime Minister is the leader of the majority party in the Parliament and the President cannot exercise his discretion in the appointment of the Prime Minister. He stays in office till the majority of the members of Lok Sabha has confidence in him. He occupies an important posi-tion in relation to the council of Ministers. He recommends the names of the persons to be included in the Council of Ministers. He allocates portfolios among them and can ask any minister to tender resignation. He can drop a minister while reshuffling the ministry. He coordinates the administration of various departments. He is the chief link between the President and the Council. He is the leader of the majority party and so, he has a great influence on the Parliament and the party. The Prime Minister enjoys such extensive powers as have been described as the virtual ruler of the country.

THE SOLAR SYSTEM: SOME FACTS

Number of Planets: 8—Mercury, Venus, Earth, Mars, Jupiter, Saturn, Uranus and Neptune.

Largest most

Massive planet .... Jupiter

Brightest planet .... Venus

Brightest star .... Sirius

Fastest orbiting planet .... Mercury

Longest (Synodic)
day .... Mercury

Most moons Jupiter-69

Planet with largest
moon .... Jupiter

Greatest average density .... Jupiter

Tallest mountain .... Earth

Strongest magnetic fields .... Jupiter

Most circular orbit .... Venus

Shortest (synodic) day .... Jupiter

Hottest planet .... Venus

No moons .... Mercury, Venus

Planet with moon with
most eccentric orbit .... Neptune

Lowest average density .... Saturn

Deepest Oceans .... Jupiter

Greatest amount of
liquid on the surface .... Earth

THE EARTH: FACTS AND DATA

Composition of the Earth: Aluminium (0.4%), Sulphur (2.7%), Silicon (13%), Oxygen (28%), Calcium (1.2%), Nickel (2.7%), Magnesium (17%), Iron (35%)

Surface area	: 510100500 sq km	Polar Circumference	: 39992 km
Land Surface (29.1%)	: 148950800 sq km	Polar diameter	: 12710 km
Ocean Surface (70.9%)	: 361149700 sq km	Equatorial radius	: 6376 km
Type of water	: 97% salt, 3% fresh	Polar radius	: 6335 km
Total area of water	: 382672000 sq km	Mass (estimated weight)	: 594×10^{19} metric tons
Equatorial diameter	: 12753 km		
Equatorial Circumference	: 40066 km	Mean distance from the Sun	: 149407000 km

Earth's orbit speed (around sun)	: 107320 kmph	Time of Rotation (on its axis)	: 23 hrs 56 min 4.09 seconds
Period of Revolution (round the sun)	: 365 days 5 hrs 48 min. 45.51 seconds	Inclination of the axis (to the plane of the ecliptic)	: 23°27'

PRINCIPAL MOUNTAIN PEAKS OF THE WORLD

	Mountains	Height in Metres	Range	Date of First Ascent
1.	Mount Everest	8,848	Himalayas	May 29, 1953
2.	K-2 (Godwin Austen)	8,611	Karakoram	July 31, 1954
3.	Kanchenjunga	8,597	Himalayas	May 25, 1955
4.	Lhotse	8,511	Himalayas	May 18, 1956
5.	Makalu I	8,481	Himalayas	May 15, 1955
6.	Dhaulagiri I	8,167	Himalayas	May 13, 1960
7.	Mansalu I	8,156	Himalayas	May 9, 1956
8.	Chollyo	8,153	Himalayas	Oct. 19, 1954
9.	Nanga Parbat	8,124	Himalayas	July 3, 1953
10.	Annapurna I	8,091	Himalayas	June 3, 1950
11.	Gasherbrum I	8,068	Karakoram	July 5, 1958
12.	Broad Peak I	8,047	Karakoram	June 9, 1957
13.	Gasherbrum II	8,034	Karakoram	July 7, 1956
14.	Shisha Pangma (Gosainthan)	8,014	Himalayas	May 2, 1964
15.	Gasherbrum III	7,952	Karakoram	Aug. 11, 1975

POPULAR NICK NAMES OF SOME FAMOUS PERSONALITIES

Nick Name	Personality	Nick Name	Personality
Andhra Kesari	T. Prakasam	Lal, Bal, Pal	Lala Lajpat Rai, Bal Gangadhar Tilak, Bipin Chandra Pal
Anna	C.N. Anna Durai		
Bang Bandhu	Sheikh Mujibur Rehman	Little Corporal	Napoleon Bonaparte
Bapu	Mahatma Gandhi	Lokmanya	Bal Gangadhar Tilak
Bard of Avon	William Shakespeare	Mahamana	Pt. Madan Mohan Malaviya
Chachaji	Jawaharlal Nehru	Maid of Orleans	Joan of Arc
Desh Bandhu	C.R. Das	Maiden Queen	Queen Elizabeth I
Frontier Gandhi	Khan Abdul Gaffar Khan	Missile Man	A.P.J. Abdul Kalam
Fuhrer	Adolf Hitler	Man of Destiny	Napoleon Bonaparte
G.B.S.	George Bernard Shaw	Netaji	Subhash Chandra Bose
Grand Old Man of India	Dadabhai Naoroji	Nightingale of India	Sarojini Naidu
Grand Old Man of Britain	Gladstone	Panditji	Jawaharlal Nehru
Guru Dev	Rabindra Nath Tagore	Punjab Kesari	Lala Lajpat Rai
Guruji	M.S. Golwalkar	Shastriji	Lal Bahadur Shastri
Iron Man of India	Sardar Patel	Uncle Ho	Ho Chi Minh
Lok Nayak	Jayaprakash Narayan	Wizard of the North	Walter Scott
Lady with the Lamp	Florence Nightingale		

FAMOUS INTERNATIONAL ORGANISATIONS, HEADQUARTERS AND YEAR OF ESTABLISHMENT

International Organisations	Headquarters	Year of Establishment
United Nations Organisations (U.N.O.)	New York	1945
International Monetary Fund (I.M.F.)	Washington	1945
World Health Organisation (W.H.O.)	Geneva	1948
Food & Agricultural Organisation (FAO)	Rome	1943
International Labour Organisation (ILO)	Geneva	1919
UNESCO	Paris	1946
International Court of Justice	The Hague	—
Universal Postal Union (UPU)	Berne	1874
International Civil Aviation Organisation (ICAO)	Montreal	1947
UNIDO	Vienna	1967
International Atomic Energy Agency (IAEA)	Vienna	1957
International Finance Corporation (IFC)	Washington	1956
United Nations Development Programme (UNDP)	New York	—
UNICEF	New York	1946
International Maritime Organisation (IMO)	London	1948
World Meteorological Organisation (WMO)	Geneva	1951
International Telecommunication Union (ITU)	Geneva	1947
Arab League	Tunis	1945
Commonwealth of Nations	London	1931
World Trade Organisation (WTO)	Geneva	1995
International Development Association (IDA)	Washington D.C.	1960
International Bank for Reconstruction and Development (IBRD)	Washington D.C.	1946
World Intellectual Property Organisation (WIPO)	Geneva	1967
Organisation of Islamic Conference (OIC)	Mecca (Saudi Arabia)	1971
European Economic Community (EEC)	Geneva	1957
Red Cross	Geneva	1863
Interpol	Lyons (France)	1923
Asian Development Bank (ADB)	Manila	1966
North Atlantic Treaty Organisation (NATO)	Brussels	1949
Association of South East Asian Nations (ASEAN)	Jakarta	1967

BHARAT RATNA AWARD WINNERS

1.	Dr. S. Radhakrishnan	1954	17.	K. Kamraj*	1976	33. M.S. Subbalakshmi	1998
2.	C. Rajagopalachari	1954	18.	Mother Teresa	1980	34. C. Subramaniam	1998
3.	Dr. C.V. Raman	1954	19.	Acharya Vinoba Bhave*	1983	35. Jaya Prakash Narayan*	1999
4.	Dr. Bhagwan Das	1955	20.	Khan Abdul Ghaffar Khan	1987	36. Prof. Amartya Sen	1999
5.	Dr. M. Visvesvaraya	1955	21.	M.G. Ramachandran*	1988	37. Pt. Ravi Shankar	1999
6.	Jawaharlal Nehru	1955	22.	Dr. B.R. Ambedkar*	1990	38. Gopinath Bardoloi	1999
7.	Govind Ballabh Pant	1957	23.	Dr. Nelson R. Mandela	1990	39. Lata Mangeshkar	2001
8.	Dr. D.K. Karve	1958	24.	Rajiv Gandhi*	1991	40. Bismillah Khan	2001
9.	Dr. Bidhan Chandra Roy	1961	25.	Sardar Vallabhbhai Patel*	1991	41. Bhimsen Joshi	2008
10.	Purushottam Das Tandon	1961	26.	Morarji R. Desai	1991	42. C.N.R. Rao	2014
11.	Dr. Rajendra Prasad	1962	27.	Maulana Abdul Kalam Azad*	1992	43. Sachin Tendulkar	2014
12.	Dr. Zakir Hussain	1963	28.	Jehangir Ratanji Dadabhai Tata	1992	44. Madan Mohan Malaviya*	2015
13.	Dr. Pandurang Vaman Kane	1963	29.	Satyajit Roy	1992	45. Atal Bihari Vajpayee	2015
14.	Lal Bahadur Shastri*	1966	30.	Gulzari Lal Nanda	1997	46. Nanaji Deshmukh*	2019
15.	Indira Gandhi	1971	31.	Mrs. Aruna Asaf Ali*	1997	47. Bhupen Hazarika*	2019
16.	V.V. Giri	1975	32.	Dr. A.P.J. Abdul Kalam	1998	48. Pranab Mukherjee	2019

* Posthumous

ART AND CULTURE

☞ Classical Dances

Dance	State	Famous Artists
Bharat Natyam	Tamil Nadu	Yamini Krishnamurthy, Rukmini Devi Arundale, Swapna Sundari, Sonal Mansingh, Vaijanti Mala, Mrinalini Sarabhai, Chandralekha, Indrani, Ram Gopal, Bal Saraswati
Kathakali	Kerala	Gopinath, K.K. Nayar, Kunju-Kurup, T.K. Chandu
Kuchipudi	Andhra Pradesh/ Telangana	Sapna Sundari, Raja Reddy, Shobha Nayar, Radha Reddy, Vedantam Satyanarayan, Vimpanti Chinna Satyam.
Kathak	North India	Birju Maharaj, Gopi Krishna, Shambhu Maharaj, Sitara Devi, Vishnu Sharma, Durga Lal, Shobhana Narayan
Odissi	Odisha	Kelucharan Mahapatra, Indrani Rehman, Madhavi Mudgal, Pratima Bedi, Samyukta Panigrahi, Sonal Mansingh, Debudas
Manipuri	Manipur	Uday Shankar, Bipin Singh, Suryamukhi, Darohra Jhaveri

☞ Famous Folk Dances

State	Folk Dance	State	Folk Dance
Andhra Pradesh/ Telangana	Dandari, Banjara	Kerala	Mohini Attam, Padayuni
Assam	Bihu, Keli Gopal, Sataria	Madhya Pradesh	Lota Nritya, Jawara
Bihar	Chhau, Magahi, Durga dance	Maharashtra	Tamasha, Dahi Handi, Gof, Deepak Dindi
W. Bengal	Kirtan, Kalatri, Asweabadh, Brita, Kalidance	Manipur	Dhol Cholam
Chhattisgarh	Saila, Karama, Bhagoria	Meghalaya	Nongakarem
Gujarat	Garba, Rasalila, Tippani, Dandia,	Nagaland	Bamboo dance
		Odisha	Chhau, Maya Shabari, Dalachai
Haryana	Damyal, Lahoor	Punjab	Gidda, Bhangra, Panihari
Himachal Pradesh	Dussehra dance, Hikat, Notio	Rajasthan	Thumar, Kathaputali, Tera Tali
		Tamil Nadu	Terukalathu, Kabalatam, Kargam, Pulivesham
Jammu & Kashmir	Dumhal	Tripura	Hazagiri
Jharkhand	Jhau, Ghumakudia, Jadur, Sarhul, Soharai, Karama, Vaima, Loojhari, Jat-Jatin, Vidayat	Uttar Pradesh	Rasalila, Nautanki, Thali, Dhurang, Jhumela, Huraka, Bol.
		Uttarakhand	Kajari, Karan
Karnataka	Yakshagan, Dolu Kunitha	Goa	Dhode Modini

MUSIC

Main Schools of Classical Music

- There are two main schools of classical music, namely, the Hindustani and the Carnatic. The Hindustani school of classical music is in vogue in north-western India, eastern India and northern parts of the South India.

Musical Instruments

- *They are:* Tabla, Mridangam, Pakhawaj, Chandai, Dholak, Veena, Sitar, Sarod, Gootuvadhyam, Sarangi, Flute, Nadaswaram, Shehnai, Shringi and Turahi.

FAMOUS INTERNATIONAL AIR SERVICES

Air Service	Name of Country	Air Service	Name of Country
Air India	India	Lufthansa Airlines	Germany
British Overseas	Britain	Iraqi Airways	Iraq
Airways Corporation		National Airlines	Iran
Trans World Airlines	America	Quantas Airlines	Australia
Russian Airlines	Russia	Hong-Kong Airlines	Hong-Kong
Japan Airlines	Japan	Egypt Airlines	Egypt
Pakistan International Airlines	Pakistan	Slovak Airlines	Slovakia
Malaysia Airlines	Malaysia	S.I.A.	Singapore
Royal Nepal Airlines	Nepal	Garuda Airways	Indonesia
Swiss Airways	Switzerland	Bangladesh Viman Sewa	Bangladesh
Air France	France	Air Lanka	Sri Lanka
Kuwait Airways	Kuwait	Elitalia Airlines	Italy
Pan American World Airways	America	Air Canada	Canada
K.L.M. Royal Airlines	The Netherlands (Holland)		

FAMOUS RELIGIONS, FOUNDERS, HOLY BOOKS & PLACES OF WORSHIP

Religion	Founder	Holy Books	Place of Worship
Hinduism	Hinduism has no one Founder. (This religion is based upon the religion of original Aryan Settlers)	Ramayan, Vedas, Puranas and Geeta	Temple
Sikh	Guru Nanak Dev	Guru Grantha Sahib	Gurdwara
Christianity	Jesus Christ	Bible	Church
Islam	Prophet Mohammed	Koran (Quran)	Mosque
Parsi	Zoroaster	Zend Avesta	Fire Temple
Jainism	Adinath Rishavdev	Jain Granth	Jain Temple
Buddhism	Gautam Buddha	Tripitaka	Buddha Temple
Jew	Moosa	Torah	Synagogue

INTELLIGENCE AGENCIES OF SOME PROMINENT COUNTRIES

Country	Intelligence Agency	Country	Intelligence Agency
India	Research & Analysis Wing (RAW), Intelligence Bureau (I.B.), Central Bureau of Investigation (C.B.I.)	Russia	K.G.B. (Komitel Gosudarstvennoy Bezopasnosty) (Committee for State Security)
Pakistan	Inter Service Intelligence (I.S.I.)	Canada	Security Intelligence Service
U.S.A.	Central Intelligence Agency, Federal Bureau of Investigation	S. Africa	Bureau of State Security
		Iran	Sabak
Britain	Military Intelligence (M.I.)-5 and 6, Special Branch, Ultra, Joint Intelligence Organisation	Iraq	Al-Mukhabarat
		Australia	Australian Security and Intelligence Organisation
Israel	Mosad		
Egypt	Mukhabarat	France	S.D.E.C.E.
		Spain	C.E.S.I.D.
Japan	Nicho	Cuba	D.G.I.

SOME PROMINENT RACES OF THE WORLD

Races	Country	Races	Country	Races	Country	Races	Country
Veddas	Sri Lanka	Pygmy	Congo Basin	Eskimo	Canada, Tundra Region	Bushman	Kalahari Desert
Somaid	West Siberia	Bantu	Central and South Africa	Lapps	European Tundra	Red Indian	North America
Masai	East Africa						
Muree	New Zealand	Tartars	Siberia				
Yakoot	Russian Tundra	Baddu	Arab's Desert	Hausa	Nigeria		
Papuans	New Guyana	Semang	Malaysia	Kirghiz	Steppes (Russia)		

FAMOUS STRAITS OF THE WORLD

Strait	Between	Country
Malacca Strait	Andaman Sea and South China Sea	Indonesia
Palk Strait	Mannar and Bay of Bengal	India-Sri Lanka
Magellan Strait	Pacific and South Atlantic Ocean	Chile
Dover Strait	English Channel and North Sea	England-France
Berring Strait	Berring Sea and Chukasi Sea	Alaska-Russia
Sugaroo Strait	Japan Sea and Pacific Ocean	Japan
Sunda Strait	Java and Indian Ocean	Indonesia
Gibralter Strait	Mediterranean Sea and Atlantic Ocean	Spain
Harmuj Strait	Persia and Bay of Oman	Oman-Iran
Hudson Strait	Bay of Hudson and Atlantic Ocean	Canada

FAMOUS NEWSPAPERS OF THE WORLD

Newspaper	Place of Publishing	Language	Newspaper	Place of Publishing	Language
Daily News	New York (America)	English	Hindu, Hindustan, Times of India, Tribune, Statesman, Indian Express, Economic Times	India	English
Guardian	London (Britain)	English			
Pravada	Moscow (Russia)	Russian			
Al-Ahram	Cairo (Egypt)	Arabic			
Merdeca	Jakarta (Indonesia)	Indonesian			
Times	London (Britain)	English	Hindustan, Nav Bharat Times, Dainik Bhaskar, Dainik Jagaran, Punjab Kesari	India	Hindi
People's Daily	Beijing (China)	Chinese			
New Statesman	Britain	English			
Daily Mirror	Britain	English			

IMPORTANT BOUNDARY LINES

Boundary Line	Countries	Boundary Line	Countries
Durand Line	Pakistan and Afghanistan	17th Parallel	The line which defined the boundary between North Vietnam and South Vietnam before the two were united.
Hindenberg Line	Germany-Poland		
Maginot Line	France and Germany		
Mannerhein Line	Russia-Finland		
Mc Mahon Line	India-China		
Order Niesse Line	Germany-Poland		
Radcliff Line	India-Pakistan	38th Parallel	North Korea and South Korea
Seigfrid Line	Germany-France		
24th Parallel	India-Pakistan	49th Parallel	U.S.A. and Canada

SIGNALS/SIGNS AND MEANING

Signal/Sign	Meaning	Signal/Sign	Meaning
Red Triangle	Family Planning	White Flag	Treaty or Surrender
Red Cross	Medical Help	Yellow Flag	Vehicles with patients of contagious diseases
Red Light	Danger, 'Stop' for the movement of vehicles	Two Bones across with a Skull	Danger of electricity
Green Light	Go	Half mast flown Flag	National mourning
Olive Branch	Peace	Lotus and culture	Sign of civilization
White Pigeon or Dove	Peace	Wheel (Chakra)	Sign of Progress
Black Strip on Arm	(i) Opposition (ii) Sorrow	A blind folded woman with scale in hand	Sign of Justice
Black Flag	Opposition		
Red Flag	(i) Danger (ii) Revolution	Reversed flown	National calamity flag

NATIONAL EMBLEMS OF IMPORTANT COUNTRIES

Country	National Emblem	Country	National Emblem
America	Golden Rod	New Zealand	Kiwi, Fern Southern Cross
Australia	Kangaroo	Norway	Lion
Ireland	Shamrock	Nepal	Kukri
Italy	White Lily	Pakistan	Crescent
Israel	Candelabrum	Poland	Eagle
Iran	Rose	France	Lily
Canada	White Lily	Belgium	Lion
Great Britain	Rose	Bangladesh	Water Lily
Chile	Candor and Huemul	Mongolia	The Soyombo
Germany	Corn Flower	Russia	Double headed eagle
Japan	Chrysanthemum	Lebanon	Cedar Tree
Zimbabwe	Zimbabwe Bird	Sudan	Secretary Bird
Denmark	Beach	Syria	Eagle
Turkey	Crescent and Star	India	Lioned Capital
The Netherlands	Lion		

THE CONTINENTS OF THE WORLD

Name	Area (In sq. km.)	Population (2017) (In million)	Per cent of the world's population
Asia	4,40,30,000	4,504	59.66
Africa	2,97,85,000	1,256	16.64
Europe	1,04,98,000	742	9.83
North America	2,42,55,000	582	7.71
South America	1,77,98,000	424	5.62
Australia	76,87,120	40.69	0.54
Antarctica	1,33,38,500	NA	NA

COMPUTER

The computer is the system of that electronic device through which various informations are processed on the basis of a definite set of instructions called program and mathematical (numerical) and non-mathematical both types of informations are processed.

The first mechanical computer was composed or fabricated by Blaise Pascal in 1642 and it is called Pascalene. But in 1833, Charles Babbage first time conceived an automatic calculator or computer. Charles Babbage is called the father of modern computer. Herman made an electronic tabulating machine based on punch cards which operates automatically.

In 1937, first mechanical computer mark-I was fabricated by Howard Akeen. The most outstanding contribution in the development of modern computer goes to John Wan Newmaan who brought the 2nd revolution in the area of computer in 1951. He discovered EDVAC (Electronic Discrete Variable Automatic Computer) and utilised the stored program and the binary number system in the computer.

FUNCTIONS OF COMPUTER

1. Collection and composition (input) of datas;
2. Storage of datas.
3. Processing of datas.
4. Retrieval or output of the proccessed informations and datas.

UNITS OF COMPUTER

1. Input unit.
2. Central processing unit–CPU.
3. External Memory unit.
4. Output unit.

The CPU of the computer is called brain of the computer and sometimes CPU is also called Micro Processor of the computer. The data is entered through the input unit in the computer and through the central processing unit with the help of External Memory Unit datas are arranged and processed. Ultimately by the output unit these datas or informations are issued or released.

PARTS OF COMPUTER

- **Monitor :** The monitor of the computer is like a television in which the picture appears in the form of doted points on the screen and these are called pixcels.
- **Hard Disc and Floppy Disc :** The Hard Disc is the permanent disc in the computers while the Floppy Disc is the disc utilised when datas or informations are to be transferred from one computer to another.
- **Mouse :** The mouse of the computer is like the remote control of TV through which computer is directly regulated or controlled without utilising the key-board.
- **Printer :** The printer is a device which prints any documents or processed informations of the computer.

SOME HIGH LEVEL LANGUAGES

1. **FORTRAN :** This language was developed for solving the mathematical formulae very quickly and conveniently.
2. **COBOL :** This language was developed for the commerical purposes. For the processing of this language a group of sentences is selected called paragraph and all paragraphs composed are called a section, while all sections composed are called a division.
3. **BASIC :** In basic a definite part of the prescribed instruction is only inserted in the computer.
4. **ALGOL :** This was basically fabricated and designed for the complex algebraic calculations.
5. **PASCAL :** It is an amplified and modified form of ALGOL.
6. **COMAL :** This computer language is used for the students of secondary level.
7. **LOGO :** This language is used for children and kids for drawing Graphic line diagrams.
8. **PROLOG :** This language is developed in 1973 in France and this language is used for Artificial Intelligence which is capable and equivalent to the logical program.

9. FORTH : This language was invented by Charles Mure which is frequently used in all types of the works in the computer.

COMPUTER VIRUS

The computer virus is an electronic code which is used to abolish or erradicate the inclusive informations or programs of the computer. Some important computer viruses are Micheleanjalo, Dork Avangor, kilo, filip, Macmug, Scores, Casecade, Jeruslem, Date crime, Coloumbs crime, Internet virus, Pachcom, Pach EXE, COM-EXE, Marizuana, C-brain, bloody, Chenge Mungu and Desi etc.

COMPUTER NETWORKING

There are two types of networkings which are usually occur—Local Area Networking (LAN) and Wide Area Networking (WAN). By LAN all the computers of the same buildings are connected like the computers of university premises, computers of offices etc.

By WAN all the comptuers of a large area are connected like the computers of all the offices of a city or town etc. In India a very large computer network namely INDONET has been installing through which all the main towns and cities has to be interlinked.

COMPUTER TERMINOLOGY

- **Bit :** The bit is a unit of measurement of the electronic data. One bit is either 0 or 1 but not both. On composing 8 bits, 1 byte is formed.
- **Bug :** The Bug is the error in the computer program or system and its eradication is called Debug.
- **Byte :** Total eight bits compose a byte. Thus 8 bits = 1 byte.
- **CD-ROM :** A CD like of music CD in which data can be stored substantially called CD-ROM. In a CD with comparison to floppy extremely more datas can be stored but one problem in it is that one time recorded data can not be deleted or modified.
- **Chip :** It is a thin slice on which by a special mechanism a circuit is designed which is normally made from Silicon.
- **Memory System :** The place where computer data and program are temporarily kept is called Memory system. Usually memory is implied from RAM.
- **Modem :** The device which converts digital signals into analogue signals and vice-versa is called Modem.

- **RAM :** It is Random Access Memory (a place) where datas to be processed are kept temporarily and it is unstable memory.
- **ROM :** It is Read Only Memory and it is stable or Non-valatile memory which doesn't ended after power off.
- **Scanner :** It is a device through which graphic image is transformed to digital image and the scanners are of usually two types one desktop and another hand operating.

PROGRAMING

Computers perform phenomenal feats of calculation, but they do not do so in a complicated way. They actually carry out very simple operations, such as addition and subtraction. They achieve their fantastic computing power by carrying out these operations at incredible speed.

The programme, or set of instructions for operating the computer, is therefore written as a sequence of very simple steps. (See box below) Several computer languages have been developed for different applications, including BASIC, COBOL, FORTRAN and PASCAL. Writing programmes is very skilled and time-consuming work. But for most typical computer applications ready-written programmes are available, called "packages".

☞ **How A Programme Works**

Without a programme to tell it what to do and how to do it, a computer is unable to function. If, for example, you wanted to know how many times the word 'the' appears in this paragraph, or in the whole book, it would not be enough merely to put the text into a computer and then ask it how many times the word appears. For the computer to accomplish the calculations it has to be told what to do in simple steps. The instructions might be:

1. Scan the text until a space followed by 'T' or 't' is found.
2. If the next letter is not 'h', go back to step 1.
3. If the letter is 'h', is the next letter 'e'?
4. If not, go back to step 1. If it is, go to step 5.
5. If 'e' is followed by a space, add 1 to the total.
6. Go back to step 1.

A full computer programme for this operation would need to be broken down into even more simple steps, but a series of such programmes could enable a computer to analyse any amount of text in great detail.

DEFENCE

The Supreme Command of the Armed Forces is vested in the hands of the President of the Country. The responsibility for national defence, however, rests with the Cabinet. All important questions having a bearing on defence are decided by the Cabinet Committee on Political Affairs, which is presided over by the Prime Minister. The Defence Minister is responsible to Parliament for all matters concerning the Defence Services. All the administrative and operational control of Armed Forces are exercised by the Ministry of Defence. The three services – Army, Navy and Air Force function through their respective service headquarters headed by the chief of Staff.

COMMISSIONED RANKS IN DEFENCE SERVICES

Army	Navy	Air Force
General	Admiral	Air Chief Marshal
Lieutenant-General	Vice-Admiral	Air Marshal
Major-General	Rear-Admiral	Air Vice-Marshal
Brigadier	Commodor	Air Commodor
Colonel	Captain	Group Captain
Lieutenant-Colonel	Commander	Wing Commander
Major	Lt.Commander	Squadron Leader
Captain	Lieutenant	Flight Lieutenant
Lieutenant	Sub-Lieutenant	Flying Officer

INTERNAL SECURITY ORGANISATIONS OF INDIA

S. No	Name of Organisation	Year of Creation	Headquarters
1.	Assam Rifles (A.R.)	1835	Shillong
2.	Central Reserve Police Force (C.R.P.F.)	1939	New Delhi
3.	National Cadet Corps (N.C.C.)	1948	New Delhi
4.	Territorial Army	1948	In different States
5.	Indo-Tibetan Border Police	1962	New Delhi
6.	Home Guard	1962	In different States
7.	Coast Guard	1978	New Delhi
8.	Border Security Force (B.S.F.)	1965	New Delhi
9.	Central Industrial Security Force (C.I.S.F.)	1969	New Delhi
10.	National Security Guard	1984	New Delhi
11.	Police	—	In different States

COMMANDER-IN-CHIEFS OF INDIA

1. General Roy Bucher   Jan. 1, 1948 — Jan. 14, 1949
2. General K. M. Kariappa   Jan. 15, 1949 — Jan. 14, 1953
3. General Maharaj Rajendra Sinhji   Jan. 15, 1953 — March 31, 1955
4. First Marshal of the Indian Air Force Arjan Singh

FIRST CHIEFS OF STAFF OF INDIAN FORCES

1. General Maharaj Rajendra Sinhji (Army Staff)   April 1, 1955 — May 14, 1955
2. Vice Admiral R.D. Katari (Naval Staff)   April 22, 1958 — June 4, 1962
3. Air Marshal Sri Thomas Elmherst (Air Staff)   Aug. 15, 1947 — Feb. 21, 1950

ARMY INSTITUTES

1. Sainik Schools upto +2 Level — 18 places in India
2. Rashtriya Indian Military College (prepare for entrance to N.D.A) — Dehradun
3. National Defence Academy (three services) — Khadakwasla, Pune
4. Indian Military Academy (Army) — Dehradun
5. Officers Training Academy (3 services) Short Courses — Chennai
6. National Defence College — New Delhi
7. The College of Combat — Mhow
8. The College of Military Engineering — Kirkee
9. Military College of Telecommunication Engineering — Mhow
10. The armoured Corps Centre and School — Ahmed Nagar
11. The School Artillery — Deolali
12. The Infantry School — Mhow and Belgaum
13. College of Material Management — Jabalpur

AIR FORCE INSTITUTIONS

Air Force Academy	Hyderabad
Helicopter Training School	Hakimpet
Flying Instructors School	Tambaram, Chennai
The College of Air Warfare	Secunderabad
Air Force Administrative College	Coimbatore
Air Force Technical College	Jalahalli

DEFENCE PRODUCTION UNITS

1. Bharat Dynamites Ltd. — Hyderabad
2. Praga Tools — Hyderabad
3. Mishra Dattu Nigam — Hyderabad
4. Bharat Electronics Ltd. — Bangalore
5. Bharath Earthmovers Ltd. — Bangalore
6. Heavy Vehicles Ltd. — Avadi, Chennai
7. Garden Reach Ship Builders and Engineers Ltd. — Kolkata
8. Mazagaon Dock — Mumbai
9. Goa Shipyard — Marmugao
10. Hindustan Shipyard Ltd. — Vishakhapatnam
11. Hindustan Aeronautics Ltd. — Bangalore, Hyderabad, Nasik, Koraput, Kanpur, Lucknow

☞ Indian Army Commands

Command	HQ Location	Command	HQ Location
Eastern Command	Kolkata	Western Command	Chandigarh
Northern Command	Udhampur	Southern Command	Pune
Central Command	Lucknow	Training Command	Shimla
South-Western Command	Jaipur		

☞ Indian Air Force Commands

Command	HQ Location	Command	HQ Location
Western Air Command	New Delhi	South-Western Air Command	Gandhinagar
Central Air Command	Allahabad	Eastern Air Command	Shillong
Southern Air Command	Thiruvananthapuram	Training Command	Bengaluru

☞ Indian Navy Commands

Command	HQ Location	Command	HQ Location
Eastern Naval Command	Vishakhapatnam	Western Naval Command	Mumbai
Southern Naval Command	Cochin		

☞ Missile and Other Weapons

Name	Class	Range	Name	Class	Range
∗ Agni I	SRBM	850 km	∗ Brahmos	Supersonic Cruise Missile	290 km
∗ Agni II	MRBM	2500 km			
∗ Agni III	IRBM	3500 km-5500 km	∗ Brahmos 2	Hypersonic Cruise Missile	290 km
∗ Agni IV *or* Agni II Prime	IRBM	4000 km	∗ Prithvi I	SRBM	150 km
			∗ Prithvi III	SRBM	350 km
∗ Agni V	ICBM	5000 km-6000 km	∗ Sagarika	SLBM	700 km-2200 km
∗ Agni VI	ICBM	8000 km-10000 km	∗ Shaurya	TBM	700 km-2200 km
∗ Agni 3SL	ICBM	5200 km-11600 km	∗ Astra	Air to Air Missile	80 km-100 km
∗ Dhanush	SRBM	350 km			
∗ Nirbhay	Subsonic Cruise Missile	1000 km	∗ Barak-I	SRSAM	12 km
			∗ Barak-8	SRSAM	90 km

MULTIPLE CHOICE QUESTIONS

1. Match List-I with List-II and select the correct answer from the codes given below the lists:
   List-I
   (*a*) Napoleon Bonaparte
   (*b*) Jean Jacques Rousseau
   (*c*) Croce
   (*d*) Madame Roland
   List-II
   1. 'A history is contemporary history'
   2. 'Liberty what crimes are committed in thy name'
   3. 'Man is born free but everywhere he is in chains.'
   4. 'I am the Child of Revolution'
   Codes :

	(a)	(b)	(c)	(d)
A.	1	2	3	4
B.	4	3	1	2
C.	3	4	2	1
D.	3	4	1	2

2. Abraham Lincon was elected the President of United States in:
   A. 1862   B. 1860
   C. 1875   D. 1855

3. Who was known as the 'Prince of Humanists'?
   A. Francisco Petrarch   B. Dante
   C. Boccacio   D. Erasmus

4. D-Day is the day when:
   A. Germany declared war on Britain
   B. US dropped the atom bomb on Hiroshima.
   C. Allied Troops landed in Normandy
   D. Germany surrendered to the allies

5. Whose teachings inspired the French Revolution?
   A. Locke
   B. Rousseau
   C. Hegel
   D. Plato

6. At a time when empires in Europe were crumbling before the might of Napoleon which one of the following Governor-Generals kept the British flag flying high in India?
   A. Warren Hastings   B. Lord Cornwallis
   C. Lord Wellesley   D. Lord Hastings

7. Which one of the following statements regarding Fascism in Italy is *not* true?
   A. The Fascists came to power as a result of popular uprising
   B. In 1926, all political parties except Mussolini's party were banned
   C. The Fascists suppressed the Socialist movement
   D. The Fascists were hostile to the Communists

8. The fall of Czar Nicholas-II is known as:
   A. Bloody Sunday
   B. Bolshevik Revolution
   C. February Revolution
   D. October Revolution

9. Industrial Revolution took place first in:
   A. France   B. Germany
   C. United Kingdom   D. Japan

10. The British Prime Minister at the outbreak of World War II was :
    A. Churchill   B. Baldwin
    C. Attlee   D. Chemberlain

11. The 'Great Depression' (1929) economic crisis was met by adopting the policy of
    A. Stimulus   B. Marshall Plan
    C. New Deal   D. Open Door

12. The slogan "No taxation without representation" was raised during the:
    A. American War of Independence
    B. Russian Revolution
    C. French Revolution
    D. Indian Freedom struggle

13. In the nineteenth century the people of Europe started moving from the villages to the cities due to the impact of :
A. Epidemics
B. War
C. Industrialisation
D. Population explosion in villages

14. The important cause of the Civil War in America was:
A. Abolition of slavery
B. Quest for freedom
C. Industrialisation
D. Rebellion by the native Americans

15. Industrial Revolution could not have come about without:
A. Merchant capitalism
B. The Enclosure Movement
C. The services of the proletariat class
D. An agricultural revolution

16. Consider the following statements :
The French Revolution came about mainly due to the :
1. Extreme poverty of the people
2. Impact of the works of great writers
3. Cruelty of the rulers
4. Impact of impulsive reaction
Which of the above statements are correct?
A. 1, 2 and 4   B. 2 and 3
C. 1, 3 and 4   D. 1, 2, 3 and 4

17. Asia's oldest and largest Buddhist monastery is situated in :
A. Tawang (Arunachal Pardesh)
B. Lhasa (Tibet)
C. Trincomallee (Sri Lanka)
D. Ulan Bator (Mongolia)

18. Who was the main architect of the Russian Revolution?
A. Karl Marx   B. Lenin
C. Stalin   D. Tolstoy

19. V.I. Lenin is associated with :
A. Russian Revolution of 1917
B. Chinese Revolution of 1949
C. German Revolution
D. French Revolution of 1789

20. Which one of the following statements is *not* correct?
A. Voltaire believed in Natural Religion
B. Rousseau wrote *Social Contract*
C. Montesquieu authored *The Spirit of Laws*
D. Necker believed in 'General Will'

21. 6th April, 1930 is well known in the history of India because this date is associated with............
A. Dandi March by Mahatma Gandhi
B. Quit India Movement
C. Partition of Bengal
D. Partition of India

22. Which ruler enforced the system of 'Price Control' in India?
A. Mohammad Tughlak
B. Razia Begum
C. Alauddin Khilji
D. Sher Shah Suri

23. The concept of 'Din-e-Elahi' was founded by which king?
A. Dara Shikoh   B. Akbar
C. Sher Shah Suri   D. Shahjahan

24. Who are supposed to be the earliest inhabitants of India? Where did they come from?
A. Aryans from Central Asia
B. Dravidians from Mediterranean
C. Negroids from Africa
D. Bhils and the Santhals from West Asia

25. The one chief characteristic of temple architecture of the Gupta Age was :
A. Absence of dome
B. Huge size
C. Beautiful carvings
D. absence of a covered courtyard for the gathering of worshippers

26. The Rigveda consists of :
A. 1000 hymns   B. 2028 hymns
C. 1028 hymns   D. 1038 hymns

27. The central point in Ashoka's dharma was :
A. royalty to kings
B. peace and non-violence
C. respect to elders
D. religious tolerance

28. The social evil which was conspicuously absent during ancient India was :
A. *Sati*-System
B. *Devadasi*-System
C. Polygamy
D. *Purdah*-System

29. Which, among the following, can be accepted as a novelty introduced by Mughal emperors to their buildings?
A. Domes
B. Minarets
C. Arches
D. Attached gardens

30. The first ruler of India who defeated Muhammud of Ghur was :
A. Mularaja II of Gujarat
B. Prithviraja Chauhan of Delhi
C. Jayachand of Kannauj
D. Parmaldeva of Bundelkhand

31. What important event happened in India in 1911?
A. Bengal was partitioned
B. Non-Cooperation movement was launched
C. India's capital was shifted from Calcutta to Delhi
D. Mahatma Gandhi presided over the Congress session

32. The first phase of the Congress Party (1885-1905) was characterized by its efforts to secure:
A. limited independence
B. complete freedom
C. Indianization of services
D. constitutional reforms

33. The Muslim League demanded a separate homeland for the Indian Muslims openly for the first time at its annual session held in Lahore in the year :
A. 1931 A.D.
B. 1936 A.D.
C. 1940 A.D.
D. 1941 A.D.

34. Under whose governorship did the East India Company secure the Diwani Rights in Bengal, Bihar and Odisha from Emperor Shah Alam?
A. Lord Cornwallis
B. Lord William Bentinck
C. Lord Clive
D. Lord Wellesley

35. The Simon Commission was generally boycotted by the Indian political parties. What was the reason for this general non-cooperation?
A. the Commission aimed at dividing the people
B. it was an 'all white' Commission
C. it came after the Jallianwala Bagh carnage
D. it was an eye wash

36. Aligarh Muslim University was founded by :
A. Dr. Saifuddin Kitchlu
B. Mohammad Ali Jinnah
C. Sir Syed Ahmed Khan
D. Maulana Mohammad Ali

37. Ibn Batutah was an African traveller visiting India during the time of :
A. Alivardi Khan
B. Ala-ud-din Khalji
C. Iltutmish
D. Mohammad-bin-Tughlaq

38. The battle of Wandiawash was fought in :
A. 1726
B. 1760
C. 1818
D. 1857

39. The abolition of *Sati* by government regulation was at the time of :
A. Warren Hastings
B. Lord Wellesley
C. Lord Bentinck
D. Lord Ahmerst

40. Pick out the wrong combination :
A. Dilwara Temple : Mt. Abu
B. Pashupati Temple : Kathmandu
C. Padmanabh Temple : Bangalore
D. Minakshi Temple : Madurai

41. Match the following:
(a) Chanhudaro
(b) Kalibangan
(c) Lothal
(d) Surkotada
1. Alleged discovery of the skeleton of horse.
2. Bead making.
3. Traces of a dock and ship on seal.
4. Evidence of ploughing the fields.
The Correct code is :

	(a)	*(b)*	*(c)*	*(d)*
A.	2	4	3	1
B.	2	1	3	4
C.	1	2	3	4
D.	2	1	4	3

42. Match the Harappan settlements with the banks of rivers on which they were located :

(a) Harappa		1. Ravi
(b) Mohenjodaro		2. Indus
(c) Ropar		3. Sutlej
(d) Kalibangan		4. Ghaggar
(e) Lothal		5. Bhogava

Codes :

	(a)	(b)	(c)	(d)	(e)
A.	1	2	3	4	5
B.	1	2	3	5	4
C.	2	1	3	5	4
D.	2	1	4	3	5

43. The Goddess 'Kannagi' whose many temples were erected during the 'Sangam Age' was the goddess of :
A. Chastity   B. Love
C. Prowess   D. Wisdom

44. The Jain goal of life is to attain deliverance from the fetters of mudane existence, the way to which lies through three jewels. Which one of the following was not included among the 'three jewels' of Jainism?
A. Right faith   B. Right action
C. Right knowledge D. Right conduct

45. The most striking feature of the Ashokan pillar is polish. Name the Ashokan pillar which is considered to be the most graceful of all Ashokan pillars.
A. Sarnath
B. Rampurva
C. Laurya-Nandangarh
D. Rummindei

46. Which are the correct statements?
1. The land grants, started in Satavahana period, paved the way for feudal developments in India.
2. Silk and spices were the Chief Indian export articles of Indo-Roman trade.
3. The Guptas issued the largest number of gold coins in ancient India.
4. The first memorial of a 'SATI' dated 510 A.D. is found at Eran in Madhya Pradesh.
A. 1 and 2   B. 1, 3, and 4
C. 1 and 4   D. 1, 2, 3 and 4

47. Who among the following patronised the 'Gandhara' (Indo-Greek style) School of Art?
A. Ashoka, the Great
B. Harsha Vardhana
C. Kanishka
D. Chandragupta Vikramaditya

48. The Sultanate of Delhi had five ruling dynasties. The dynasty having longest and shortest period were :
A. Ilbari and Khalji
B. Tughlaq and Khalji
C. Tughlaq and Sayyid
D. Ilbari and Lodis

49. Which one of the following events took place at the last during reign of Muhammad-bin-Tughlaq?
A. Introduction of token currency
B. Increase of land-revenue in Doab
C. Transfer of Capital from Delhi to Devagiri.
D. Conquest of Khurasan and Iraq

50. The most learned medieval Muslim ruler who was well versed in various branches of learning including astronomy, mathematics and medicine was :
A. Jalaluddin Khilji
B. Sikander Lodi
C. Ghiyasuddin Tughlaq
D. Muhammad-bin-Tughlaq

51. The 'Sufis' had 12 silsilas. They propounded the idea of Union with God through:
A. Love   B. Rituals
C. Fasts   D. Prayers

52. Match the following:

(a) Peshwa	1. Foreign affairs
(b) Panditrao	2. Audit and accounts
(c) Amatya	3. Providing grants to scholars
(d) Sumant	4. General supervision
	5. Military affairs

Select the correct code :

	(a)	(b)	(c)	(d)
A.	2	3	4	5
B.	4	1	2	3
C.	4	3	2	1
D.	3	1	4	2

53. The Regulating Act of 1773 can be regarded as the first measure to :
A. assert the right of British Parliament to legislate for India
B. separate the legislature from the executive
C. separate the judiciary from the executive
D. centralise law-making

54. What was the exact constitutional status of the Indian Republic on 26th January, 1950?
A. A Democratic Republic
B. A Sovereign, Democratic Republic
C. A Sovereign, Secular, Democratic Republic
D. A Sovereign, Socialist, Secular, Democratic Republic

55. When the British obtained the grant of Diwani of Bengal, Bihar and Odisha they acquired the right to :
A. maintain law and order in these territories
B. administer civil justice and collect revenue in these territories
C. collect revenue and establish revenue administration in these territories
D. militarily defend these territories

56. Which of the following were responsible for the growth of nationalism in India during the British rule?
1. Economic exploitation of India.
2. Impact of western education.
3. Role of the Press.
Select the correct answer using the codes given below :
Codes:
A. 1, 2 and 3
B. 1 and 2
C. 2 and 3
D. 1 and 3

57. Which one of the following nationalist leaders has been described as being radical in politics but conservative on social issues?
A. G.K. Gokhale
B. B.G. Tilak
C. Lala Lajpat Rai
D. Madan Mohan Malviya

58. Provincial Autonomy in British India was envisaged by the :
A. Act of 1909
B. Act of 1919
C. Act of 1935
D. Act of 1947

59. Dyarchy means :
A. double government
B. a government in which the centre is very powerful
C. a government based on division of power between centre and provinces
D. None of the above

60. The Indian National Congress observed 'Independence Day' for the first time on 26th January in :
A. 1920
B. 1925
C. 1930
D. 1947

61. ....is situated near the banks of Sabarmati River
A. Bhavnagar
B. Aurangabad
C. Ahmedabad
D. Rajkot

62. Sericulture is:
A. science of the various kinds of serum
B. artificial rearing of fish
C. art of silkworm breeding
D. study of various cultures of a community

63. The most abundant constituents of earth's crust are:
A. Igneous rocks
B. Sedimentary rocks
C. Metamorphic rocks
D. Granite

64. Indian Standard Time is based on:
A. $80°E$ longitude
B. $82\frac{1}{2}°E$ longitude
C. $110°E$ longitude
D. $25°E$ longitude

65. Tides in the oceans are caused by :
A. Gravitational pull of the moon on the earth's surface including sea water
B. Gravitational pull of the sun on the earth's surface only and not on the sea water
C. Gravitational pull of the moon and the sun on the earth's surface including the sea water
D. None of these

66. Nagarjunasagar Project is situated on the river:
A. Tungabhadra
B. Cauvery
C. Krishna
D. Godavari

67. The difference between the Indian Standard Time and the Greenwich Mean Time is:
    A. − 3½ hours   B. + 3½ hours
    C. − 5½ hours   D. + 5½ hours

68. Which of the following dams is not on Narmada river?
    A. Indira-Sagar Project
    B. Maheshwar Hydel Power Project
    C. Jobat Project
    D. Koyna Power Project

69. Which of the following statements is **not true** about the availability of water on the earth, the crisis for which is going to increase in the years to come?
    A. About 97.5 per cent of the total volume of water available on the earth is salty
    B. 80 per cent of the water available to us for use comes in bursts as monsoons
    C. About 2.5 per cent of the total water available on the earth is polluted water and cannot be used for human activities
    D. Possibility is that some big glaciers will melt in the coming ten-fifteen years and sea level will rise by 3-4 metres all over the earth

70. Which of the following is **not** a cash crop?
    A. Jute   B. Paddy
    C. Cashewnut   D. Sugarcane

71. Through which States does Cauvery River flow?
    A. Gujarat, M.P., Tamil Nadu
    B. Karnataka, Kerala, Tamil Nadu
    C. Karnataka, Kerala, Andhra Pradesh
    D. M.P., Maharashtra, Tamil Nadu

72. Indian Standard Time is the local time of 82½°E which passes through :
    A. Guntur   B. Delhi
    C. Allahabad   D. Kolkata

73. The 17th parallel defines the boundary between:
    A. North and South Korea
    B. USA and Canada
    C. North and South Vietnam
    D. China and Russia

74. During the period of south-west monsoon, Tamil Nadu remains dry because:
    A. the winds do not reach this area
    B. there are no mountains in this area
    C. it lies in the rain shadow area
    D. the temperature is too high to let the winds cool down

75. Which country does top in producing cocoa?
    A. Cote d'Ivoire   B. Brazil
    C. Ivory Coast   D. Nigeria

76. The biggest reserves of thorium are in :
    A. India   B. China
    C. The Soviet Union   D. U.S.A.

77. The Girnar Hills are situated in which of the following states?
    A. Gujarat   B. Karnataka
    C. Madhya Pradesh   D. Maharashtra

78. During December 22nd the sun is vertically over:
    A. Tropic of Cancer
    B. Tropic of Capricorn
    C. The Equator
    D. None of the above

79. Photosphere is described as the :
    A. Lower layer of atmosphere
    B. Visible surface of the sun from which radiation emanates
    C. Wavelength of solar spectrum
    D. None of the above

80. Broadly, there are three layers of the earth of the crust, the mantle and the core. The crust forms what percentage of the volume of the earth?
    A. 0.5%   B. 2.5%
    C. 7.5%   D. 12.5%

81. The grassland of Argentina is known as :
    A. Pampas   B. Campos
    C. Savanna   D. None of the above

82. Different seasons are formed because :
    A. Sun is moving around the earth
    B. of revolution of the earth around the Sun on its orbit
    C. of rotation of the earth around its axis
    D. All of the above

83. Eskers and Drumlins are features formed by:
A. underground water
B. running water
C. the action of wind
D. glacial action

84. Match List-I and List-II and select the correct answer using the codes given below the Lists :

List-I *(Rivers)*	List-II *(Towns)*
(a) Ghaghara	1. Lucknow
(b) Brahmaputra	2. Hoshangabad
(c) Narmada	3. Ahmedabad
(d) Sabarmati	4. Guwahati
	5. Ayodhya

	(a)	*(b)*	*(c)*	*(d)*
A.	4	5	1	2
B.	5	4	2	3
C.	5	4	3	1
D.	3	5	2	1

85. Which of the statements as regards the consequences of the movement of the earth is not correct?
A. Revolution of the earth is the cause of the change of seasons.
B. Rotation of the earth is the cause of days and nights.
C. Rotation of the earth causes variation in the duration of days and nights.
D. Rotation of the earth effects the movement of winds and ocean currents.

86. The world is divided into :
A. 12 time zones
B. 20 time zones
C. 24 time zones
D. 36 time zones

87. The 'Kiel' canal links the :
A. Pacific and Atlantic Oceans
B. Mediterranean Sea and Red Sea
C. Mediterranean Sea and Black Sea
D. North Sea and Baltic Sea

88. Match the following :

List-I	List-II
(a) Himadri	1. Outer Himalayas
(b) Shivalik	2. Inner Himalayas
(c) Himanchal	3. Middle Himalayas
(d) Sahyadri	4. Western Ghats

Codes:

	(a)	*(b)*	*(c)*	*(d)*
A.	1	2	3	4
B.	4	2	3	1
C.	2	1	3	4
D.	1	2	3	4

89. The term 'Regur' refers to:
A. Laterite soils
B. Black Cotton soils
C. Red Soils
D. Deltaic Alluvial Soils

90. Location of sugar industry in India is shifting from north to south because of:
A. cheap labour
B. expanding regional market
C. cheap and abundant supply of power
D. high yield and high sugar content in sugarcane

91. Consider the following statements :
1. Ozone is found mostly in the Stratosphere.
2. Ozone layer lies 55-75 km above the surface of the earth.
3. Ozone absorbs ultraviolet radiation from the Sun.
4. Ozone layer has no significance for life on the earth.
Which of the above statements are correct?
A. 1 and 3 B. 2 and 4
C. 2 and 3 D. 1 and 4

92. Match List-I with List-II and select the correct answer using the codes given below the Lists :

List-I *(Crops)*	List-II *(Producer)*
(a) Banana	1. Brazil
(b) Cocoa	2. Cote d'Ivoire
(c) Coffee	3. India
(d) Tea	4. China

Codes :

	(a)	*(b)*	*(c)*	*(d)*
A.	2	3	1	4
B.	3	2	1	4
C.	3	2	4	1
D.	2	3	4	1

93. Darjeeling and Dharamsala would be the right places to visit if one wanted to get a clear view respectively of :
A. Kanchanjunga and Dhauladhar ranges
B. Nandadevi and Dhauladhar ranges
C. Kanchanjunga and Nandadevi ranges
D. Nandadevi and Nanga Parvat

94. Atmosphere exists because:
A. The Gravitational force of the Earth
B. Revolution of the Earth
C. Rotation of the Earth
D. Weight of the gases of atmosphere

95. Victoria lake is located in the continent:
A. Africa
B. Asia
C. North America
D. South America

96. The famous Lagoon Lake of India is :
A. Dal Lake   B. Chilka Lake
C. Pulicat Lake   D. Mansarover

97. Where are most of the earth's active volcanoes concentrated?
A. Indian Ocean   B. Pacific Ocean
C. Aral Sea   D. Atlantic Ocean

98. Through which of the following states does the river Chambal flow?
A. U.P., M.P., Rajasthan
B. M.P., Gujarat, U.P.
C. Rajasthan, M.P., Bihar
D. Gujarat, M.P., U.P.

99. Which country is called the sugar bowl of the world?
A. Cuba   B. India
C. Argentina   D. USA

100. The area covered by forest in India is about:
A. 46%   B. 33%
C. 23%   D. 21.54%

101. A closed economy is the one which :
A. does not permit emigration or immigration
B. permits emigration but no immigration
C. engages in no foreign trade
D. engages in no foreign and domestic trade or transit

102. In a developed economy the major share of employment originates in the :
A. primary sector   B. tertiary sector
C. secondary sector   D. any of the above

103. The Economic and Social Commission for Asia and Pacific (ESCAP) is located at :
A. Bangkok   B. Kuala Lumpur
C. Manila   D. Singapore

104. Commercial vehicles are not produced by which of the following companies in India?
A. TELCO   B. Ashok Leyland
C. DCM Daewoo   D. Birla Yamaha

105. In India, the Public Sector is most dominant in:
A. transport
B. steel production
C. commercial banking
D. organised term-lending financial institutions

106. The main argument advanced in favour of small scale and cottage industries in India is that:
A. cost of production is low
B. they require small capital investment
C. they advance the goal of equitable distribution of wealth
D. they generate a large volume of employment

107. The most serious economic problems of India are:
A. Poverty and unemployment
B. Stagnation, not poverty
C. Unemployment, not poverty
D. Underdevelopment, not poverty

108. Which of the following is not one of the three central problems of an economy?
A. What to produce
B. How to produce
C. When to produce
D. For whom to produce

109. If saving exceeds investment, the national income will:
A. fall   B. rise
C. fluctuate   D. remain constant

110. In which of the following industries in India are the maximum number of workers employed?
A. Sugar
B. Jute
C. Textiles
D. Iron and Steel

111. Terrace Cultivation is practiced mostly:
A. in urban areas
B. on slopes of mountains
C. on tops of hills
D. in undulating tracts

112. Which of the following is a Selective Credit Control method?
A. Bank Rate
B. RBI directives
C. Cash Reserve Ratio
D. Open market operations

113. Which of the following taxes is not shared by the Central Government with the States?
A. Union excise duties
B. Customs duty
C. Income tax
D. Estate duty

114. ICICI is the name of a:
A. Financial Institution
B. Chemical Industry
C. Cotton Industry
D. Chamber of Commerce and Industry

115. Structural Unemployment arises due to
A. Deflationary conditions
B. Heavy industry bias
C. Shortage of raw material
D. Inadequate productive capacity

116. Which of the following is the largest single source of the government's earning from tax revenue?
A. Excise duties
B. Customs duties
C. Corporation tax
D. Income tax

117. The largest public sector bank in India is:
A. Central Bank of India
B. Punjab National Bank
C. State Bank of India
D. Indian Overseas Bank

118. Which of the following statements best explains the term contraband goods?
A. Goods produced only for exports
B. Goods produced in joint sector only
C. Goods for the trading of which licence is not required
D. Goods that are forbidden, from export, import or even possession, by law

119. Price in the market is fixed by:
A. Stock exchange rates
B. The demand and supply ruling in the market at a particular time
C. The Finance Minister
D. None of the above

120. Devaluation of currency helps to promote:
A. National Income
B. Savings
C. Imports at lower cost
D. Exports

121. Balanced economic growth can be achieved only if:
A. All the sectors of economy grow at the same rate
B. Population growth is arrested
C. All the inter dependent sectors grow in harmony
D. Basic and heavy industries are assigned highest priority

122. Which one of the following contributes most to the National Income in India?
A. Agricultural Sector
B. Industrial Sector
C. Foreign Trade Sector
D. Tertiary Sector

123. 'MODVAT' stands for:
A. Ad Valorem tax on output
B. Deduction of cost of inputs from the value of output
C. Reduction in import duties
D. Imposition of tax on professions

124. Largest revenue in India is obtained from:
A. Excise duties
B. Corporation tax
C. Income tax
D. None of the above

125. The term 'devaluation' means:
    A. Reducing the value of a currency in terms of another currency
    B. Increasing the value of a currency
    C. Revising the value of a currency
    D. None of the above

126. Per capita net availability of pulses has shown a tendency of:
    A. Increase over time
    B. Decrease over time
    C. Constant over time
    D. First increase then decrease

127. National Income is the same as:
    A. Net national product at market price
    B. Net domestic product at market price
    C. Net national product at factor cost
    D. Net domestic product at factor cost

128. Which one of the following is not an example of indirect tax?
    A. Sales tax   B. Excise duty
    C. Customs duty   D. Expenditure tax

129. The major aim of devaluation is to:
    A. encourage imports
    B. encourage exports
    C. encourage both exports and imports
    D. discourage both exports and imports

130. Structural unemployment arises due to:
    A. deflationary conditions
    B. heavy industry bias
    C. shortage of raw materials
    D. inadequate productive capacity

131. When was the Family Planning Programme officially started in India?
    A. 1950   B. 1952
    C. 1956   D. 1962

132. When was the Reserve Bank of India nationalised?
    A. 1947   B. 1949
    C. 1950   D. 1951

133. Which of the following is *not* a feature of the Indian economy?
    A. High rate of population growth
    B. Disguised unemployment
    C. Lowest rate of adult literacy
    D. High rate of exports

134. The 'Relative Deprivation' approach for measuring poverty has been adopted by:
    A. developing countries
    B. developed countries
    C. under-developed countries
    D. None of the above

135. One of the main factors that led to rapid expansion of Indian exports is:
    A. Imposition of import duties
    B. Liberalisation of the economy
    C. Recession in other countries
    D. Diversification of exports

136. Sustainable economic development means an increase in the rate of growth of real:
    A. total and per capita product
    B. total and per capita product and level of literacy rate
    C. total and per capita product and life expectancy at birth
    D. total and per capita product, taking into account the cost of degradation of the quality of environment in this process

137. Functional unemployment occurs when:
    A. unemployed have no qualification for job
    B. people frequently change their job
    C. people were thrown out from job due to recession
    D. None of these

138. Which among the following does **not** have a 'free trade zone'?
    A. Kandla   B. Mumbai
    C. Visakhapatnam   D. Thiruvanantpuram

139. Sun Belt of USA is important for which one of the following industries?
    A. Cotton textile
    B. Petrochemicals
    C. Hi-tech electronics
    D. Food Processing

140. Commercial banking system in India is
    A. unit banking   B. branch banking
    C. mixed banking   D. None of the above

141. Who gives recognition to political parties in India?
    A. Parliament

B. President
C. Supreme Court
D. Election Commission

142. The Quorum of the Legislative Council is :
A. one-fourth of its total membership
B. one-third of its membership
C. one-tenth of its membership
D. 25

143. The Indian Constitution is:
A. federal
B. unitary
C. a happy mixture of the federal and unitary
D. federal in normal times and unitary in times of emergency

144. Universal adult franchise implies a right to vote to all:
A. adult residents of the State
B. adult male citizens of the State
C. residents of the State
D. adult citizens of the State

145. When a resolution prefering a charge against the President has been passed by a specified majority in the House, it is sent to the other House for investigation. If, as a result of such an investigation, a resolution is passed through a specified majority by the other House, declaring that the charge has been sustained, the President shall leave his office. The specified special majority must not be less than :
A. two-third of the members present and voting
B. one-third of the members present and voting
C. three-fourth of the members present and voting and two-third of the total membership
D. two-third of the total membership

146. Which one of the following judicial powers of the President of India has been *wrongly* listed?
A. he appoints the Chief Justice and other judges of the Supreme Court
B. he can remove the judges of the Supreme Court on grounds of misconduct

C. he can consult the Supreme Court on any question of law or fact which is of public importance
D. he can grant pardon, reprieves and respites to persons punished under Union Law

147. The Vice-president of India can be removed from his office before the expiry of his term if :
A. the Rajya Sabha passes a resolution by a majority of its members and the Lok Sabha agrees with the resolution
B. if the Supreme Court of India recommends his removal
C. the President so desires
D. None of the above

148. The Chief Justice of a High Court in India is appointed by the :
A. Governor of the State
B. Prime Minister of India
C. Chief Justice of the Supreme Court
D. President of India

149. Which of the following statements is constitutionally not true about the passing of the Union Budgets, Railway Budgets and Finance Bill in India?
1. Under the law, Finance Bill should be adopted by both the Houses of the Parliament within 45 days of its introduction.
2. If the Finance Bill is not adopted within specified period, the government loses its authority to levy the taxes proposed in the budgets.
3. In the absence of full budget, a vote-on-account gives the power to the government to spend.
4. Government cannot raise revenues without a proper approval of the Finance Bill
A. Only 2   B. Only 3
C. Only 4   D. Only 1, 2 and 3

150. Normally, on whose advice the President's Rule is imposed in a State?
A. Chief Minister
B. Legislative Assembly
C. Governor
D. Chief Justice of High Court

151. Which Article of the Indian Constitution deals with Amendment procedure?
A. Article 368
B. Article 358
C. Article 367
D. All of these

152. Government is the agency through which the will of :
A. the state is expressed
B. the people is expressed
C. the head of the state is expressed
D. the majority is expressed

153. In a unitary system of government :
A. The centre is all powerful
B. The centre is weaker than the states
C. The centre and states stand at par
D. The states and centre are supreme in their respective spheres

154. In Cabinet System of Government the real executive authority rests with :
A. The Council of Ministers
B. The Prime Minister
C. The Constitution
D. The Parliament

155. The Head of the State under a parliamentary government:
A. is an elected representative
B. is a hereditary person
C. is a nominated person
D. may be any one of the above

156. In the event of a ministerial proposal being defeated on the floor of the legislature, under the parliamentary system :
A. the government waits for a general no-confidence motion
B. the minister concerned is taken to task by the Prime Minister
C. the minister is forced to resign
D. the whole Council of Ministers resign

157. The "due process of law" is an essential characteristic of the judicial system of:
A. UK
B. France
C. USA
D. India

158. Under the Constitution it is :
A. obligatory for the President to accept the advice of the Council of Ministers but is not obliged to follow it
B. obligatory for the President to accept the advice of the Council of Ministers
C. not obligatory for the President to seek or accept the advice of the Council of Ministers
D. obligatory for the President to seek the advice of the Council of Ministers if his own party is in power

159. Which one of the following statements is correct?
A. the Presiding Officer of Rajya Sabha is elected every year
B. the Presiding Officer of Rajya Sabha is elected for a term of two years at a time
C. the Presiding Officer of Rajya Sabha is elected for a term of six years
D. the Vice-President of India is the ex-officio Presiding Officer of Rajya Sabha

160. The introduction of "no confidence" motion in the Lok Sabha requires the support of at least:
A. 50 members
B. 70 members
C. 60 members
D. 80 members

161. The High Court comes under :
A. State List
B. Union List
C. Concurrent List
D. None of the above

162. Which one of the following has been wrongly listed as a Fundamental Duty of the Indian citizens?
A. to develop scientific temper, humanism and spirit of inquiry and reform
B. to work for raising the prestige of the country in the international sphere
C. to protect and improve the natural environment
D. to strive towards excellence in all spheres of individual and collective activity

163. Which one of the following is not a Fundamental Duty as outlined in Article 51A of the Constitution?
A. to abide by the Constitution and respect its ideals
B. to defend the country and render national service when called upon to do so

C. to work for the moral upliftment of the weaker sections of society
D. to preserve the rich heritage

164. The main characteristics of the Directive Principles of State Policy given in the Indian Constitution are :
A. not enforceable by any court
B. fundamental in the governance of the country
C. 'Like instruments, instructions, political manifesto and a code of moral precepts which have to guide governors of the country'
D. no law can be passed, which is opposed to these principles

165. Of the following which are true?
A. In a State, the Legislative Council is dominant with regard to non-financial bills and the Legislative Assembly with regard to financial (money) bills
B. Vidhan Parishad can virtually block legisla-tion even if the same is passed by the Vidhan Sabha
C. In case of a tie between the two Houses, the Governor is duty-bound to call a joint session of the two Houses to have the issue settled on a majority verdict
D. If a Bill is twice approved by the Vidhan Sabha, it becomes law even if rejected by the Vidhan Parishad

166. Which one of the following types of emergency can be declared by the President?
A. Emergency due to threat of war and external aggresion
B. Emergency due to break-down of constitu-tional machinery in a State
C. Financial emergency on account of threat to the financial credit of India
D. all the three emergencies

167. The chairman of which of the following parliamentary committees is invariably from the members of ruling party?
A. Committee on public undertakings
B. Public accounts committee
C. Estimates committee
D. Committee on delegated legislation

168. Which of the following is not a formally prescribed device available to the members of parliament?
A. Question hour
B. Zero hour
C. Half-an-hour discussion
D. Short duration discussion

169. Which of the following is not a tool of executive control over public administration?
A. Power of appointment and removal
B. Line agencies
C. Appeal to public opinion
D. Civil services code

170. If the Speaker of the State Legislative Assembly decides to resign, he should submit his resignation to the:
A. Judges of the High Court
B. Deputy Speaker
C. Chief Minister
D. Finance Minister

171. The Constitution of India provides for the nomination of two members of Lok Sabha by the President to represent:
A. the Parsis
B. men of eminence
C. the business community
D. the Anglo-Indian community

172. India is a Federal State because of:
A. dual judiciary
B. dual citizenship prevalent here
C. share of power between the Centre and the States
D. rigid Constitution

173. Residuary Subjects are those subjects which are:
A. contained in the State list
B. contained in the Union list
C. contained in the Concurrent list
D. not covered by any of the three lists

174. Which of the following writs can be issued, by the Supreme Court, to enforce Fundamental Rights?
A. Writ of Habeas Corpus
B. Writ of Mandamus
C. Writ of Quo Warranto
D. All of these

175. When the offices of both the President and the Vice-President of India are vacant, who will discharge their functions?
A. Prime Minister
B. Home Minister
C. Chief Justice of India
D. The Speaker

176. The Supreme Court tenders advice to the President of India on a matter of law or fact:
A. on its own
B. only when such advice is sought
C. only if the matter relates to some basic issue
D. only if the issue poses a threat to the unity and integrity of the country

177. Six months shall **not** intervene between two sessions of the Indian Parliament because :
A. it is the customary practice
B. it is the British convention followed in India
C. it is an obligation under the Constitution of India
D. None of the above

178. The States of the Indian Union can be recognised or their boundaries altered by:
A. the Union Parliament by a simple majority in the ordinary process of legislation
B. two-thirds majority of both the Houses of Parliament
C. two-thirds majority of both the Houses of Parliament and the consent of the legislatures of concerned States
D. an executive order of the Union government with the consent of the concerned State governments

179. The Basic Feature theory of the Constitution of India was propounded by the Supreme Court in the case of :
A. Minerva Mills Vs. Union of India
B. Golaknath Vs. State of Punjab
C. Maneka Gandhi Vs. Union of India
D. Keshavananda Vs. State of Kerala

180. Which one of the following writs is issued by a court in case of illegal detention of a person?
A. Habeas corpus
B. Mandamus
C. Certiorari
D. Quo-warranto

181. Name the instrument with the help of which a sailor in a submarine can see the objects on the surface of the sea.
A. Telescope
B. Periscope
C. Gycroscope
D. Stereoscope

182. 'HEMOPHILLIA' is the disease of ....
A. liver
B. blood
C. brain
D. bones

183. Vitamin A is abundantly found in ....
A. Brinjal
B. Tomato
C. Carrot
D. Cabbage

184. .... is not soluble in water.
A. Vitamin A
B. Vitamin B
C. Vitamin C
D. None of these

185. The blood vessels with the smallest diameter are called ....
A. capillaries
B. arterioles
C. venules
D. lymphatics

186. Out of the following .... has the greatest elasticity.
A. steel
B. rubber
C. aluminium
D. annealed copper

187. Cooking gas is a mixture of which of the following two gases?
A. Carbon Dioxide and Oxygen
B. Butane and Propane
C. Carbon Monoxide and Carbon Dioxide
D. Methane and Ethylene

188. The substance most commonly used as a food preservative is:
A. sodium carbonate
B. tartaric acid
C. acetic acid
D. benzoic acid

189. Normally, the substances that fight against diseases in human systems are known as:
A. dioxyribonucleic acids
B. carbohydrates
C. enzymes
D. antibodies

190. The SI unit of temperature is ....
A. Kelvin
B. Celsius
C. Fahrenheit
D. None of the above

191. One of the common fungal diseases of man is :
A. plague
B. ringworm
C. cholera
D. typhoid

192. A clear sky is blue because:
A. red light is scattered more than blue
B. ultraviolet light has been absorbed
C. blue light is scattered more than red
D. blue light has been absorbed

193. Jenner introduced the method of making people immune to :
A. small pox   B. rabies
C. cholera   D. polio

194. The largest cell in the human body is :
A. Nerve cell   B. Live cell
C. Muscle cell   D. Kidney cell

195. What is the device that steps up or steps down the voltage?
A. Dynamo   B. Conductor
C. Inductor   D. Transformer

196. The protein deficiency disease is known as :
A. Kwashiorker   B. Cirrhosis
C. Eczema   D. Clycoses

197. Iron deficiency causes :
A. rickets   B. anaemia
C. cirrhosis   D. goitre

198. Blood group of an individual is controlled by :
A. Haemoglobin   B. Shape of RBC
C. Shape of WBC   D. Genes

199. In a normal man the amount of blood pumped out by the heart per minute is about :
A. 1 litre   B. 3 litres
C. 4 litres   D. 5 litres

200. Red/green colour blindness in man is known as :
A. Protanopia
B. Deutetanopia
C. Both A and B above
D. Marfan's syndrome

201. The blue colour of the water in the sea is due to :
A. Reflection of the blue light by the impurities in sea water
B. Reflection of the blue sky by sea water and scattering of blue light by water molecules
C. Absorption of other colours by water molecules
D. None of the above

202. The image formed on the retina of the eye is:
A. upright and real
B. larger than the object
C. small and inverted
D. enlarged and real

203. Unit of loudness of sound is:
A. bel   B. decibel
C. phon   D. none of these

204. Oil rises up the wick in a lamp :
A. because oil is volatile
B. due to the capillary action phenomenon
C. due to the surface tension phenomenon
D. because oil is very light

205. The 'stones' formed in human kidney consist mostly of :
A. calcium oxalate
B. sodium acetate
C. magnesium sulphate
D. calcium

206. We hear the sound later, while the light is seen earlier:
A. because light's speed is more than that of sound
B. because lights travel in a straight direction while sound in a zigzag direction
C. because sound's frequency is lower than light
D. All of the above

207. Which part of an eye is transplanted?
A. Cornea   B. Retina
C. Iris   D. Sciera

208. The Universal donor group of blood is:
A. O   B. A
C. B   D. AB

209. The green colour of the leaf is due to :
A. Presence of Chloroplast
B. Presence of Chromium
C. Presence of Nicoplast
D. Presence of excess of oxygen

210. Voice of a child is more shrill than that of an elderly person because:
A. the pitch of the child's voice is higher than that of the person
B. the pitch is lower
C. the child is more energetic
D. None of the above

ANSWERS

1	2	3	4	5	6	7	8	9	10
B	C	D	C	B	C	A	C	C	D

11	12	13	14	15	16	17	18	19	20
C	A	C	A	A	D	A	B	A	D

21	22	23	24	25	26	27	28	29	30
A	C	B	C	D	C	B	D	D	B

31	32	33	34	35	36	37	38	39	40
C	D	C	C	B	C	D	B	C	C

41	42	43	44	45	46	47	48	49	50
A	A	A	B	C	D	C	B	B	D

51	52	53	54	55	56	57	58	59	60
A	C	A	B	B	A	B	C	A	C

61	62	63	64	65	66	67	68	69	70
C	C	B	B	C	C	D	D	D	B

71	72	73	74	75	76	77	78	79	80
B	C	C	C	A	A	A	B	B	A

81	82	83	84	85	86	87	88	89	90
A	B	D	B	C	C	D	C	B	D

91	92	93	94	95	96	97	98	99	100
A	B	A	A	A	B	B	A	A	D

101	102	103	104	105	106	107	108	109	110
C	B	A	D	D	D	A	C	D	C

111	112	113	114	115	116	117	118	119	120
B	B	B	A	D	A	C	D	B	D

121	122	123	124	125	126	127	128	129	130
C	A	A	B	A	D	C	D	B	D

131	132	133	134	135	136	137	138	139	140
B	B	D	A	B	D	B	D	D	C

141	142	143	144	145	146	147	148	149	150
D	C	D	D	D	B	A	D	C	C

151	152	153	154	155	156	157	158	159	160
A	B	A	A	A	D	C	B	D	A

161	162	163	164	165	166	167	168	169	170
B	B	C	B	D	D	C	B	B	B

171	172	173	174	175	176	177	178	179	180
D	C	D	D	C	B	C	A	D	A

181	182	183	184	185	186	187	188	189	190
B	B	C	A	A	A	B	D	D	A

191	192	193	194	195	196	197	198	199	200
B	C	A	A	D	A	B	D	D	A

201	202	203	204	205	206	207	208	209	210
B	B	B	B	A	A	A	A	A	A

1904

GENERAL INTELLIGENCE AND REASONING

SERIES

Directions : *In each of the following series determine the order of the letters. Then from the given options select the one which will complete the given series.*

1. BMK, DLM, FKO, HJQ, ?
   - A. JIR
   - B. JIT
   - C. JHS
   - D. JIS

2. A, CD, FGH, ?
   - A. IJKL
   - B. KLMN
   - C. JKLM
   - D. LMNO

3. BXJ, ETL, HPN, KLP, ?
   - A. PHR
   - B. NIR
   - C. NHR
   - D. MHR

4. PUF, QVG, RWH, ?
   - A. SXI
   - B. SYZ
   - C. SXJ
   - D. SVI

5. DEF, HIJ, MNO, ?
   - A. RTV
   - B. STU
   - C. PTU
   - D. SRU

Directions : *Which of the following groups of letters will complete the given series?*

6. ab---b-bbaa-
   - A. babba
   - B. abaab
   - C. abbab
   - D. baaab

7. aa-ab--aaa-a
   - A. baaa
   - B. abab
   - C. aaab
   - D. aabb

8. -baa-aab-a-a
   - A. baab
   - B. abab
   - C. aaba
   - D. aabb

9. -a cca-ccca-acccc-aaa
   - A. ccaa
   - B. acca
   - C. caac
   - D. caaa

10. c-bbb--abbbb-abbb-
    - A. abccb
    - B. bacbb
    - C. aabcb
    - D. abacb

Directions : *In the following questions, select the number(s) from the given options for completing the given series.*

11. 3, 9, 27, 81, 243, ?
    - A. 486
    - B. 729
    - C. 972
    - D. 359

12. 1, 6, 12, 19, 27, ?
    - A. 38
    - B. 35
    - C. 36
    - D. 54

13. 2, 6, 14, 30, 62, ?
    - A. 126
    - B. 128
    - C. 120
    - D. 130

14. 8, 48, 16, 96, 32, ?
    - A. 192
    - B. 150
    - C. 64
    - D. 288

15. 2, 8, 14, 24, 34, 48, ?
    - A. 66
    - B. 62
    - C. 58
    - D. 64

Directions : *In the given series find the number which is wrong.*

16. 5, 25, 120, 625, 3125, 15625
    - A. 15625
    - B. 625
    - C. 120
    - D. 5

17. 4, 8, 11, 22, 18, 36, 24, 50
    - A. 8
    - B. 22
    - C. 36
    - D. 24

18. 2, 4, 12, 24, 72, 142, 432
    - A. 432
    - B. 12
    - C. 142
    - D. 72

19. 2, 3, 4, 4, 6, 8, 9, 12, 16
    - A. 3
    - B. 9
    - C. 6
    - D. 12

20. 97, 91, 86, 83, 79, 77, 76, 76
    - A. 86
    - B. 76
    - C. 91
    - D. 83

4

ANSWERS

1	2	3	4	5	6	7	8	9	10
D	C	C	A	B	D	C	B	D	A

11	12	13	14	15	16	17	18	19	20
A	B	A	A	B	C	A	C	B	D

SOME SELECTED EXPLANATORY ANSWERS

1. The letters in one group correspond to the letters in the next group in the manner +2, –1, +2 respectively.

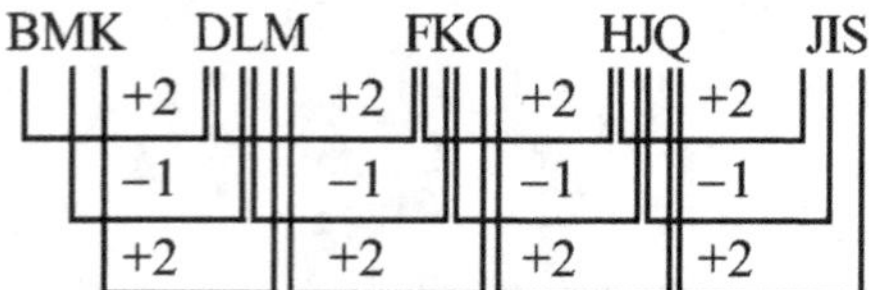

2. The letters are in natural sequence and from one group to the next one letter is dropped. Also the number of letters in groups is increased by one.

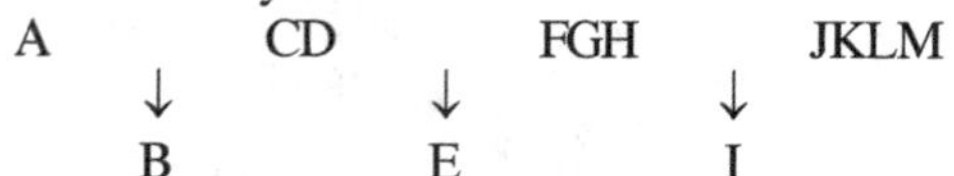

3. The letters in one group correspond to the letters in the next group in the manner +3, – 4, +2 respectively, *i.e.,*

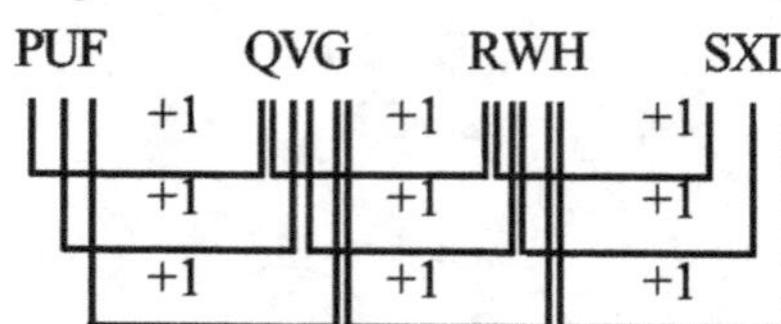

4. The three letters in each group are moved one step forward.

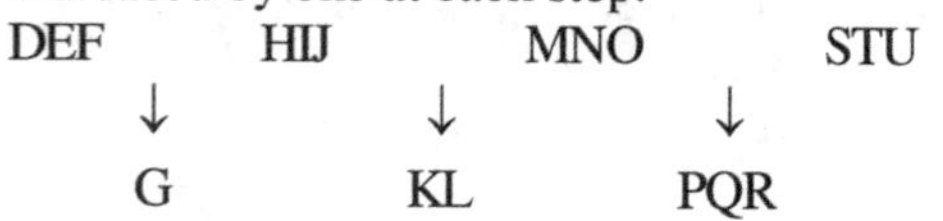

5. The letters are in natural order. The number of letters dropped in between the groups is increased by one at each step.

DEF	HIJ	MNO	STU
↓	↓	↓	
G	KL	PQR	

6. The series is abbaab, abbaab

7. The series is aaaaba, aaaaba

8. The series is aba, aba, aba, aba

9. The series is c,a,cc,aa, ccc, aaa, cccc, aaaa

10. The series is cabbbb, cabbbb, cabbbb

11. The numbers in the series are multiplied by 3 to get the next numbers.

12. The difference between the numbers in the series increases by 1, after beginning from 5, *i.e.,*

1	6	12	19	27	36
+5	+6	+7	+8	+9	

13. The difference between the numbers in the series doubles each time, after beginning from 4, *i.e.,*

2	6	14	30	62	126
+4	+8	+16	+32	+64	

14. *Explanation I* : The sequence in the series is × 6, ÷ 3 which is repeated.

8	48	16	96	32	192
×6	÷3	×6	÷3	×6	

Explanation II : There are two alternate series and the numbers are multiplied by 2.

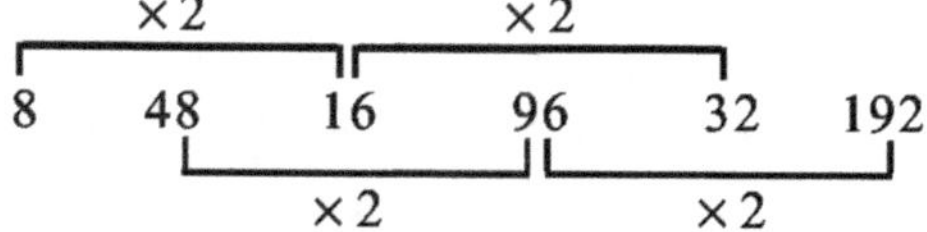

Series I : 8, 16, 32
Series II : 48, 96, 192

15. The sequence in the series is :

2	8	14	24	34	48	62
+6	+6	+10	+10	+14	+14	

The difference increases by 4 at alternate step.

16. The numbers in the series are multiplied by 5 to get the next number.

∴ 125 should be in place of 120.

17. Two numbers form a pair. The first number increases by 7 for the next pair and the second number is the double of first number.

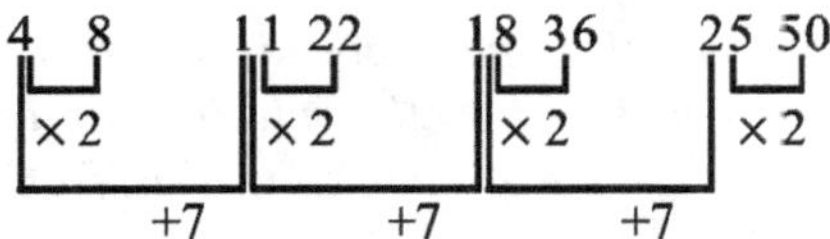

∴ 25 should be in place of 24.

18. There are two alternate series and in each series, the numbers are multiplied by 6 to get the next number.

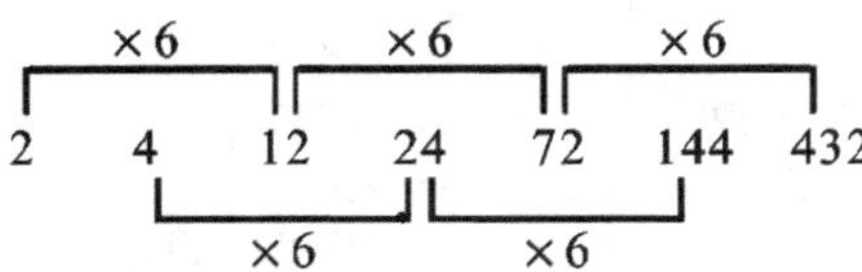

∴ 144 should be in place of 142.

19. There are three alternate series and in each series, the numbers are multiplied by 2 to get the next number.

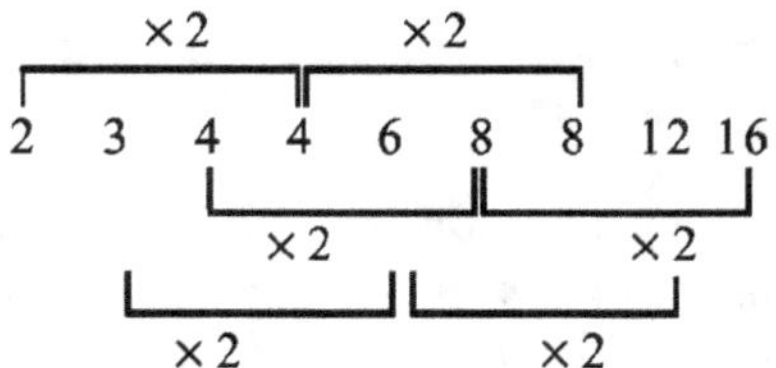

Series I : 2, 4, 8
Series II : 3, 6, 12
Series III : 4, 8, 16

∴ 8 should be in place of 9.

20. The difference between the consecutive numbers in the series decreases by 1 at each step.

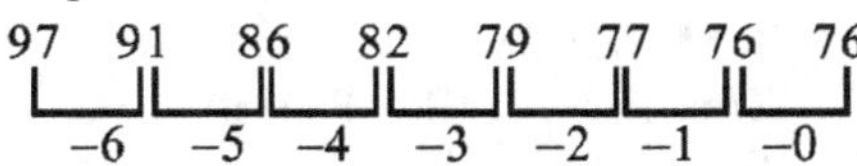

∴ 82 should be in place of 83.

ANALOGIES OR RELATIONSHIPS

1. ADULT : BABY : : FLOWER : ?
   - A. Seed
   - B. Bud
   - C. Fruit
   - D. Butterfly
2. WRITER : READER : : PRODUCER : ?
   - A. Creator
   - B. Contractor
   - C. Creature
   - D. Consumer
3. ENTRANCE : EXIT : : LOYALTY : ?
   - A. Treachery
   - B. Patriotism
   - C. Fidelity
   - D. Reward
4. MOTHER : MATERNAL : : FATHER : ?
   - A. Eternal
   - B. Detrimental
   - C. Paternal
   - D. Formidable

5. GFC : CFG : : RPJ : ?
   - A. JRP
   - B. JPR
   - C. PJR
   - D. RJP
6. BCF : DEG : : MNQ : ?
   - A. OPR
   - B. PQS
   - C. OPP
   - D. QRT
7. NATION : ANITNO : : HUNGRY : ?
   - A. HNUGRY
   - B. UNHGYR
   - C. YRNGUH
   - D. UHGNYR
8. SSTU : MMNO : : AABC : ?
   - A. GGHH
   - B. IJKK
   - C. XXYZ
   - D. NOOP

ANSWERS

1	2	3	4	5	6	7	8
B	D	A	C	B	A	D	C

SOME SELECTED EXPLANATORY ANSWERS

1. The youngone of an adult is a baby and that of a flower is a bud.
2. A writer aims to please the readers by his writings, a producer aims to please the consumers by his products.
3. The related words are opposites.
4. Relations on the mother's side are maternal and on the father's side paternal.
5. The letters of the first group are reversed.

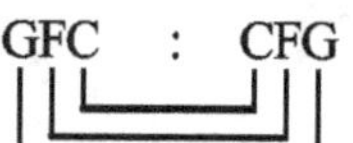

6. The three letters are moved 2, 2 and 1 steps forward respectively.

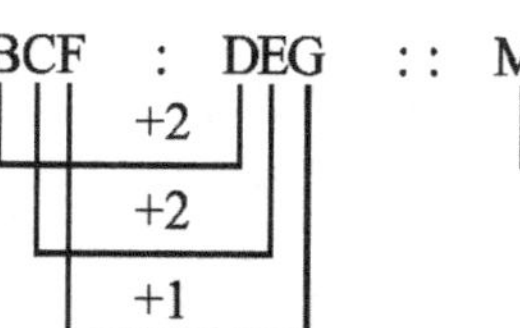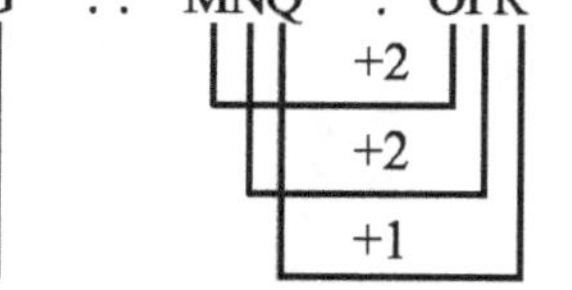

7. The word is divided in sections of two letters and the letters are reversed.

8. The first letter in each group is repeated and followed by two consecutive letters.

ODD ONE OUT

Directions : *Three of the following four in each question are alike in a certain way and so form a group. Select the group of letters that does not belong to that group.*

1. A. ACE   B. LOR
   C. GIK   D. VXZ

2. A. TSR   B. LKJ
   C. PQO   D. HGF

3. A. EF LM   B. KJ SR
   C. XW HG   D. ED YX

4. A. JOPK   B. BOPC
   C. QOPR   D. TOPS

5. A. DfH   B. MoQ
   C. UwY   D. lnO

6. A. JKkL   B. OPpQ
   C. DEEf   D. VWwX

7. A. BdfH   B. FHJL
   C. RTvX   D. uVwX

8. A. DFHEG   B. TWXUV
   C. OQSPR   D. JLNKM

9. A. FEUV   B. DCXW
   C. BAZY   D. HGTS

10. A. UTSR   B. XYZW
    C. ONML   D. IHGF

ANSWERS

1	2	3	4	5	6	7	8	9	10
B	C	A	D	D	C	D	B	A	B

SOME SELECTED EXPLANATORY ANSWERS

1. The sequence in each group is +2. Only option B has sequence in +3, *i.e.,*

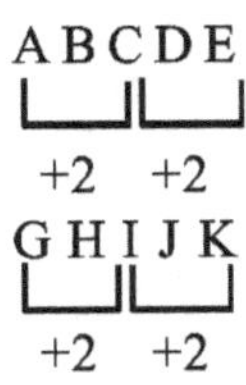

2. The sequence of alphabet in each group is in reverse order. Only option C has sequence in disturbed order.

3. Two consecutive alphabet in each group are in reverse sequence (–1), *i.e.,*

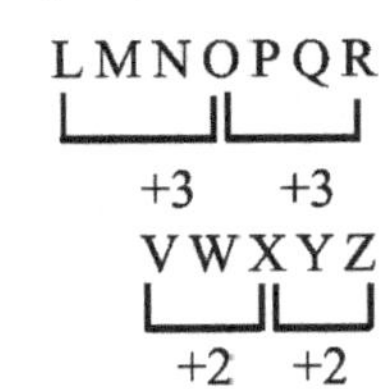

Only in option (A) the sequence is in natural order (+1), *i.e.,*

4. In each group, letters 'OP' are common. The two corner alphabet are in natural order (+1); *i.e.,*

JOPK ;   BOPC ;   QOPR
  +1   +1   +1

Only in option (D) they are in reverse order (–1); *i.e.,*

TOPS
 –1

5. In other groups, only the alphabet in the centre is of lower case. In this option letter 'L' on the left is also in lower case.

6. In other groups, the third letter which is a repeat of the second alphabet is in lower case.

7. In each group, the sequence of the alphabet, irrespective of the case, is +2; *i.e.,*

$$B\ D\ f\ H\ ;\quad F\ H\ J\ L\ ;\quad R\ T\ v\ X$$
$$+2\ +2\ +2\qquad +2\ +2+2\qquad +2\ +2\ +2$$

Only in option (D) the sequence is in natural order (+1), *i.e.,*

$$u\ V\ w\ X$$
$$+1\ +1\ +1$$

8. In each group; the alphabet at positions-first, fourth, second, fifth and third, form a natural sequence.

In option (B), the alphabet at positions first, fourth, fifth, second and third, form the natural sequence.

9. In each group, two alphabets in the corner and two alphabets in the centre correspond to their reverse order positioned alphabet. *i.e.,*

natural order → A B C D E F G H I J K L M
reverse order → Z Y X W V U T S R Q P O N
natural order → N O P Q R S T U V W X Y Z
reverse order → M L K J I H G F E D C B A

As such—

D corresponds with W and
C corresponds with X.
B corresponds with Y and
A corresponds with Z.
H corresponds with S and
G corresponds with T.

Similarly,

F should correspond with U and
E should correspond with V;
i.e. letters 'UV' should be written as 'VU'

10. In each group, the alphabet are in reverse order. In option (B), the order is disturbed.

————————

CODING AND DECODING

Directions : *In the following questions select the right option which indicates the correct code for the word or letter given in the question.*

1. If CHAIR is coded as FKDLU then RAID is coded as :
   - A. ULGD
   - B. ULKG
   - C. ULDG
   - D. UDLG

2. If CONDEMN is coded as CNODMEN, then TEACHER is coded as :
   - A. TEACHER
   - B. TAEECHR
   - C. TCAEEHR
   - D. TAECEHR

3. In a code language COME is written as XLNV and ABLE as ZYOV. How will MOLLY be written in that code?
   - A. NLOBO
   - B. NLBOO
   - C. LNOOB
   - D. NLOOB

4. In a certain code PROFESSION is written as EFORPNOISS. In the same code DICTIONARY will be written as :
   - A. YRANOITCID
   - B. ITCIDYRANO
   - C. ITCIDYRNAO
   - D. ITCDIYARNO

5. JUNE is coded as NXPF, how will STAY be coded in the same manner?
   - A. WWCZ
   - B. WVCZ
   - C. WWDB
   - D. VWZC

Directions : *In the following questions study the coded patterns and then select the right option from the given alternatives.*

6. In a certain language, (a) 'go ju mi' stands for 'plenty of money'; (b) pao ju go nei vu' for 'money creates lots of problems'; (c) 'kol vu nei' for 'problems create tension'; and (d) 'sol tun ju haw' for 'still money is needed'. Which of the following words stand for 'money'?
   - A. nei
   - B. ju
   - C. haw
   - D. go

7. In a certain language, (a) 'FOR' stands for 'old is gold'; (b) 'ROT' stands for 'gold is pure'; (c) 'ROM' stands for 'gold is costly'. How will 'pure old gold is costly' be written?
   - A. TFROM
   - B. FOTRM
   - C. FTORM
   - D. TOMRF

8. In a certain code '415' means 'milk is hot'; '18' means 'hot soup'; and '895' means 'soup is tasty'. What number will indicate the word 'tasty'?
   - A. 9
   - B. 8
   - C. 5
   - D. 4

9. In a certain code '643' means 'she is beautiful', '593' means 'he is handsome', and '567' means 'handsome meets beautiful'. What number will indicate the word 'meets'?
   - A. 5
   - B. 3
   - C. 7
   - D. 6

10. In a certain code language, (a) 'dugo hui mul zo' stands for 'work is very hard'; (b) 'hui dugo ba ki' for 'Bingo is very smart'; (c) 'nano mul dugo' for 'cake is hard', and (d) 'mul ki qu' for 'smart and hard'. Which of the following words stand for 'Bingo'?
    - A. jalu
    - B. dugo
    - C. ki
    - D. ba

ANSWERS

1	2	3	4	5	6	7	8	9	10
D	D	D	B	A	B	A	A	C	D

SOME SELECTED EXPLANATORY ANSWERS

2. In this word, the second and third letters interchange their places and the fifth and sixth letters do the same. Other letters retain their position.

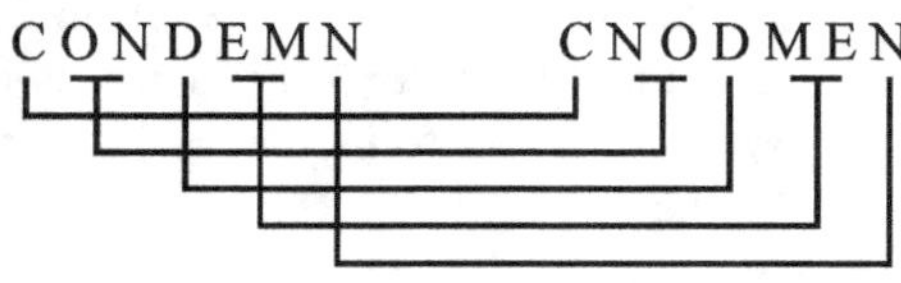

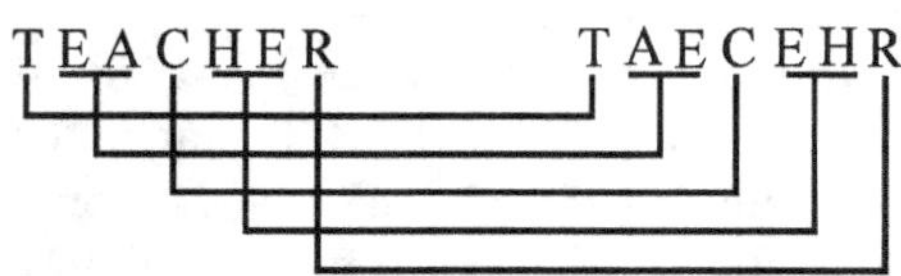

3. The letters of the word are coded by their represented letters in the reverse series.

C	O	M	E	→	letters in natural series
X	L	N	V	→	letters in reverse series
↓	↓	↓	↓		
3rd	15th	13th	5th	→	position of letters
A	B	L	E	→	letters in natural series
Z	Y	O	V	→	letters in reverse series
↓	↓	↓	↓		
1st	2nd	12th	5th	→	position of letters

Similarly,

M	O	L	L	Y	→	letters in natural series
N	L	O	O	B	→	letters in reverse series
↓	↓	↓	↓	↓		
13th	15th	12th	12th	25th	→	position of letters

4. The word is divided into two equal parts and the letters of each part are written backwards.

Similarly,

5. The word is coded by moving the letters +4, +3, +2, and +1 steps respectively.

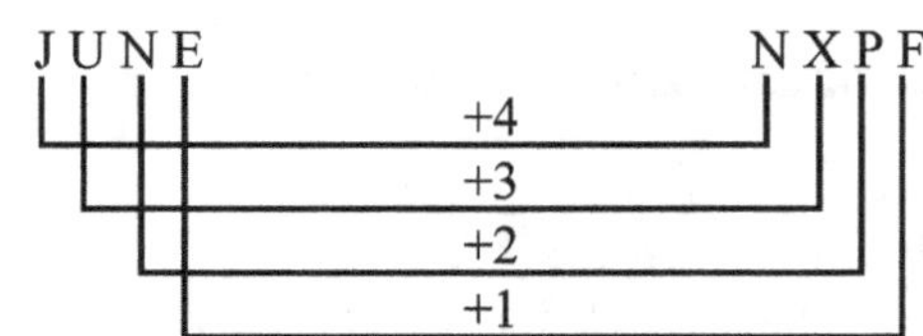

Similarly,

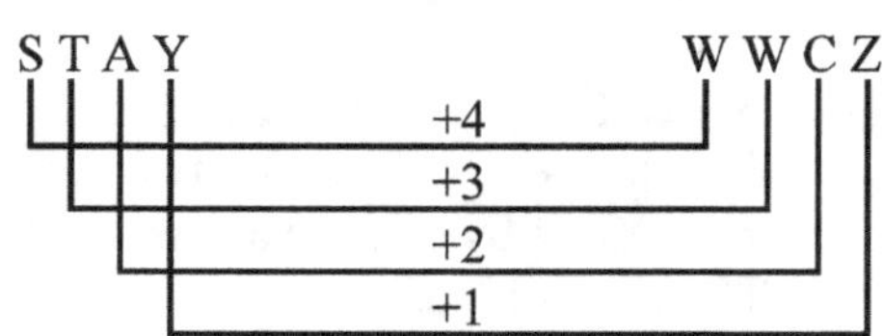

6.

	Code	Sentence
1.	go *ju* mi	plenty of *money*
2.	pao *ju* go nei vu	*money* creates lots of problems
3.	kol vu nei	problems create tension
4.	sol tun *ju* haw	still *money* is needed

In 1st, 2nd and 4th codes and their sentences the word 'ju' is repeated and so is 'money'.

8.

	Code	Sentence
1.	415	milk is hot
2.	18	hot soup
3.	895	soup is *tasty*

From 3rd code and its sentence neither number '9' is repeated nor the word 'tasty'.

9.

	Code	Sentence
1.	643	she is beautiful
2.	593	he is handsome
3.	567	handsome *meets* beautiful

From 3rd code and its sentence, neither number '7' nor the word 'meets' is repeated.

10.

	Code	Sentence
1.	*dugo* hui mul zo	work *is very* hard
2.	hui *dugo* **ba** ki	**Bingo** *is very* smart
3.	nano mul *dugo*	cake is *hard*
4.	mul *ki* qu	*smart* and hard

From 2nd code and its sentence, neither 'ba' nor 'Bingo' is repeated.
(Words repeated are in italics)

1. Among five friends, A is heavier than B; C is lighter than D; B is lighter than D but heavier than E. Who among them is the heaviest?
   A. B
   B. C
   C. A
   D. Can't say

2. Pune is bigger than Jhansi, Sitapur is bigger than Chittor. Raigarh is not as big as Jhansi, but is bigger than Sitapur. Chittor is not as big as Sitapur. Which is the smallest?
   A. Jhansi
   B. Pune
   C. Chittor
   D. Sitapur

3. Ajay works more than Ram. Alok works as much as Raju. Pankaj works less than Alok. Ram works more than Alok. Who works the most of all?
   A. Ajay
   B. Ram
   C. Alok
   D. Raju

4. Vipul is taller than Hans. Hans is taller than Anand. Alok is taller than Ashok. Ashok is taller than Hans. Who among them is the tallest?
   A. Vipul
   B. Alok
   C. Ashok
   D. Cannot be determined

5. Pramod is taller than Gopal. Gopal is shorter than Madhu. To find out who among them is the tallest, which of the following further informations is necessary?
   A. Madhu is taller than Gopal.
   B. Madhu is shorter than Pramod's brother
   C. Pramod is taller than Madhu.
   D. Pramod is taller than Madhu's brother.

6. Among five friends P, Q, R, S and T, who is the youngest? To arrive at the answer which of the following information given in the statements (a) and (b) is sufficient?

(a) R is younger than P and T.
(b) S is younger than Q.
   A. Only (a) alone is sufficient
   B. Either (a) or (b) is sufficient
   C. Both (a) and (b) together are needed
   D. Both (a) and (b) together are not sufficient

7. Sushma is richer than Rashmi whereas Anand is richer than Priya. Arun is as rich as Rashmi. Shoba is richer than Sushma.
   Which of the following statements is correct according to the above propositions?
   A. Rashmi is poorer than Priya.
   B. Priya is richer than Arun
   C. Arun is poorer than Sushma.
   D. Anand is richer than Rashmi

8. A is elder to B while C and D are elder to E who lies between A and B. If C be elder to B, which one of the following statements is necessarily true?
   A. E is elder to B
   B. A is elder to C
   C. C is elder to D
   D. D is elder to C

9. Vikram is taller than Rajan but shorter than Annie. Jamal is taller than Annie. Sita is taller than Vikram. Rajan is shorter than Sita. Who is the shortest of all in the group?
   A. Sita
   B. Rajan
   C. Vikram
   D. Cannot be determined

10. Suresh is as much older than Kamal as he is younger than Prabodh. Navin is as old as Kamal. Which of the following statements is wrong?
   A. Suresh is older than Navin
   B. Kamal is younger than Suresh
   C. Prabodh is not the oldest
   D. Navin is younger than Prabodh

ANSWERS

1	2	3	4	5	6	7	8	9	10
D	C	A	D	C	D	C	A	B	C

SOME SELECTED EXPLANATORY ANSWERS

1. The five friends in descending order of weight are : A/D, B/C, E or A/D, B, C/E. Either A or D is the heaviest.

2. The order of cities in descending order of size is : Pune, Jhansi, Raigarh, Sitapur, Chittor.

3. On the basis of doing work, the descending order will be : Ajay, Ram, Alok/Raju, Pankaj.

4. On the basis of height, the descending order will be Vipul/Alok, Ashok, Hans, Anand. Either Vipul or Alok is the tallest.

5. According to the information both Pramod and Madhu are taller than Gopal. Option (c) decides who is the tallest.

6. Statements are not inter-related.

7. On the basis of wealth, the descending order will be :
   1. Shobha, Sushma, Rashmi/Arun
   2. Anand, *and* Priya
   (The two statements are not inter-related.)

8. The order in descending seniority will be : A/C/D, E, B.

9. On the basis of height the descending order will be :
   Jamal/Sita, Annie, Vikram, Rajan.

   or

   Jamal, Sita/Annie, Vikram, Rajan.

10. On the basis of age the descending order will be : Prabodh, Suresh, Kamal/Navin.

PLACE ARRANGEMENT

Directions : *In the following questions, understand the arrangement pattern and then select the right answer from the given options :*

1. Five boys are sitting in a row. Raghu is not adjacent to Shyam or Amit. Ajay is not adjacent to Shyam. Raghu is adjacent to Mayank. If Mayank is at the middle in the row, then Ajay is adjacent to whom out of the following?
   - A. Amit
   - B. Raghu
   - C. Mayank
   - D. Shyam

2. Mini is to the right of Rajni but to the left of Ananta. Saya is to the right of Mini but to the left of Jaya. Who is on the extreme left if all the girls are facing North?
   - A. Jaya
   - B. Mini
   - C. Rajni
   - D. Saya

3. Kittu is in-between Mohan and Sohan. Raju is to the left of Sohan and Shyam is to the right of Mohan. If all of the friends are sitting facing South, then who is on their extreme right?
   - A. Mohan
   - B. Sohan
   - C. Kittu
   - D. Shyam

4. A, B, C, D and E are running one behind the other. C is not near E and A is not near D. B is next to A and E is not near D. Who is in the middle?
   - A. B
   - B. E
   - C. A
   - D. Cannot be said

5. O, P, Q, R, S and T are standing on a bench according to their height. P is taller than O but shorter than S. Only S is taller than T. R is shorter than P but taller than Q. Who is the shortest?
   - A. O
   - B. Q
   - C. P
   - D. Cannot be said

ANSWERS

1	2	3	4	5
B	C	D	A	D

SOME SELECTED EXPLANATORY ANSWERS

1. The order of sitting is :
   Amit, Shyam, Mayank, Ajay, Raghu
   or
   Ajay, Raghu, Mayank, Amit, Shyam

2. The order in which the girls are positioned is :
   Rajni, Mini, Ananta, Saya, Jaya
   or
   Saya, Jaya, Ananta
   or
   Saya, Ananta, Jaya

3. The order of sitting while facing South is:
   Shyam, Mohan, Kittu, Sohan, Raju.

4. The positions while running behind the other is :

E		E	
A		A	
B	*or*	B	
C		D	
D		C	

5. In descending order of height, the standing positions are :

S		S
T		T
P	*or*	P
R		R
O		Q
Q		O

Either O or Q is the shortest. The information given is not enough to clarify the answer.

DIRECTION SENSE

Directions : *In the following questions, select the right answer from the given options to depict the correct direction/distance.*

1. Kittu walks towards East and then towards South. After walking some distance he turns towards West and then turns to his left. In which direction is he walking now?
   A. North B. South
   C. East D. West

2. A person is driving towards West. What sequence of directions should he follow so that he is driving towards South?
   A. left, right, right B. right, right, left
   C. left, left, left D. right, right, right

3. Richa drives 8 km to the South, turns left and drives 5 km. Again, she turns left and drives 8 km. How far is she from her starting point?
   A. 3 km B. 5 km
   C. 8 km D. 13 km

4. Dingi runs 40 km towards North then turns right and runs 50 km. He turns right and runs 30 km, and once again turns right and runs 50 km. How far is he from his starting point?
   A. 90 km B. 50 km
   C. 10 km D. 5 km

5. Debu walks towards East then towards North and turning 45° right walks for a while and lastly turns towards left. In which direction is he walking now?
   A. North B. East
   C. South-East D. North-West

ANSWERS

1	2	3	4	5
B	D	B	C	D

SOME SELECTED EXPLANATORY ANSWERS

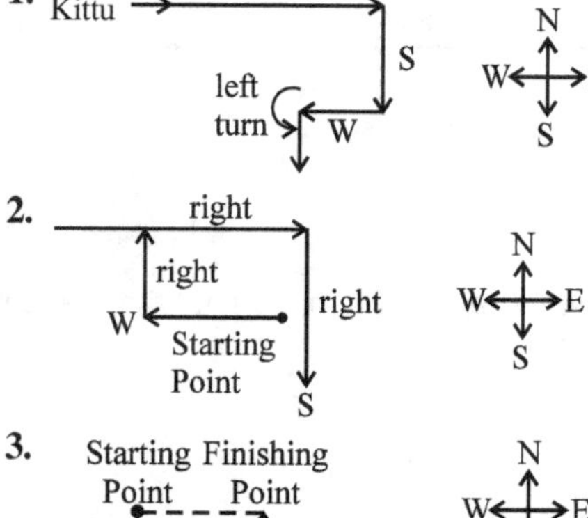

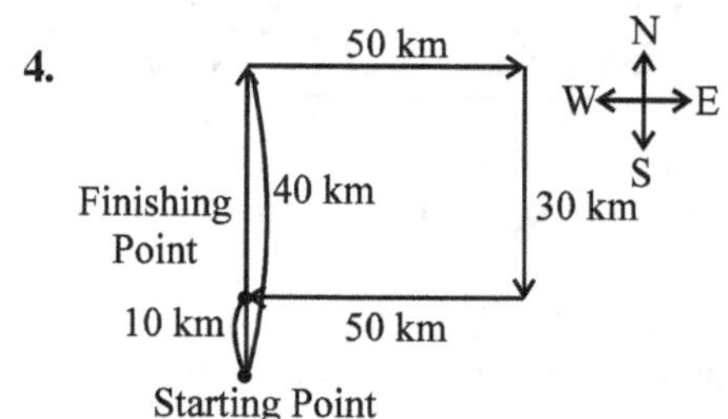

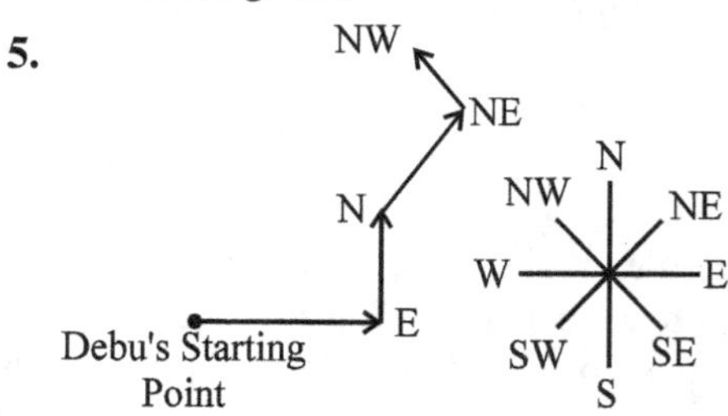

BLOOD RELATIONSHIPS

Directions : *In each of the following questions keenly study the relationship mentioned between the persons, and then from the given options select the right relationship as the answer.*

1. 'A' is the father of 'B' and 'C'. 'B' is the son of 'A' but 'C' is not the son of 'A'. What is 'C's' relation with 'A'?
   A. Daughter   B. Son
   C. Niece   D. Nephew

2. A lady said, "The person standing there is my grandfather's only son's daughter". How is the lady related to the standing person?
   A. Sister   B. Mother
   C. Aunt   D. Cousin

3. Ravi is the brother of Amit's son's son. What is Amit's relation to Ravi?
   A. Cousin   B. Father
   C. Grandfather   D. Son

4. Mayank said, "My mother is the sister of Rajat's brother." What is Rajat's relation with Mayank?
   A. Cousin   B. Maternal uncle
   C. Uncle   D. Brother-in-law

5. Introducing Lily, Raghav said, "Her father is my mother's only son". How is Lily related to Raghav?
   A. Aunt   B. Daughter
   C. Mother   D. Sister

ANSWERS

1	2	3	4	5
A	A	C	B	B

SOME SELECTED EXPLANATORY ANSWERS

1. 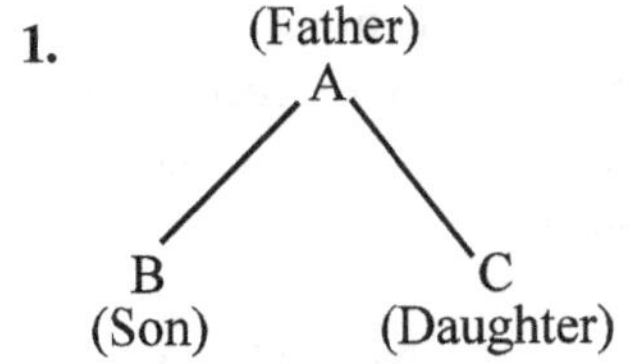

'C' is not the son of 'A', but 'A' is the father of 'C'. So, 'C' is the daughter of 'A'.

2. Grand father

Lady's grandfather's son is lady's father and father's daughter will only be lady's sister.

4. 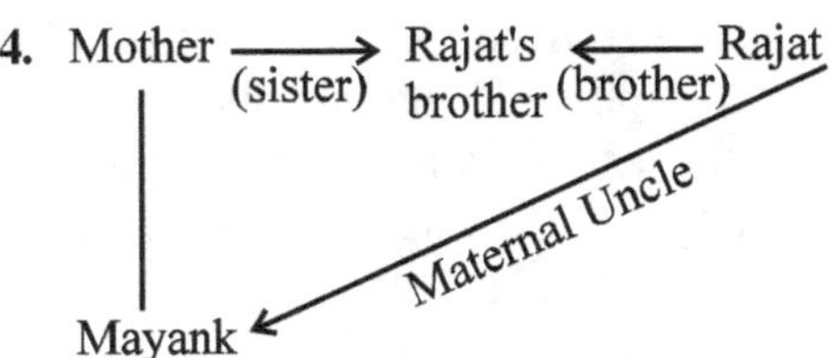

Mayank's mother is the sister of Rajat's brother. So Rajat is also the brother of Mayank's mother. Relation of the brother with his sister's child is maternal. So Rajat is Mayank's maternal uncle.

CALENDAR, CLOCK, TIME, DISTANCE

1. If the day before yesterday was Thursday, when will Sunday be?
   A. Tomorrow
   B. Day after tomorrow
   C. Today
   D. Two days after today

2. There are twenty people working in an office. The first group of five works between 8:00 A.M. and 2:00 PM. The second group of ten works between 10:00 AM to 4:00 PM. And the third group of five works between 12 noon to 6:00 PM. There are three computers in the office which all the employees frequently use. During which of the following hours the computers are likely to be used most?
   A. 1:00 PM - 3:00 PM
   B. 12 noon - 2:00 PM
   C. 2:00 PM - 4:00 PM
   D. 10:00 AM - 12 noon

3. If the seventh day of a month is three (3) days earlier than Friday, what day will it be on the nineteenth day of the month?
   A. Sunday
   B. Monday
   C. Wednesday
   D. Friday

4. Radha remembers that her father's birthday is after 16th but before 21st of March, while her brother Mangesh remembers that his father's birthday is before 22nd but after 19th of March. On which date is the birthday of their father?
   A. 19th
   B. 20th
   C. 21st
   D. Cannot be determined

5. A man is three (3) years older than his wife and four (4) times as old as his son. If the son attains an age of fifteen (15) years after three (3) years, what is the present age of the mother?
   A. 60 years
   B. 51 years
   C. 48 years
   D. 45 years

6. A clock is so placed that at 12 noon its minute hand points towards north-east. In which direction does its hour hand point at 1.30 P.M.?
   A. East
   B. West
   C. North
   D. South

7. If in the above question clock is turned through an angle of 135° in an anticlockwise direction, in which direction will its minute hand point at 8.45 P.M.?
   A. East
   B. West
   C. North
   D. South

8. A couple married in 1980 had two children, one in 1982 and the other in 1984. Their combined ages will equal the years of the marriage in?
   A. 1986
   B. 1985
   C. 1987
   D. 1988

9. Manoj left home for the bus stop 15 minutes earlier than the usual time. It takes 10 minutes to reach the stop. He reached the stop at 8.40 a.m. What time does he usually leave home for the bus stop?
   A. 8.30 a.m.
   B. 8.55 a.m.
   C. 8.45 p.m.
   D. None of these

10. Mamuni went to the movies nine days ago. She goes to the movies only on Thursday. What day of the week is today?
    A. Sunday
    B. Tuesday
    C. Thursday
    D. Saturday

11. If Thursday was the day after the day before yesterday five days ago, what is the least number of days ago when Sunday was three days before the day after tomorrow?
    A. Two days ago
    B. Three days ago

C. Four days ago
D. Five days ago

12. 1.12.91 is the first Sunday. Which is the fourth Tuesday of December 91?
A. 31.12.91   B. 24.12.91
C. 17.12.91   D. 26.12.91

13. If the third day of a month is Monday, which of the following will be the fifth day from 21st of that month?
A. Tuesday   B. Monday
C. Wednesday   D. Thursday

14. Keshav runs a factory in three shifts of eight hours each with 210 employees. In each shift minimum of 80 employees are required to run the factory effectively. No employee can be allowed to work for more than 16 hours a day. At least how many employees will be required to work for 16 hours every day?
A. 30
B. 60
C. Data inadequate
D. None of these

15. If 15 horses eat 15 bags of gram in 15 days, in how many days will one horse eat one bag of grain?
A. 15 days   B. 1/15 days
C. 1 day   D. 30 days

16. A century leap year is divisible by :
A. 4   B. 16
C. 40   D. 400

17. If the fifth day of a month is Friday, which of the following will be the Seventh day from 10th of that month?
A. Tuesday   B. Monday
C. Wednesday   D. Thursday

18. Day after tomorrow is my birthday. On the same day next week falls 'Holi'. Today is Monday. What will be the day after 'Holi'?
A. Wednesday   B. Thursday
C. Friday   D. Saturday

19. A clock shows the time as 3 : 30 p.m. If the minute hand gains 2 minutes every hour, how many minutes will the clock gain by 4 a.m.?
A. 23 Minutes   B. 24 Minutes
C. 25 Minutes   D. 26 Minutes

20. Two brothers were expected to return home on the same day. Rajat returned 3 days earlier but Rohit returned 4 days later. If Rajat returned on Thursday, what was the expected day when both the brothers were to return home and when did Rohit Return?
A. Wednesday, Sunday
B. Thursday, Monday
C. Sunday, Thursday
D. Monday, Friday

ANSWERS

1	2	3	4	5	6	7	8	9	10
A	B	A	B	A	A	D	A	D	D

11	12	13	14	15	16	17	18	19	20
A	B	C	D	A	D	C	B	C	C

SOME SELECTED EXPLANATORY ANSWERS

1. Thursday —Day-before-yesterday
Friday —Yesterday
Saturday —Today
Sunday — Tomorrow

2. 1. 5 people work between 8 a.m. to 2 p.m.
2. 10 people work between 10 a.m. to 4 p.m.
3. 5 people work between 12 noon to 6 p.m.

So, computers are used most between 12 noon to 2 p.m.

3. 7th day is 3 days earlier than Friday so, 10th day is Friday, so also is 17th.

∴ 19th day will be 2nd day ahead of Friday, *i.e.,* Sunday.

4. Father's birthday

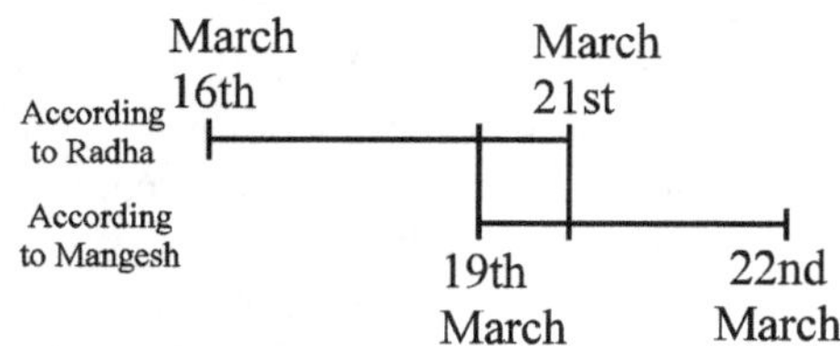

∴ Their father's birthday is on 20th March.

5. Present age of son is 15 – 3 = 12 years. Age of the man is 4 times the age of son, *i.e.*,

12 × 4 = 48 years

Man is 3 years elder to his wife/son's mother.

So Age of the mother is 48 – 3 = 45 years

6.  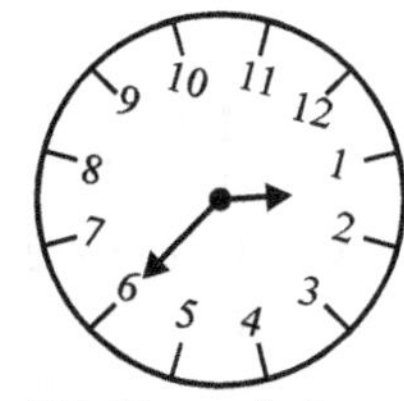

At 12 noon   At 1.30 p.m. the hour hand will point towards East.

7. 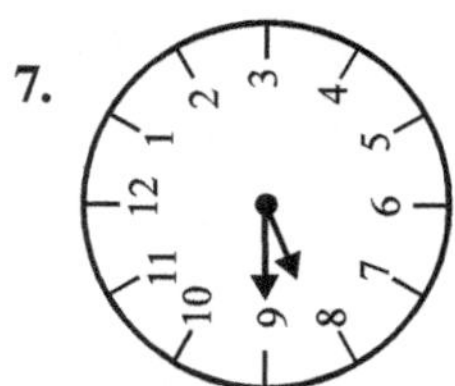

After rotating the clock in earlier question, its minute hand will point towards South at 8:45 p.m.

8. 1982 —   2 years later — 1st child
1984 —   4 years later — 2nd child
Total age of children — 2 years.
1985 — 5 years later — Total age of children: 4 years.
1986 —   6 years later — Total age of children : 6 years.

9. Manoj reached the bus stop at 8.40 a.m. He left his home at 8:40 – 10 minutes = 8:30 a.m. He left 15 minutes earlier than usual, so his actual time of leaving home is 8:30 am + 15 minutes = 8:45 a.m.

10. Mamuni goes to the movies on Thursday, so nine days ago was Thursday.

∴ Two days ago was also Thursday. So, today is Saturday.

11. Day after the day-before-yesterday five days ago is the 6th day which is Thursday. And so, the 3rd day will be Sunday. Three days before the day-after-tomorrow is Yesterday which is the 1st day of the five days. So, two days ago was Sunday.

12. First Sunday is on 1st December
First Tuesday is on 3rd December
3 weeks later, Fourth Tuesday will be on 3 + (7 × 3) = 24th December.

13. 3rd day of the month is Monday
5th day from 21st is 26th
26 – 3 = 23 days
23 days later, 23/7 leaves 2 days.
So, two days ahead of Monday will be Wednesday.

14. 80 employees are required for double shift.

15. 15 horses eat 15 bags of grain in 15 days
15 horses eat 1 bag of grain in 1 day
1 horse eats 1 bag of grain in 15 days

16. A leap year is divisible by 4 and a century leap year is divisible by 400.

17. Seventh day from 10th is 17th.
5th day is Friday. Next Friday is on 12th, 17 – 12 = 5, 5 days ahead of Friday will be Wednesday. So, 17th is Wednesday.

18. Today is Monday
Day-after-tomorrow is Wednesday
Next week 'Holi' is also on Wednesday
So, Day after Holi is Thursday.

19. Hours between 3:30 p.m. and 4 a.m. are — 12½ hours. Number of minutes gained will be 12½ × 2 = 25 minutes.

20. Rajat returned on Thursday. 3 days later was the day of expected return, *i.e.*, Sunday. Rohit returned 4 days after Sunday, *i.e.*, Thursday.

ROWS AND RANKS

1. In a row of trees, one tree is fifth from either end of the row. How many trees are in the row?
   - A. 11
   - B. 8
   - C. 10
   - D. 9

2. Jaya ranks 5th in a class of 53. What is her rank from the bottom in the class?
   - A. 49th
   - B. 48th
   - C. 47th
   - D. 50th

3. Mohan ranks twenty-first in a class of sixty-five students. What will be his (Mohan's) rank if the lowest candidate is assigned rank 1?
   - A. 44th
   - B. 45th
   - C. 46th
   - D. Data inadequate

4. If Rahul finds that he is 12th from the right in a line of boys and 4th from the left, how many boys should be added to the line such that there are 28 boys in the line?
   - A. 12
   - B. 14
   - C. 20
   - D. 13

5. In a row of boys, Rajan is tenth from the right and Suraj is tenth from the left. When Rajan and Suraj interchange their positions, Suraj will be twenty-seventh from the left. Which of the following will be Rajan's position from the right?
   - A. Tenth
   - B. Twenty-sixth
   - C. Twenty-ninth
   - D. None of these

6. Mahesh and Suresh are ranked 11th and 12th respectively from the top in a class of 41 students. What will be their respective ranks from the bottom?
   - A. 32nd and 33rd
   - B. 29th and 30th
   - C. 30th and 31st
   - D. 31st and 30th

7. Uma ranked 8th from the top and 37th from bottom in a class. How many students are there in the class?
   - A. 47
   - B. 46
   - C. 45
   - D. None of these

8. In a queue, Sadiq is 14th from the front and Joseph is 17th from the end, while Jane is in between Sadiq and Joseph. If Sadiq be ahead of Joseph and there be 48 persons in the queue, how many persons are there between Sadiq and Jane?
   - A. 5
   - B. 6
   - C. 7
   - D. 8

9. Rohan ranked eleventh from the top and twenty-seventh from the bottom among the students who passed the annual examination in a class. If the number of students who failed in the examination was 12, how many students appeared for the examination?
   - A. 48
   - B. 49
   - C. 50
   - D. Cannot be determined

10. Some boys are sitting in a row. P is sitting fourteenth from the left and Q is seventh from the right. If there are four boys between P and Q, how many boys are there in the row?
    - A. 19
    - B. 21
    - C. 25
    - D. 23

ANSWERS

1	2	3	4	5	6	7	8	9	10
D	A	B	D	D	D	D	C	B	C

SOME SELECTED EXPLANATORY ANSWERS

1. 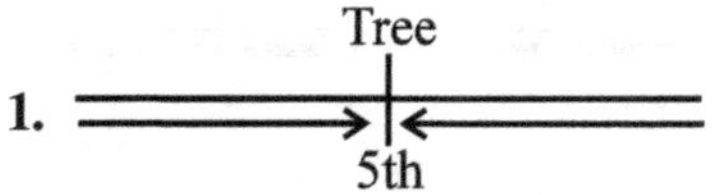

Total number of trees in the row are :
(5 + 5) –1 =9

2. 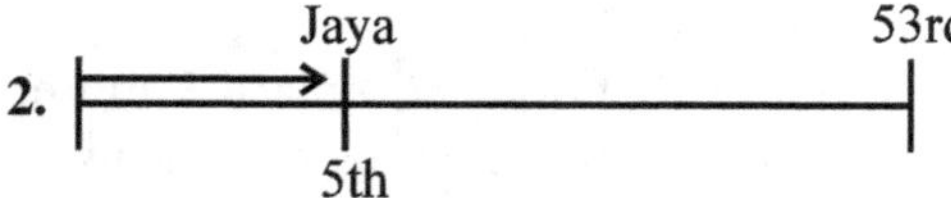

Jaya's rank from the bottom is :
(53 – 5) +1 = 49th.

3. 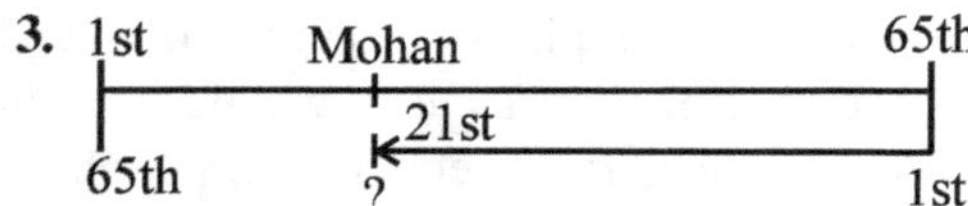

Note : Mohan's rank from the last or the question asked means the same.
Mohan's rank is (65 – 21) +1 = 45th

4. 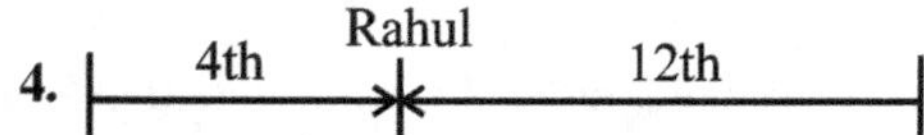

The number of boys in the line are :
(4 + 12) – 1 = 15
To make a line of 28 boys, (28 –15) *i.e.* 13 more boys are needed.

5. 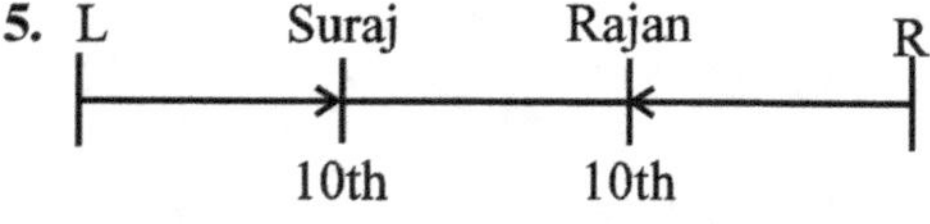

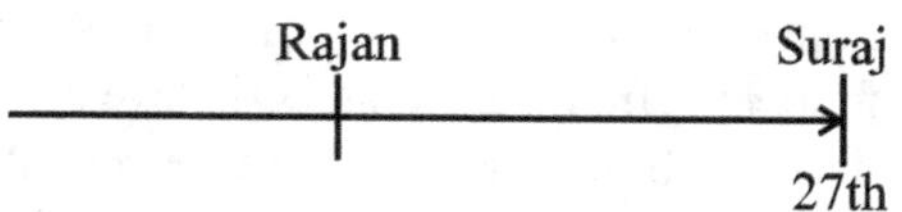

As the position of boys is equal from both ends, Rajan will also be 27th from the right after changing positions.

6. 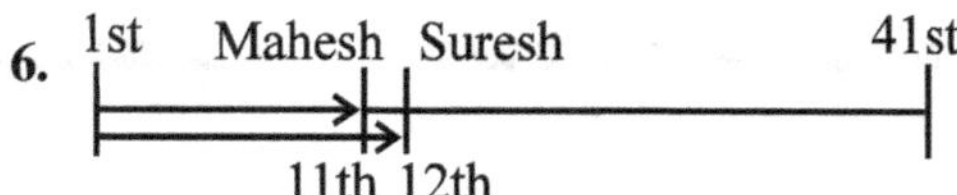

Mahesh's position from bottom is :
(41 – 11) + 1 = 31st
Suresh's position from bottom is :
(41 – 12) +1 = 30th

7. 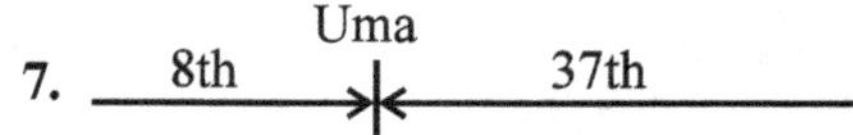

Total number of students in the class are :
(8 + 37) – 1 = 44

8. 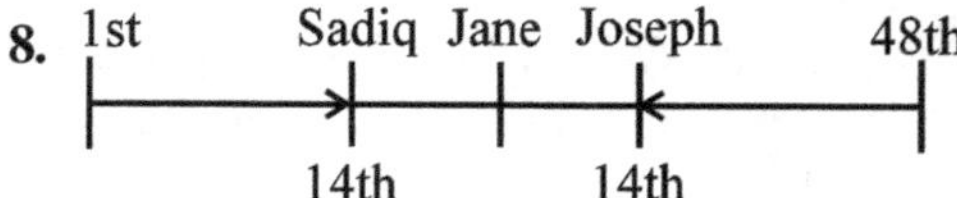

Sadiq's position from last is :
(48 – 14) + 1 = 35th
Number of persons between Sadiq and Joseph are (35 – 17) – 1 = 17
Jane is in-between Sadiq and Joseph *i.e.,* she's at 9th position from both the boys.
∴ there are 8 persons between Sadiq and Jane.
Note : (8 + 8) – 1 = 17

9. 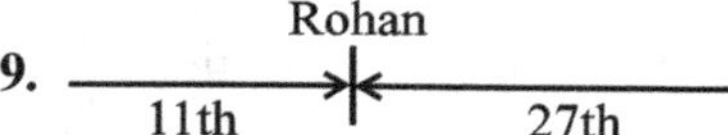

Number of students who passed the examination (11+ 27) – 1 = 37
Those who failed = 12
Total number of students who appeared in the examination = 37 + 12 = 49.

10. 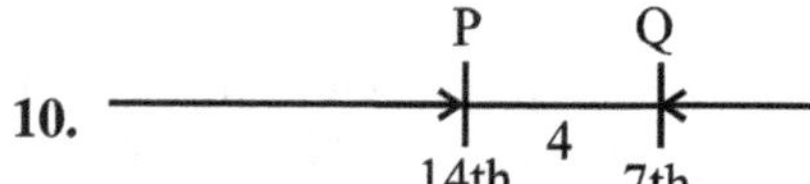

The number of boys in the row are :
(14 + 4 + 7) = 25

NUMBER PROBLEMS

1. How many 6's are there in the following series of numbers which are preceded by 7 but not immediately followed by 9?

   6 7 9 5 6 9 7 6 8 7 6 7 8 6 9 4 6 7 7 6 9 5 7 6 3
   A. One   B. Two
   C. Three   D. Four

2. In a chess tournament each of six players will play every other player exactly once. How many matches will be played during the tournament?
   A. 12   B. 15
   C. 30   D. 36

3. How many 4's are there in the following series which are preceded by 7, but are not preceded by 8?

   3 4 5 7 4 3 7 4 8 5 4 3 7 4 9 8 4 7 2 7 4 1 3 6

4. How many even numbers are there in the following series of numbers, each of which is immediately preceded by an odd number, but not immediately followed by an even number?

   5 3 4 8 9 7 1 6 5 3 2 9 8 4 3 5
   A. Nil   B. 1
   C. 2   D. 3

5. If all the numbers from 1 to 51 which are exactly divisible by 3 are arranged in descending order, which of the following numbers will come at the seventh and tenth places from the top?
   A. 33 & 27   B. 33 & 21
   C. 21 & 30   D. 33 & 24

Additional options (for question above):
A. 1   B. 2
C. 3   D. 4

ANSWERS

1	2	3	4	5
C	B	D	C	D

SOME SELECTED EXPLANATORY ANSWERS

1. 6 7 9 5 6 9 7 6 8 7 6 7 8 6 9 4 6 7 7 6 9 5 7 6 3

2. When all the players have to play with each other then the method of calculating the number of matches to be played is $\dfrac{n(n-1)}{2}$ where 'n' is the number of players playing the match. So, the number of matches played will be :

   $(6 \times 5) \div 2 = 30 \div 2 = 15$

3. 3 4 5 7 4 3 7 4 8 5 4 3 7 4 9 8 4 7 2 7 4 1 3 6

4. 5 3 4 8 9 7 1 6 5 3 2 9 8 4 3 5

5. The numbers divisible by 3 in descending order are :

   51, 48, 45, 42, 39, 36, 33, 30, 27, 24, 21,
                                     7th   10th

   18, 15, 12, 9, 6, 3.

SYMBOL SUBSTITUTION

1. If "+" means "–"; "–" means "×"; "×"means "÷" and "÷" means "+", then
   $15 \times 5 \div 10 + 5 - 3 = ?$
   A. 9.5   B. 0
   C. – 2   D. 24

2. If "+" means "–"; "–" means "×"; "×"means "÷" and "÷" means "+", then
   $15 \times 3 \div 15 + 5 - 2 = ?$
   A. 0   B. 10
   C. 20   D. 6

3. If "+" means "÷"; "×" means "–"; "÷"means "+" and "–" means "×", then
   $16 \div 8 \times 6 - 2 + 12 = ?$

A. 22   B. 24
C. 23   D. 20

4. If "+" means "×"; "–" means "÷"; "÷"means "+" and "×" means "–", then what will be the value of $20 \div 40 - 4 \times 5 + 6 = ?$
   A. 60   B. 1.67
   C. 150   D. 0

5. If "+" means "×"; "–" means "÷"; "×"means "–" and "÷" means "+", then
   $5 + 8 - 4 \times 2 \div 9 = ?$
   A. 15   B. 13
   C. 17   D. 11

ANSWERS

1	2	3	4	5
C	B	C	D	C

SOME SELECTED EXPLANATORY ANSWERS

1. $15 \div 5 + 10 - 5 \times 3$
   $3 + 10 - 15 = - 2$

2. $15 \div 3 + 15 - 5 \times 2$
   $5 + 15 - 10 = 10$

3. $16 + 8 - 6 \times 2 \div 12$

   $16 + 8 - 1 = 23$

4. $20 + 40 \div 4 - 5 \times 6$
   $20 + 10 - 30 = 0$

5. $5 \times 8 \div 4 - 2 + 9$
   $10 - 2 + 9 = 17$

MISSING NUMBERS

Directions : *In each question given below which one number can be placed at the sign of interrogation?*

1.

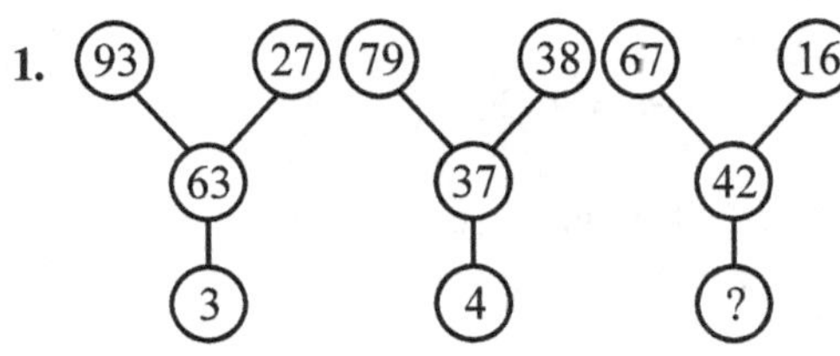

A. 5   B. 6
C. 8   D. 9

2.

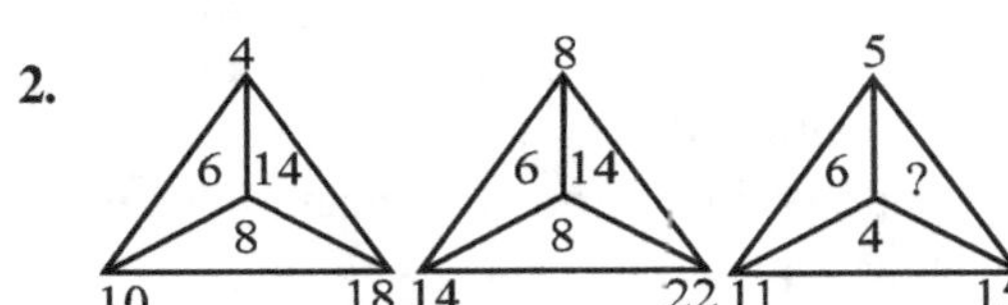

A. 8   B. 14
C. 10   D. 6

3.

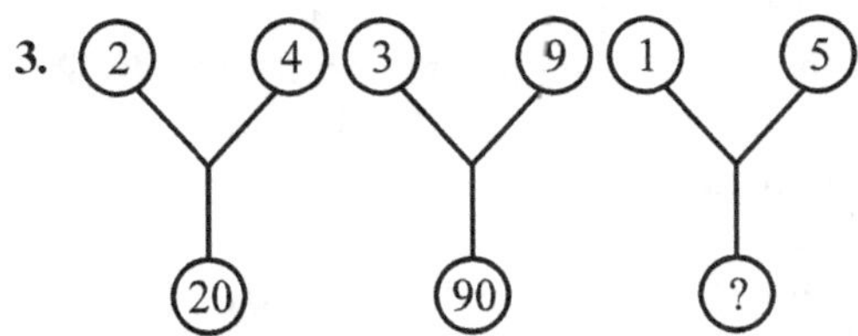

A. 20   B. 25
C. 26   D. 75

4.

27	22	50
13	12	26
9	2	?

A. 12   B. 39
C. 18   D. 24

5.

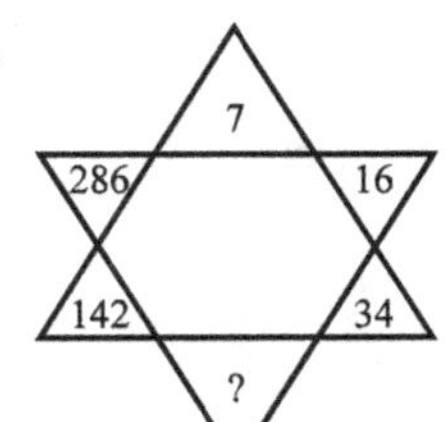

A. 25   B. 47
C. 37   D. 41

6.

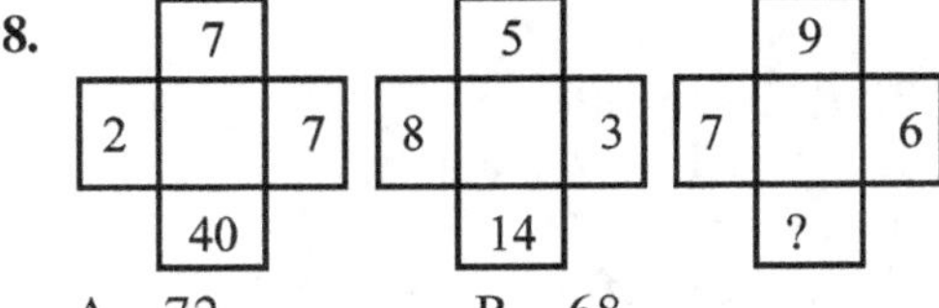

A. 70   B. 68
C. 56   D. 92

7.

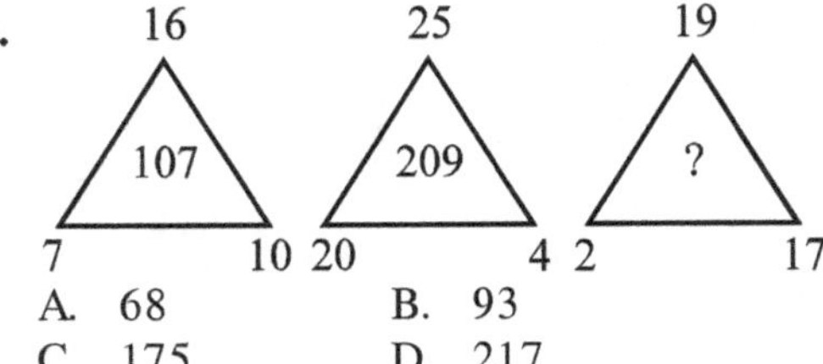

A. 41   B. 37
C. 29   D. 25

8.

A. 72   B. 68
C. 82   D. 96

9.

42	(21)	22
78	(?)	84
162	(18)	99

A. 12   B. 13
C. 60   D. 72

10.

A. 68   B. 93
C. 175   D. 217

ANSWERS

1	2	3	4	5	6	7	8	9	10
D	C	C	A	D	A	C	B	B	A

SOME SELECTED EXPLANATORY ANSWERS

1. The sum of numbers on right and centre subtracted from the number on the left gives the number at the bottom, *i.e.,*
$$93 - (27 + 63) = 3$$
$$79 - (38 + 37) = 4, \text{ similarly}$$
$$67 - (16 + 42) = 9$$

2. The number inside each triangle is the difference of the numbers at its base *i.e.*
$$10 - 4 = 6, \ 18 - 4 = 14 \text{ and } 18 - 10 = 8$$
$$14 - 8 = 6, \ 22 - 8 = 14 \text{ and } 22 - 14 = 8, \text{ similarly}$$
$$11 - 5 = 6, \ 15 - 5 = 10 \text{ and } 15 - 11 = 4.$$

3. The sum of squares of two numbers at the top gives the third number below, *i.e.,*
$$2^2 + 4^2 = 20$$
$$3^2 + 9^2 = 90, \text{ similarly}$$
$$1^2 + 5^2 = 26$$

4. The sum of numbers in 1st and 2nd column plus 1 is the number in the 3rd column, *i.e.,*
$$27 + 22 + 1 = 50$$
$$13 + 12 + 1 = 26, \text{ similarly}$$
$$9 + 2 + 1 = 12$$

5. The product of numbers on either side of the triangle plus the number at the base is the number inside the triangle, *i.e.,*
$$(5 \times 3) + 4 = 19$$
$$(6 \times 4) + 5 = 29, \text{ similarly}$$
$$(7 \times 5) + 6 = 41$$

6. Clockwise starting from number 7, the next number is obtained by doubling the number and adding 2, *i.e.,*
$$(7 \times 2) + 2 = 16$$
$$(16 \times 2) + 2 = 34 \ldots, \text{ similarly}$$
$$(34 \times 2) + 2 = 70$$
$$(70 \times 2) + 2 = 142$$
$$(142 \times 2) + 2 = 286$$

7. The difference between the numbers in opposite sectors is 13, *i.e.,*
$$26 - 13 = 13$$
$$68 - 55 = 13, \text{ similarly}$$
The missing number is $42 - 13 = 29$
$(42 + 13 = 55$ is not given as option)

8. The number at the bottom is obtained by subtracting the sum of two numbers in the centre grid line from the square of the number at the top, *i.e.,*
$$7^2 - (2 + 7) = 40$$
$$5^2 - (8 + 3) = 14, \text{ similarly}$$
$$9^2 - (7 + 6) = 68$$

9. The number inside the brackets is obtained by multiplying the number on the left by 2 and then dividing the product by the sum of digits of number on the right, *i.e.,*
$$(42 \times 2) \div (2 + 2) = 21$$
$$(162 \times 2) \div (9 + 9) = 18, \text{ similarly}$$
$$(78 \times 2) \div (8 + 4) = 13$$

10. Subtracting the sum of squares of two numbers at the base from the square of number at the apex gives the number inside the triangle, *i.e.,*
$$16^2 - (7^2 + 10^2) = 107$$
$$25^2 - (20^2 + 4^2) = 209, \text{ similarly}$$
$$19^2 - (2^2 + 17^2) = 68$$

ALPHABET PROBLEMS

Directions : *The following questions are based on alphabet series in natural or reverse order and the combinations that can be made by changing the position of alphabet in given words.*

1. Which alphabet comes immediately before the sixth alphabet from the left extreme in alphabetical series?
   - A. U
   - B. E
   - C. F
   - D. V

2. Which letter is midway between G and S?
   - A. L
   - B. N
   - C. M
   - D. No letter

3. Which letter should be ninth letter to the left of ninth letter from the right if the first half of the alphabet is reversed?
   - A. I
   - B. D
   - C. F
   - D. E

4. If the alphabet is in reverse order, which letter will be eighth letter to the left of the seventh letter counting from the right end?
   - A. O
   - B. P
   - C. N
   - D. Q

5. What will be the fifth letter to the right of the thirteenth letter from the right?
   - A. R
   - B. S
   - C. I
   - D. O

ANSWERS

1	2	3	4	5
B	C	D	A	B

SOME SELECTED EXPLANATORY ANSWERS

1. 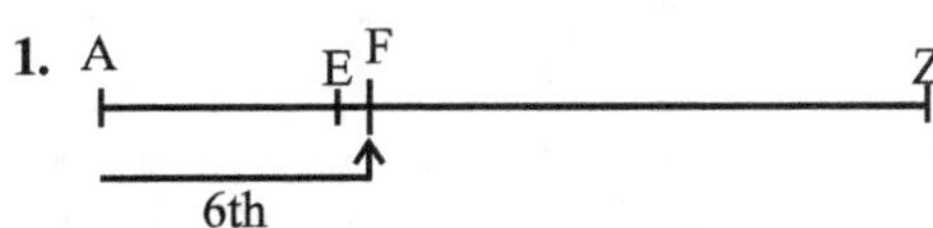

Sixth letter from left is 'F' and letter immediately before 'F' is 'E'.

2. 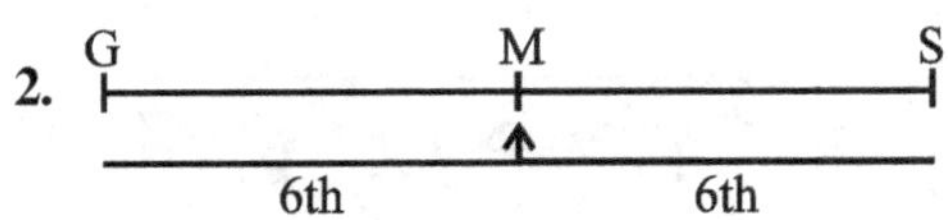

'M' is midway between G and S.

3. MLKJIHGFEDCBANOPQRSTUVWXYZ

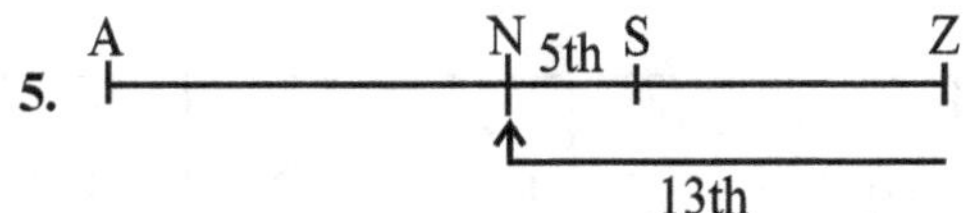

4. ZYXWVUTSRQPONMLKJIHGFEDCBA

5.

13th letter from right is 'N' and 5th letter to the right of 'N' is 'S'.

NON-VERBAL SERIES

Directions (Q. 1–10) : *In each of the following questions which one of the five answer figures given below should come after the problem figures if the sequence are continued?*

Problem Figures   **Answer Figures**

1.

2.

3.

4.

5.

6.

7.

Problem Figures   **Answer Figures**

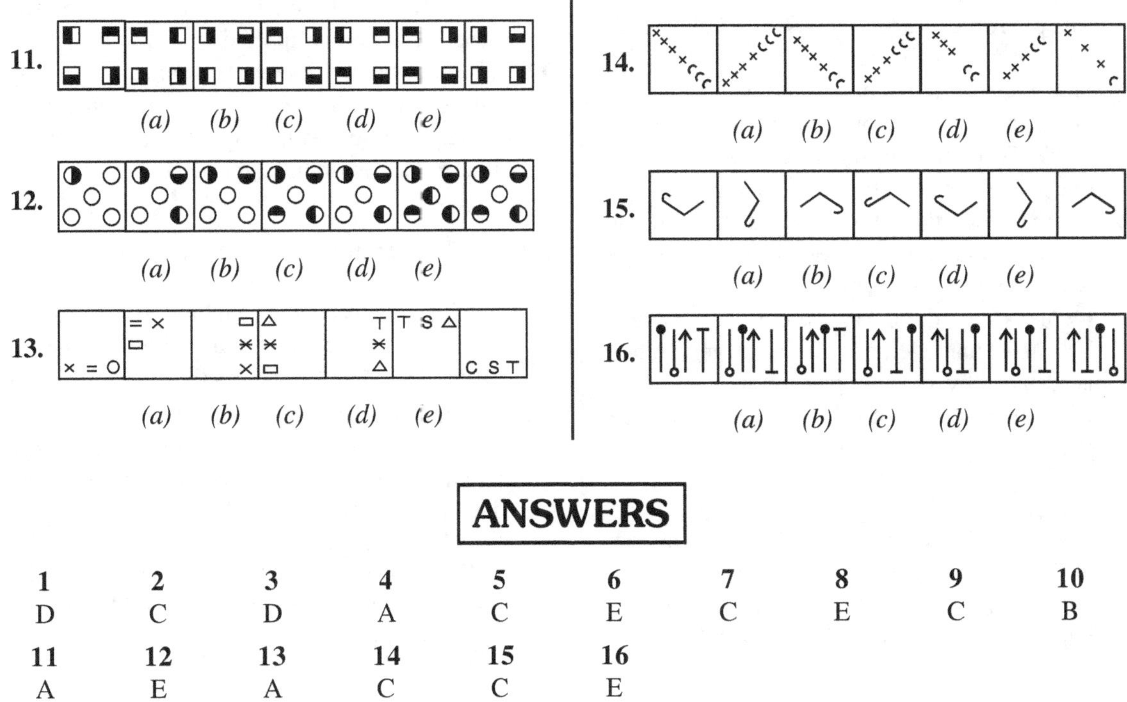

Directions (Q. 11-20) : *In each of these questions, a series begins with an unmarked figure on the extreme left in the row of figures. One and only one of the five lettered figures in the series does not fit into the series. The two unmarked figures, one on the extreme left and the other on the extreme right fit into the series. Take as many aspects into account as possible of the figures in the series and find out the one and only of the five marked figures which does not fit into the series. The letter of that figure is the answer.*

ANSWERS

1	2	3	4	5	6	7	8	9	10
D	C	D	A	C	E	C	E	C	B

11	12	13	14	15	16
A	E	A	C	C	E

SOME SELECTED EXPLANATORY ANSWERS

1. In each step, all the elements move to the adjacent corner (of the square boundary) in a CW direction and the element that reaches the upper-left corner gets vertically inverted.

2. We can label the arcs as shown . The arcs get inverted in the sequence (1 & 2), (3, 4 & 5), (6 & 1), (2, 3 & 4), (5 & 6), ...

3. All the elements move half-a-side of the square boundary in ACW direction in each step. Also, first, third and fifth elements are replaced by new elements in one step and second, fourth and sixth elements are replaced by new elements in the next step. The two steps are repeated alternately.

4. In each step, the dot moves one space CW and the arrow moves two spaces CW.

5. One arc and four arcs get inverted alternately.

6. The number of parts increases by one along with the number of sides in the figure.

7. The pin rotates 45°CW and 90°CW alternately and moves one space (each space is equal to half-a-side of the square) and two spaces CW alternately. The arrow rotates 90°ACW and 45°ACW alternately and moves two spaces and one space.

8. In one step, the two elements interchange positions and the smaller element gets enlarged while the larger element gets reduced in size. In the next step, the smaller element is replaced by a new small element and the larger element is replaced by a new large element.

9. In each step, the elements move in the order

10. The upper-left element gets laterally inverted in first, third, fifth. .... steps; the upper-right element gets rotated through 180° is first, fourth, seventh,.... steps; the lower-left element gets laterally inverted in second, fourth, sixth, ... steps; the lower-right element gets rotated through 180° in third, sixth,... steps and the pin at the middle-right position gets laterally inverted in every second step.

11. The shade in the top left square is moved one step clockwise till figure B and then reversed, the process is repeated. The shade in the top right square is moved one step anticlockwise till figure D and then reversed. The shade in the bottom left square is moved one step clockwise in alternate figures and the shade in bottom right square is moved one step clockwise after two figures. In figure 'A' the rule is isolated by the shade in the bottom left square.

12. In alternate figures a new circle is shaded clockwise. The pattern of the shade is also moved clockwise. In figure 'E' right half of the circle in the centre should have been shaded.

13. The three elements are placed either horizontally or vertically. In option 'A' neither of the placements can be applied.

14. The placement of elements is same in alternate figures. The number and type of elements is same in two subsequent figures. In this manner, figure 'C' should have four crosses and two C shapes.

15. (c): The element is moved one step anticlockwise and the arc at one end is turned outside and inside alternately. In figure 'C' the element should be on the right side with the arc turned outside on the top side.

16. The left most element, line segment with the dot is moved one step towards right till figure C where it reaches the extreme right position. This process is repeated from figure D where the element on the extreme left, line segment with a circle, is moved. In figure 'E' the placement of the elements does not follow the rule of the series.

ARITHMETICAL AND NUMERICAL ABILITY

NUMBER SYSTEM

1. There are four numbers A, B, C and D. Average of the first three i.e., A, B and C is 15 and that of B, C and D is 16. If the last number, i.e., D is 19, then the first number is—
   A. 15   B. 16
   C. 17   D. 18

2. Of the three numbers, the first is twice the second and thrice the third. If the average of three is 22, the three numbers are—
   A. 12, 18, 36   B. 18, 12, 36
   C. 36, 12, 18   D. 36, 18, 12

3. If a person is standing on the sixth number in the queue from both the ends, the total persons in the queue are—
   A. 9   B. 11
   C. 12   D. 13

4. A number 'x' when multiplied by 5 and added to three times its own gives 64, the number is—
   A. 8   B. 12
   C. 14   D. 18

5. A number which when multiplied by 11 is as much above 180 as it was originally below it. The number is—
   A. 25   B. 30
   C. 40   D. 45

6. The sum of a number and its reciprocal is thrice the difference of the number and its reciprocal. Find the number.
   A. $\sqrt{2}$ B. $\sqrt{3}$
   C. $\sqrt{5}$ D. $\sqrt{7}$

7. A boy was asked to find $\dfrac{7}{9}$ of a fraction. He made a mistake of dividing the fraction by $\dfrac{7}{9}$ and so got an answer which exceeded the correct answer by $\dfrac{8}{21}$. Find the correct answer.
   A. $\dfrac{2}{3}$ B. $\dfrac{5}{7}$
   C. $\dfrac{7}{12}$ D. $\dfrac{7}{15}$

8. There are 408 boys and 312 girls in a school, which are to be divided into equal sections of either boys or girls alone. Find the maximum number of boys or girls that can be placed in a section. Also find the total number of sections thus formed.
   A. 10, 20   B. 24, 30
   C. 24, 40   D. 30, 30

9. The sum of all possible two-digit number formed from three different one-digit natural numbers, when divided by the sum of the original three numbers is equal to—
   A. 11   B. 18
   C. 22   D. 36

10. There are four prime numbers written in ascending order. The product of the first three is 385 and that of the last three is 1001. The last number is—
    A. 19   B. 17
    C. 13   D. 11

11. If the number 357 ★ 25 ★ is divisible by both 3 and 5, then the missing digits in the unit's place and thousandth place respectively are—
    A. 0, 4   B. 5, 4
    C. 5, 6   D. 0, 6

12. The difference between two numbers is 1365. When the larger number is divided by the smaller one, the quotient is 6 and the remainder is 15. The smaller number is:

A. 360   B. 295
C. 270   D. 240

13. When a number is divided by 31, the remainder is 29. When the same number is divided by 16, what will be the remainder?
A. 15   B. 13
C. 11   D. Data inadequate

14. In dividing a number by 585, a student applied the method of short division. He divided the number successively by 5, 9 and 13 (factor of 585) and got the remainders 4, 8 and 12. If he had divided the number by 585, the remainder would have been:
A. 584   B. 292
C. 144   D. 24

15. When a number divided by 6 leaves a remainder 3. When the square of the same number is divided by 6, the remainder is:
A. 3   B. 2
C. 1   D. zero

ANSWERS

1	2	3	4	5	6	7	8	9	10
B	D	B	A	B	A	C	B	C	C

11	12	13	14	15
C	C	D	A	A

SOME SELECTED EXPLANATORY ANSWERS

1. $\dfrac{A+B+C}{3} = 15,$

or, $A + B + C = 15 \times 3 = 45$ ... (i)

$\dfrac{B+C+D}{3} = 16,$

or $B + C + D = 48$ ... (ii)

$D = 19$

$\therefore\ B + C + 19 = 48$

or, $B + C = 48 - 19 = 29$

But, $A + B + C = 45$

Putting the value of $B + C = 29$ in the above equation (i), we get $A + 29 = 45$

$\therefore\ A = 45 - 29 = 16.$

2. Let the third number $= x$

$\therefore$ First number $= 3x$

Second number $= \dfrac{3x}{2}$

$\therefore\ \dfrac{1}{3}\left[x+3x+\dfrac{3x}{2}\right] = 22 \Rightarrow \dfrac{11}{2}x = 66$

$\Rightarrow x = \dfrac{66 \times 2}{11} = 12 = $ Third number,

$12 \times 3 = 36 = $ First number,

$\dfrac{12 \times 3}{2} = 18 = $ Second number.

3. If the person is standing at sixth number in the queue from both sides, that means there are five persons ahead and five persons behind him. Hence, total number of persons in the queue is $5 + 1 + 5 = 11.$

4. $5 \times x + 3x = 64 \qquad \Rightarrow 8x = 64$

$\therefore \qquad x = \dfrac{64}{8} = 8.$

5. Let the number is x

$\therefore \qquad 180 - x = 11x - 180$

$\Rightarrow \quad 180 + 180 = 11x + x$

$\Rightarrow \qquad 360 = 12x,$

$\Rightarrow \qquad x = \dfrac{360}{12} = 30.$

6. Let the no. $= x$ then its reciprocal $= \dfrac{1}{x}$

By the question, $\left(x+\dfrac{1}{x}\right) = 3\left(x-\dfrac{1}{x}\right)$

$$\Rightarrow \qquad \frac{x^2+1}{x} = \frac{3(x^2-1)}{x}$$
$$\Rightarrow \qquad x^2 + 1 = 3x^2 - 3$$
$$\Rightarrow \qquad 3x^2 - x^2 = 3 + 1$$
$$\therefore \qquad x = \sqrt{2}.$$

7. Let the required fraction $= x$

then, by the question $\quad x \div \dfrac{7}{9} - x \times \dfrac{7}{9} = \dfrac{8}{21}$

$$\Rightarrow \qquad x \times \frac{9}{7} - \frac{7x}{9} = \frac{8}{21}$$

$$\Rightarrow \qquad \frac{32x}{63} = \frac{8}{21}$$

$$\Rightarrow \qquad x = \frac{8}{21} \times \frac{63}{32} = \frac{3}{4}$$

Hence, the correct answer $= \dfrac{3}{4} \times \dfrac{7}{9} = \dfrac{7}{12}$.

8.
```
        312) 408(1
             312
             ———
         96) 312 (3
             288
             ———
         24) 96 (4
             96
             ——
              ×
```

$\therefore$ Maximum number of girls or boys that can be placed in a section $= 24$ and total

number of such section $= \dfrac{408}{24} + \dfrac{312}{24}$

$$= 17 + 13 = 30$$

9. Let three different one digit natural numbers be x, y and z.
Then, sum of all possible two digits numbers
$= (10x + y) + (10y + x) + (10x + z)$
$\qquad\quad + (10z + x) + (10y + z) + (10z + y)$
$= 22x + 22y + 22z = 22 (x + y + z)$
Hence, required number = 22.

10. Let four prime numbers be a, b, c and d respectively.

Now, $\dfrac{abc}{bcd} = \dfrac{385}{1001} \quad \Rightarrow \dfrac{c}{d} = \dfrac{5}{13}$

Hence, $a = 5$ and $d = 13$

11. 357 ★ 25 ★
For divisible by 5, the last digit must be either 0 or 5.
If last digit is 0, then other required digit will be 2 or 5 or 8
Hence, the numbers are (0, 2) or (0, 5) or (0, 8)
If last digit is 5, then other required digit will be 0 or 3 or 6 or 9
Hence, the numbers are (5, 0) or (5, 3) or (5, 6) or (5, 9)
So, correct option is (c).

12. Here, $(x + 1365) = 6x + 15$
$\Rightarrow 5x = 1350$

$$\therefore \quad x = \frac{1350}{5} = 270$$

Hence, the smaller number = 270.

13. The number $= 31x + 29$.
Here, given data is inadequate.

14.
```
     5 | a
     9 | b − 4
    13 | c − 8
       | 1 − 12
```

Now, $\quad c = 13 \times 1 + 12 = 25$
$\qquad\qquad b = 9c + 8 = 9 \times 25 + 8 = 233$
$\qquad\qquad a = 5b + 4 = 5 \times 233 + 4$
$$\qquad\qquad\qquad = 1165 + 4 = 1169$$
$1169 = 585 \times 1 + 584$
Hence, required remainder = 584.

15. The number $= 6x + 3$
Now, $(6x + 3)^2 = 36x^2 + 36x + 9$
$$= (36x^2 + 36x + 6) + 3$$
$$= 6(6x^2 + 6x + 1) + 3$$
Hence, required remainder = 3.

LCM AND HCF

1. The L.C.M. and H.C.F. of two numbers are 4284 and 32 respectively. If one of the numbers is 204, the other is
   A. 672   B. 576
   C. 676   D. 572

2. Two numbers are in the ratio of 8 : 15. If their H.C.F. is 4, the numbers are
   A. 32 and 60   B. 16 and 30
   C. 80 and 150   D. 64 and 120

3. The greatest number that will divide 366, 513 and 324 leaving the same remainder in each case is
   A. 21   B. 18
   C. 27   D. 42

4. The L.C.M. of two numbers is 45 times their H.C.F. If the sum of the L.C.M. and the H.C.F. of these two numbers is 1150 and one of the numbers is 125, then the other number is
   A. 256   B. 225
   C. 250   D. 255

5. The H.C.F. and the L.C.M. of two numbers are 50 and 250 respectively. On dividing one of these numbers by 2, 50 is obtained as quotient. The numbrs are
   A. 100, 125   B. 80, 100
   C. 125, 100   D. 200, 250

6. Three bells ring respectively at an interval of 15 seconds, 20 seconds and 24 seconds. If they ring continuously for 12 minutes then how many times, during this period, will they ring together?
   A. 2 times   B. 6 times
   C. 5 times   D. 3 times

7. If the sum of two numbers is 55 and the H.C.F. and L.C.M. of these numbers are 5 and 120 respectively. Find the sum of their reciprocals.
   A. $\dfrac{120}{11}$ B. $\dfrac{11}{120}$
   C. $\dfrac{601}{55}$ D. $\dfrac{55}{601}$

8. The LCM of two numbers is 48. The numbers are in the ratio of 2 : 3. The sum of the numbers is
   A. 64   B. 40
   C. 32   D. 28

9. Find the greatest number that will divide 43, 91 and 183 so as to leave the same remainder in each case.
   A. 13   B. 9
   C. 7   D. 4

10. The greatest possible length which can be used to measure exactly the length 7m, 3m 85cm, 12m 95 cm is
    A. 42 cm   B. 35 cm
    C. 25 cm   D. 15 cm

11. A, B and C start at the same time in the same direction to run around a circular park. A completes a round in 252 seconds, B in 308 seconds and C in 198 seconds, all starting at the same point. After what time will they meet again at the starting point?
    A. 46 minutes 12 seconds
    B. 45 minutes
    C. 42 minutes 36 seconds
    D. 26 minutes 18 seconds

12. Which of the following has most numbers of divisors?
   A. 182   B. 176
   C. 101   D. 99

13. Which is of the following is a co-primes?
   A. (23, 92)   B. (21, 35)
   C. (18, 25)   D. (16, 62)

14. Let N be the greatest number that will divide 1305, 4665 and 6905, leaving the same remainder in each case. Then find the sum of the digits in N.
   A. 8   B. 6
   C. 5   D. 4

15. The greatest number which one dividing 1657 and 2037 leaves remainder 6 and 5 respectively, is:
   A. 305   B. 235
   C. 127   D. 123

ANSWERS

1	2	3	4	5	6	7	8	9	10
A	A	A	B	A	B	B	B	D	B

11	12	13	14	15
A	B	C	D	C

SOME SELECTED EXPLANATORY ANSWERS

1. 1st number × 2nd number = LCM × HCF
$\therefore$ 204 × 2nd number = 4284 × 32
$\therefore$ 2nd number $= \dfrac{4284 \times 32}{204} = 672$
$\therefore$ 2nd number = 672

2. Let the numbers be $8x$ and $15x$
$8x = 2 \times 2 \times 2 \times x$
$15x = 3 \times 5 \times x$
$\therefore$ LCM of $8x$ and $15x = 2 \times 2 \times 2 \times x \times 3 \times 5$
$= 120x$
Now, 1st number × 2nd number = HCF × LCM
$\Rightarrow$ $8x \times 15x = 4 \times 120x$
$\Rightarrow$ $120x^2 = 4 \times 120x$
$\Rightarrow$ $x = 4$
$\therefore$ Numbers are $8 \times 4 = 32$ and $15 \times 4 = 60$

3. Difference between 366 and 513 = 513 − 366
$= 147$
and difference between 513 and 324
$= 513 - 324 = 189$
$\therefore$ HCF of 147 and 189

```
        147) 189 (1
             147
        × 42) 147 (3
             126
        × 21) 42 (2
              42
              ×
```

$\therefore$ The required largest number is 21.

4. LCM of the two numbers = 45 × HCF
and   LCM + HCF = 1150
$\Rightarrow$ 45 × HCF + HCF = 1150
$\Rightarrow$ HCF(45 + 1) = 1150
$\Rightarrow$ HCF $= \dfrac{1150}{46} = 25$
$\therefore$ LCM = 45 × 25 = 1125
$\because$ 1st number × 2nd number = LCM × HCF
$\therefore$ 125 × 2nd number = 1125 × 25
$\therefore$ 2nd number $= \dfrac{1125 \times 25}{125} = 225.$

5. According to the condition of the problem, 50 is obtained on dividing one of the numbers by 2
$\therefore$ One of the numbers = 50 × 2 = 100
Now, 1st number × 2nd number = LCM × HCF
$\therefore$ 100 × 2nd number = 250 × 50
$\therefore$ 2nd number $= \dfrac{250 \times 50}{100} = 125$

Hence, numbers are 100 and 125.

6. LCM of 15, 20 and 24

5	15,	20,	24
4	3,	4,	24
3	3,	1,	6
	1,	1,	2

LCM = 5 × 4 × 3 × 2 = 120

8

$\because$ 12 minutes = 12 × 60 = 720 seconds
$\therefore$ Number of times the bells will ring together during 12 minutes

$$= \frac{720}{120} = 6 \text{ times.}$$

7. Let the number be x and y.
Then, $x + y = 55$;
$\quad xy = \text{HCF} \times \text{LCM} = 5 \times 120$
$\therefore$ Sum of their reciprocals

$$= \frac{1}{x} + \frac{1}{y} = \frac{x+y}{xy} = \frac{55}{5 \times 120} = \frac{11}{120}.$$

8. Let the two numbers be $2x$ and $3x$;
their LCM = $6x$
Now, $\quad 6x = 48 \qquad \therefore \quad x = 8$
Hence, the numbers are 2×8, $3 \times 8 = 16, 24$
Their sum = 16 + 24 = 40.

9.
```
2240) 3360 (1        1120) 5600 (5
      2240                 5600
      1120 ) 2240 (2         ×
             2240
               ×
```
Hence, N = HCF of 3360,
2240 and 5600 = 1120
Sum of digits in N = 1 + 1 + 2 + 0 = 4.

10. 7m = 700 cm;
3m 85 = 385 cm;
12m 95cm = 1295 cm
```
385) 700 (1
     385
     315) 385 (1
          315
          70) 315 (4
              280
              35 ) 70 (2
                   70
                    ×
35) 1295 (37
    105
    245
    245
      ×
```

Hence, required length = HCF of 700 cm, 385 cm, 1295 cm = 35 cm.

11.

2	252,	308,	198
2	126,	154,	99
3	63,	77,	99
3	21,	77,	33
7	7,	77,	11
11	1,	11,	11
	1,	1,	1

Hence, LCM = 2 × 2 × 3 × 3 × 7 × 11 = 2772
Hence, A, B, C will meet again at the starting point after 2772 sec. = 46 min 12 sec.

12.

Numbers	Their divisors
182	→ 1, 2, 7, 13, 14, 26, 91 and 182
176	→ 1, 2, 4, 8, 16, 22, 44, 88 and 176
101	→ 1 and 101
99	→ 1, 3, 9, 11, 33 and 99

Therefore, 176 has the most number of divisors.

13. HCF of 23 and 92 = 23
HCF of 21 and 35 = 7
HCF of 18 and 25 = 1
HCF of 16 and 62 = 2
Hence, 18 and 25 are co-prime numbers.

14. N = HCF of (4665 − 1305),
(6905 − 4665) and (6905 − 1305)
= HCF of 3360, 2240 and 5600 = 112
Sum of digit of 1 + 1 + 2 = 4.

15. Required number = HCF of (1657 − 6) and (2037 − 5) = HCF of 1651 and 2032 = 127.
```
1651) 2032 (1
      1651
      381) 1651 (4
           1524
           127) 381 (3
                381
                  ×
```

AVERAGE

1. One-third of a certain journey was covered at the rate of 25 km per hour, one-fourth at the rate of 30 km per hour and the rest at the 50 km per hour. What is the average speed per hour for whole journey?

   A. $33\dfrac{1}{3}$ kmph
   B. $44\dfrac{1}{4}$ kmph
   C. $22\dfrac{1}{2}$ kmph
   D. 33 kmph

2. A batsman has a certain average of runs for 16 innings. In the 17th innings, he makes a score of 85 runs thereby increasing his average by 3. What is the average after the 17th inning?
   A. 33 runs
   B. 34 runs
   C. 37 runs
   D. 36 runs

3. The average of 6 observations is 12. A new seventh observation is included and the new average is decreased by 1. The seventh observation is
   A. 1
   B. 3
   C. 5
   D. 6

4. The average age of 30 students in a class is 12 years. The average age of a group of 5 of the students is 10 years and that of another group of 5 of them is 14 years. The average age of the remaining students is
   A. 8 years
   B. 10 years
   C. 12 years
   D. 14 years

5. Out of the three given numbers, the first number is twice the second and thrice the third. If the average of three numbers is 121, what is the difference between the first and third number?
   A. 144
   B. 77
   C. 99
   D. 132

6. If the average marks of three batches of 55, 60 and 45 students is 50, 55 and 60, then average marks of all the students is:
   A. 55
   B. 54
   C. 54.68
   D. 55.68

7. The average of 8 numbers is 20. The average of first two numbers is $15\dfrac{1}{2}$ and that of the next three is $21\dfrac{1}{3}$. If the sixth number is less than the seventh and eighth numbers by 4 and 7 respectively, then the eighth number is:
   A. 27
   B. 25
   C. 22
   D. 18

8. A pupil's marks were wrongly entered as 83 instead of 63. Due to that the average marks for the class got increased by half. What is the number of pupils in the class?
   A. 73
   B. 40
   C. 40
   D. 10

9. A cricketer whose bowling average is 12.4 runs per wicket takes 5 wickets for 26 runs and thereby decreases his average by 0.4. The number of wickets taken by him till the last match was:
   A. 85
   B. 80
   C. 72
   D. 64

10. The average weight of a class of 24 students is 35 kg. If the weight of the teacher is included, the average rises by 400 g. What is the weight of the teacher?
    A. 55 kg
    B. 53 kg
    C. 50 kg
    D. 45 kg

11. Nine men went to a hotel. Eight of them spent Rs. 3 for each over their meals and the ninth spent Rs. 2 more than the average expenditure of all the nine. What is the total money spent by them?

A. Rs. 29.25   B. Rs. 29.50
C. Rs. 29   D. Rs. 30

12. The average age of 24 students in a class is 10. If the teacher's age is included, the average increases by one. The age of the teacher is

A. 25   B. 30
C. 35   D. 40

13. The average of 5 consecutive even numbers A, B, C, D and E is 34. What is the product of B and D?

A. 1152   B. 1368
C. 1224   D. 1088

14. The average of 50 numbers is 30. If two numbers, 35 and 40 are discarded, then the average of the remaining numbers is nearly:

A. 29.68   B. 29.27
C. 28.78   D. 28.32

15. The average monthly salary of 20 employees of an organisation is Rs. 1500. If the manager's salary is added, then the average salary increases by Rs. 100. Find the manager's monthly salary?

A. Rs. 4800   B. Rs. 3600
C. Rs. 2400   D. Rs. 2000

ANSWERS

1	2	3	4	5	6	7	8	9	10
A	C	C	C	D	C	B	B	A	D

11	12	13	14	15
A	C	A	A	B

SOME SELECTED EXPLANATORY ANSWERS

1. Let the total distance covered during journey = 60 km

$\dfrac{1}{3}$ of the distance covered during journey

$$= 60 \times \dfrac{1}{3} = 20 \text{ km}$$

$\dfrac{1}{4}$ of the distance covered during journey

$$= \dfrac{1}{4} \times 60 = 15 \text{ km}$$

∴ The distance covered during the rest of journey = 60 − (20 + 15) = 25 km

Time taken to cover 20 km at 25 km/h

$$= \dfrac{20}{25} \text{ hours} = \dfrac{4}{5} \text{ hour}$$

Time taken to cover 15 km at 30 km/h

$$= \dfrac{15}{30} \text{ hours} = \dfrac{1}{2} \text{ hour}$$

Time taken to cover 25 km at 50 km/h

$$= \dfrac{25}{50} \text{ hours} = \dfrac{1}{2} \text{ hour}$$

Total time taken $= \dfrac{4}{5} + \dfrac{1}{2} + \dfrac{1}{2}$

$$= \dfrac{9}{5} \text{ hours}$$

Hence average speed per hour $= 60 \div \dfrac{9}{5}$

$$= \dfrac{60 \times 5}{9} = \dfrac{100}{3} \text{ km/h}$$

$$= 33\dfrac{1}{3} \text{ km/h}$$

2. Average increase in the score of 17 innings = 3 runs

Total increase in the score of 17 innings = 3 × 17 = 51 runs

∴ His average of 16 innings = 85 − 51 = 34 runs

Hence, average after the 17th innings
$$= 34 + 3 = 37 \text{ runs}$$

3. Seventh observation $= (7 \times 11 - 6 \times 12) = 5$

4. Let, the required average age be x

Then, $5 \times 10 + 5 \times 14 + 20 \times x = 30 \times 12$

$\Rightarrow \qquad 20x = 360 - 120$

$\Rightarrow \qquad 20x = 240$

$\Rightarrow \qquad x = 12$

5. Let the three numbers be x, $\dfrac{x}{2}$ and $\dfrac{x}{3}$ respectively,

Now, $\dfrac{1}{3}\left(x + \dfrac{x}{2} + \dfrac{x}{3}\right) = 121$

$\Rightarrow \dfrac{11x}{6} = 121 \times 3$

$\therefore \quad x = \dfrac{121 \times 3 \times 6}{11} = 198$

Hence, required difference $= x - \dfrac{x}{3} = \dfrac{2x}{3}$

$$= \dfrac{2}{3} \times 198 = 132$$

6. Required average Marks

$$= \dfrac{55 \times 50 + 60 \times 55 + 45 \times 60}{55 + 60 + 45} = \dfrac{8750}{160} = 54.68$$

7. Let the sixth, seventh and eighth numbers are x, $x + 4$ and $x + 7$.

Sum of last three numbers

$$= 8 \times 20 - \left(2 \times \dfrac{31}{2} + 3 \times \dfrac{64}{3}\right)$$

$\Rightarrow x + x + 4 + x + 7 = 160 - 95$

$\Rightarrow 3x + 11 = 65$

$\Rightarrow 3x = 54 \qquad \therefore x = 18$

New eighth number $= x + 7 = 18 + 7 = 25$

8. Let the total number of pupils in the class be x; then,

$\dfrac{83 - 63}{x} = \dfrac{1}{2} \quad \Rightarrow \dfrac{20}{x} = \dfrac{1}{2} \qquad \therefore x = 40$

9. Let the number of wickets taken by him be x till the last match.

Then, $\dfrac{x \times 12.4 + 26}{x + 5} = 12$

$\Rightarrow 12.4x + 26 = 12x + 60$

$\Rightarrow 0.4x = 34 \quad \therefore x = \dfrac{340}{4} = 85$

10. Let the weight of the teacher be x kgs, then

$\dfrac{24 \times 35 + x}{25} = 35.4$

$\Rightarrow 840 + x = 885 \qquad \therefore x = 45 \text{ kgs}$

12. Age of the teacher $= (25 \times 11 - 24 \times 10)$ years

$$= 35 \text{ years}$$

13. Let 5 consecutive even numbers A, B, C, D and E be x, $x + 2$, $x + 4$, $x + 6$ and $x + 8$ respectively.

Now, $\dfrac{x + x + 2 + x + 4 + x + 6 + x + 8}{5} = 34$

$\Rightarrow 5x + 20 = 170$

$\Rightarrow 5x = 150 \qquad \therefore x = 30$

Then, B $= x + 2 = 30 + 2 = 32$;

D $= x + 6 = 30 + 6 = 36$

Hence, their product $= 32 \times 36 = 1152$

14. The average of remaining 48 numbers

$$= \dfrac{50 \times 30 - (35 + 40)}{48} = \dfrac{1500 - 75}{48}$$

$$= \dfrac{1425}{48} = 29.68$$

15. Let manager's salary be Rs. x, then

$\dfrac{20 \times 1500 + x}{21} = 1600$

$\Rightarrow 30{,}000 + x = 33600$

$\therefore x = \text{Rs. } 3600$

PROBLEMS BASED ON AGES

1. The ratio of ages of A and B is 3 : 11. After 3 years the ratio becomes 1 : 3. What are the ages of A and B?
   A. 9 years, 33 years
   B. 10 years, 40 years
   C. 9 years, 27 years
   D. None of these

2. Two years ago, the ratio of Ram's and Mohan's age was 3 : 2 and at present 7 : 5. What are their present ages?
   A. 14 years, 10 years
   B. 15 years, 10 years
   C. 13 years, 9 years
   D. None of these

3. The ages of Samir and Saurabh are in the ratio of 8 : 15 respectively. After 9 years the ratio of their ages will be 11 : 18. What is the difference between their ages in years?
   A. 20 years
   B. 21 years
   C. 22 years
   D. 24 years

4. The present age of father is 34 years more than that of his son. 12 years ago, father's age was 18 times the age of his son. The present age of son in years is:
   A. 12
   B. 14
   C. 16
   D. 18

5. A mother is 25 years older than her daughter. Five years ago, the age of the mother was 6 times the age of the daughter. What is the present age of mother?
   A. 25 years
   B. 29 years
   C. 32 years
   D. 35 years

6. The difference between the present ages of P and Q is 4 years. The ratio of their ages after 5 years will be 9 : 8. The present age of P is:
   A. 24 years
   B. 30 years
   C. 32 years
   D. None of these

7. Ten years ago, the age of Divya was half of the age of Namrata. If the ratio of present ages of both is 3 : 4, the sum of their present ages is:
   A. 35 years
   B. 30 years
   C. 25 years
   D. 18 years

8. The ratio between the present ages of A and B is 5 : 3 respectively. The ratio between A's age 4 years ago and B's age 4 years hence is 1 : 1. The ratio between A's age 4 years hence and B's age 4 years ago is:
   A. 4 : 1
   B. 3 : 1
   C. 2 : 1
   D. 1 : 3

9. Ram got married 8 years ago. His present age is $\frac{6}{5}$ times his age at the time of marriage. Ram's sister was 10 years younger to him at the time of his marriage. What is the present age of Ram's sister?
   A. 40 years
   B. 38 years
   C. 36 years
   D. 32 years

10. A father said to his son, "I was as old as you are at present at the time of your birth." If the father's age is 38 years now. Five years ago the age of son was:
    A. 38 years
    B. 33 years
    C. 19 years
    D. 14 years

ANSWERS

1	2	3	4	5	6	7	8	9	10
A	A	B	B	D	D	A	B	B	D

SOME SELECTED EXPLANATORY ANSWERS

1. Let the ages of A and B be $3x$ and $11x$ years; then

$$\frac{3x+3}{11x+3} = \frac{1}{3} \quad \Rightarrow \quad 9x + 9 = 11x + 3$$

$\Rightarrow 2x = 6 \quad \therefore \ x = 3$

Hence, their present age, $3x = 3 \times 3 = 9$ years; $11x = 11 \times 3 = 33$ years

2. Let the present ages of Ram and Mohan are $7x$ and $5x$ years; then

$$\frac{7x-2}{5x-2} = \frac{3}{2} \quad \Rightarrow \quad 14x - 4 = 15x - 6$$

$\therefore \ x = 2$

Hence, their present ages : $7 \times 2 = 14$ years and $5 \times 2 = 10$ years

3. Let the present ages of Samir and Saurabh are $8x$ and $15x$ years respectively; then

$$\frac{8x+9}{15x+9} = \frac{11}{18} \quad \Rightarrow \quad 144x + 162 = 165x + 99$$

$\Rightarrow 21x = 63 \quad \therefore \ x = 3$

Hence, difference of their ages = $15x - 8x = 7x$ = $7 \times 3 = 21$ years

4. Let the present ages of father and his son be $x + 34$ and x years respectively; then

$18(x - 12) = x + 34 - 12$

$\Rightarrow 18x - 216 = x + 22$

$\Rightarrow 17x = 238 \quad \therefore \ x = 14$

Hence, present age of his son = 14 years

5. Let the present ages of mother and her daughter are $(x + 25)$ and x years respectively; then

$6(x - 5) = x + 25 - 5$

$\Rightarrow \quad 6x - 30 = x + 20$

$\Rightarrow \quad\quad 5x = 50 \quad \therefore \ x = 10$

Hence, the age of the mother = $10 + 25$

$\qquad\qquad\qquad\qquad = 35$ years

6. Let the present ages of P and Q be $(x + 4)$ and x years;

then, $\dfrac{x+4+5}{x+5} = \dfrac{9}{8} \quad \Rightarrow \quad 8x + 72$

$\qquad\qquad\qquad = 9x + 45 \quad \therefore \ x = 27$

Hence, present age of P = $27 + 4 = 31$ years

7. Let the present ages of Divya and Namrata are $3x$ and $4x$ years respectively; then

$$\frac{3x-10}{4x-10} = \frac{1}{2}$$

$\Rightarrow \ 6x - 20 = 4x - 10$

$\Rightarrow \qquad 2x = 10 \quad \therefore \ x = 5$

Hence, sum of their ages = $3x + 4x = 7x$

$\qquad\qquad\qquad\qquad = 7 \times 5 = 35$ years

8. Let the present ages of A and B are $5x$ and $3x$ years respectively; then,

$$\frac{5x-4}{3x+4} = 1 \quad \Rightarrow \quad 5x - 4 = 3x + 4$$

$\Rightarrow 2x = 8 \quad \therefore \ x = 4$

Hence, their present ages are 20 years and 12 years.

So, required ratio = $(20 + 4) : (12 - 4)$

$\qquad\qquad\qquad = 24 : 8 = 3 : 1$

9. Let the present age of Ram be x years; then

$$\frac{x}{x-8} = \frac{6}{5} \quad \Rightarrow \quad 5x = 6x - 48$$

$\therefore \quad x = 48$

Hence, present age of Ram's sister

$\qquad\qquad = 48 - 10 = 38$ years.

10. Let the age of father was x years at the time of his son's birth, then present age of father and his son will be $2x$ and x years,

Now, $\qquad 2x = 38 \quad \therefore \ x = 19$ years

Hence, 5 years ago the age of son was $19 - 5$ = 14 years

CHAIN RULE

1. A fort has provision for 50 days. After 15 days a reinforcement of 150 men arrives and the provision now lasts 25 days. How many men were there in the fort?
   A. 300
   B. 225
   C. 275
   D. 200

2. In a fort there is provisions for 40 days for 275 persons. If after 16 days 125 persons leave the fort for how many more days the provisions will last?
   A. 35 days
   B. 44 days
   C. 45 days
   D. 53 days

3. 60 men could complete a work in 250 days. They worked together for 200 days. After that the work had to be stopped for 10 days due to bad weather. How many more men should be engaged to complete the work in time?
   A. 20
   B. 18
   C. 15
   D. 10

4. A contractor undertook to complete a project in 90 days and employed 60 men on it. After 60 days, he found that $\frac{3}{4}$ of the work has already been completed. How many men can he discharge so that the project may completed exactly on time?
   A. 15
   B. 20
   C. 30
   D. 40

5. A flagstaff 17.5 m high casts a shadow of length 40.25 m. The height of the building, which casts a shadow of length 28.75m under similar condition will be:
   A. 21.25 m
   B. 17.5 m
   C. 12.5 m
   D. 10 m

6. If 5 men or 9 women can do a piece of work in 19 days, then 3 men and 6 women will do the same work in how many days?
   A. 21
   B. 18
   C. 15
   D. 12

7. A certain number of men can finish a piece of work in 100 days. If there were 10 men less, it will take 10 days more for the work to be finished. How many men were there originally?
   A. 110
   B. 100
   C. 82
   D. 75

8. Some persons can do a piece of work in 12 days. Two times the number of such persons will do half of that work in:
   A. 12 days
   B. 3 days
   C. 6 days
   D. 4 days

9. 2 men and 7 boys can do a piece of work in 14 days; 3 men and 8 boys can do the same in 11 days. Then 8 men and 6 boys can do three times of this work in
   A. 30 days
   B. 4 days
   C. 21 days
   D. 18 days

10. If 3 men or 6 boys, working 7 hours a day can do a piece of work in 10 days; how many days will it take to complete a piece of work twice as large with 6 men and 2 boys working together for 8 hours a day?
    A. 9
    B. $8\frac{1}{2}$
    C. $7\frac{1}{2}$
    D. $6\frac{1}{2}$

11. If 15 men can do a certain amount of work in 20 days working 8 hours a day, in how many days will 10 men do three times the work working 6 hours a day?

   A. 120 days   B. 70 days

   C. 100 days   D. None of these

12. 40 men consume 60 kgs of rice in 15 days, then in how many days will 30 men consume 12 kgs of rice?

   A. 9 days   B. $6\dfrac{1}{4}$ days

   C. 4 days   D. $3\dfrac{1}{4}$ days

13. 56 men can complete a piece of work in 24 days. In how many days can 42 men complete the same piece of work?

   A. 48   B. 32

   C. 20   D. 16

14. Running at the same constant rate, 6 identical machines can produce a total of 270 bottles per minute. At this rate, how many bottles could 10 such machines produce in 4 minutes?

   A. 1400   B. 1600

   C. 1800   D. 2000

15. 400 persons, working 9 hours a day complete $\dfrac{1}{4}th$ of the work in 10 days. The number of additional persons, working 8 hours a day, required to complete the remaining work in 20 days, is:

   A. 275   B. 250

   C. 675   D. 200

ANSWERS

1	2	3	4	5	6	7	8	9	10
B	B	C	B	C	C	A	B	C	C

11	12	13	14	15
A	C	B	C	C

SOME SELECTED EXPLANATORY ANSWERS

1.

Days	Men
35↑	x ↓
25	$x + 150$

$$\Rightarrow \frac{x+150}{x} = \frac{35}{25} \qquad \Rightarrow 1 + \frac{150}{x} = \frac{35}{25}$$

$$\Rightarrow \frac{150}{x} = \frac{10}{25}$$

$$\therefore \; x = \frac{25}{10} \times 150 = 375$$

Required number of men = 375 – 150 = 225

2.

Persons	Days
275↑	24 ↓
150	x

$$\Rightarrow \frac{x}{24} = \frac{275}{150} \qquad \therefore \; x = \frac{275}{150} \times 24 = 44 \text{ days}$$

3.

Days	Men
50↑	60 ↓
40	x

$$\Rightarrow \frac{x}{60} = \frac{50}{40} \qquad \therefore \; x = \frac{50}{40} \times 60 = 75 \text{ men}$$

Hence, number of additional men = 75 – 60
$$= 15$$

4.

Work	Days	Men
$\dfrac{3}{4}$ ↓	60 ↑	60 ↓
$\dfrac{1}{4}$	30	x

$$\Rightarrow \frac{x}{60} = \frac{60}{30} \times \frac{1/4}{3/4}$$

$$\therefore \; x = \frac{60}{30} \times \frac{1}{3} \times 60 = 40 \text{ days}$$

Hence, number of men to be discharged
$$= 60 - 40 = 20$$

5.

Shadow (m)	Object (m)
40.25 ↓	17.5 ↓
28.75 ↓	x ↓

$$\Rightarrow \quad \frac{x}{17.5} = \frac{28.75}{40.25}$$

$$\therefore \ x = \frac{28.75 \times 17.5}{40.25} = 12.5 \text{ m}$$

6. 5 men $\equiv$ 9 women

$$\therefore \ 3 \text{ men} = \frac{9}{5} \times 3 = \frac{27}{5} \text{ women}$$

Hence, 3 men and 6 women $= \dfrac{27}{5} + 6$

$$= \frac{57}{5} \text{ women}$$

Women	Days
9 ↑	19 ↓
$\dfrac{57}{5}$ ↑	x ↓

$$\Rightarrow \quad \frac{x}{19} = \frac{9 \times 5}{57}$$

$$\therefore \ x = \frac{9 \times 5}{57} \times 19 = 15 \text{ days}$$

7.

Days	Men
100 ↑	x ↓
110 ↑	$x - 10$ ↓

$$\Rightarrow \quad \frac{x-10}{x} = \frac{100}{110} \qquad \Rightarrow \quad 110x - 1100 = 100x$$

$$\Rightarrow \ 10x = 1100 \qquad \therefore \ x = 110$$

Hence, initially the number of men = 110

8.

Work	Persons	Days
1 ↓	x ↑	12 ↓
$\dfrac{1}{2}$ ↓	$2x$ ↑	a ↓

$$\Rightarrow \quad \frac{a}{12} = \frac{x}{2x} \times \frac{1}{2} \qquad \therefore \ a = \frac{1}{4} \times 12 = 3 \text{ days}$$

9. Here, $14 \times 2 \text{ men} + 14 \times 7 \text{ boys} \equiv 11 \times 3 \text{ men}$
$$+ \ 11 \times 8 \text{ boys}$$
$$\Rightarrow 28 \text{ men} + 98 \text{ boys} \equiv 33 \text{ men} + 88 \text{ boys}$$

$\Rightarrow 5 \text{ men} = 10 \text{ boys} \quad \therefore \ 1 \text{ man} = 2 \text{ boys}$

Then, 2 men and 7 boys $\equiv$ 4 boys + 7 boys
$$= 11 \text{ boys}$$

& also, 8 men and 6 boys $\equiv$ 16 boys + 6 boys
$$= 22 \text{ boys}$$

Work	Boys	Days
1 ↓	11 ↑	14 ↓
3 ↓	22 ↑	x ↓

$$\Rightarrow \quad \frac{x}{14} = \frac{11}{22} \times \frac{3}{1}$$

$$\therefore \ x = \frac{1}{2} \times 3 \times 14 = 21 \text{ days}$$

12.

Men	Rice (kgs)	Days
40 ↑	60 ↓	15 ↓
30 ↑	12 ↓	x ↓

$$\Rightarrow \quad \frac{x}{15} = \frac{12}{60} \times \frac{40}{30}$$

$$\therefore \ x = \frac{12}{60} \times \frac{40}{30} \times 15 = 4 \text{ days}$$

14.

Machines	Time (minutes)	Bottles
6 ↓	1 ↓	270 ↓
10 ↓	4 ↓	x ↓

$$\Rightarrow \quad \frac{x}{270} = \frac{4}{1} \times \frac{10}{6}$$

$$\therefore \ x = \frac{4 \times 10}{6} \times 270 = 1800 \text{ bottles}$$

15.

Work	Hours	Days	Persons
$\dfrac{1}{4}$ ↓	9 ↑	10 ↑	400 ↓
$\dfrac{3}{4}$ ↓	8 ↑	20 ↑	x ↓

$$\Rightarrow \quad \frac{x}{400} = \frac{10}{20} \times \frac{9}{8} \times \frac{3/4}{1/4}$$

$$\therefore \ x = \frac{1}{2} \times \frac{9}{8} \times 3 \times 400 = 675$$

Hence, number of additional persons
$$= 675 - 400 = 275$$

TIME AND DISTANCE

1. Starting from a point at a speed of 4 km/hr a man reaches at a cerain place and returns back to the point from where he had started journey on bicycle at the speed of 16 km/hr. His average speed during the entire journey will be :
   A. 6.4 km/h
   B. 8.4 km/h
   C. 5.4 km/h
   D. 10 km/h

2. A motorist covers a certain distance at a average speed of 48 km/h in 45 minutes. What speed in km/h he must maintain to cover the same distance in 30 minutes?
   A. 66 km/h
   B. 79 km/h
   C. 80 km/h
   D. 72 km/h

3. A policeman saw a thief at a distance of 200 m. The policeman and the thief started running at the same time. If the policeman runs at a speed of $4\dfrac{1}{6}$ m per second and the thief at a speed of $3\dfrac{1}{3}$ m per second, after what time the policeman will catch the thief?
   A. 12 min
   B. 10 min
   C. 9 min
   D. 4 min

4. A monkey wants to climb up a glazed pole. He climbs 12 metres in 1 minute and then he slips back 3 metres in the next minute. If the pole is 63 metre high, how long does he take to climb at the top of the pole?
   A. $11\dfrac{1}{4}$ min
   B. $12\dfrac{1}{2}$ min
   C. $12\dfrac{3}{4}$ min
   D. $14\dfrac{3}{4}$ min

5. The distance between two stations A and B is 300 km. A train leaves the station A with a speed of 40 km/hr. At the same time another train departs from the station B with a speed of 50 km/hr. How much time will these two trains take to cross each other?
   A. 3 hrs 40 min
   B. 3 hrs 20 min
   C. 2 hrs 20 min
   D. 3 hrs 45 min

6. Nilesh goes to school from his village at the speed of 4 km/hr and returns from school to village at the speed of 2 km/hr. If he takes 6 hours in all, then what is the distance between the village and the school?
   A. 8 km
   B. 6 km
   C. 5 km
   D. 4 km

7. By increasing the speed of the bus by 10 km/hr the time of journey for 72 km is reduced by 36 minutes. What was the original speed of the bus?
   A. 30 km/hr
   B. 35 km/hr
   C. 40 km/hr
   D. 45 km/hr

8. A train covers a distance in 50 minutes, if it runs at a speed of 48 km/hr on an average. The speed at which the train must run to reduce the time of journey to 40 minutes will be:
   A. 70 km/hr
   B. 60 km/hr
   C. 55 km/hr
   D. 50 km/hr

9. A certain distance is covered by a vehicle at a certain speed. If half of this distance is covered by another vehicle in double the time, the ratio of the speeds of the two vehicles is:
   A. 4 : 1
   B. 1 : 4
   C. 2 : 1
   D. 1 : 2

10. A is faster than B. A and B each walk 24 km. The sum of their speeds is 7 km/hr and sum of times taken by them is 14 hours. What is the speed of A?
    A. 7 km/hr
    B. 5 km/hr
    C. 4 km/hr
    D. 3 km/hr

ANSWERS

1	2	3	4	5	6	7	8	9	10
A	D	D	C	B	A	A	B	A	C

SOME SELECTED EXPLANATORY ANSWERS

1. Average speed during the entire journey

$$= \frac{2xy}{x+y} = \frac{2\times 4\times 16}{4+16} = \frac{8\times 16}{20} = 6.4 \text{ km/hr.}$$

2. Let required speed be x km/hr; then

$$x \times \frac{1}{2} = 48 \times \frac{3}{4} \quad \therefore \quad x = 48 \times \frac{3}{4} \times 2$$
$$= 72 \text{ km/hr}$$

3. Suppose the policeman will catch the thief after t seconds

then, $\left(\dfrac{25}{6} - \dfrac{10}{3}\right)t = 200 \Rightarrow \dfrac{5}{6}t = 200$

$$\therefore \ t = \frac{200 \times 6}{5} = 240 \text{ sec} = 4 \text{ min.}$$

4. The monkey climbs 12 metres in 1 minute and then he slips back 3 metres in the next minute

$\therefore$ The monkey climbs in the first 2 minutes
$= 12 - 3 = 9$ metres

$\therefore$ In the first 12 minutes the monkey climbs
$= 9 \times 6 = 54$ metres

Remaining height of the pole to be covered by the monkey $= 63 - 54 = 9$ metre

$\therefore$ The monkey will climb the height of 9 metres in the 13th minute

$\because$ The monkey climbs 12 metres in 1 minute

$\therefore$ The monkey will climb 9 metres in $\dfrac{1}{12} \times 9$

$$= \frac{3}{4} \text{ minute}$$

$\therefore$ Time spent in climbing at the top of the

pole $= \left(12 + \dfrac{3}{4}\right)$ minutes $= 12\dfrac{3}{4}$ minutes

5. The two trains are moving in the opposite directions

$\therefore$ Relative speed $= 40 + 50 = 90$ km/hr.

$\therefore$ Time taken to cross each other $= \dfrac{300}{90} = 3\dfrac{1}{3}$

hours or, 3 hours 20 minutes.

6. Let x km be the distance between village and the school; then

$$\frac{x}{4} + \frac{x}{2} = 6 \qquad \Rightarrow \frac{3x}{4} = 6$$
$$\therefore \ x = \frac{6 \times 4}{3} = 8 \text{ km}$$

8. Let x km/hr be the required speed of the train; then

$$x \times \frac{40}{60} = 48 \times \frac{50}{60}$$
$$\therefore \ x = \frac{48 \times 50}{40} = 60 \text{ km/hr}$$

9. Let x km/hr and t hr be the certain speed and certain time.

Then, ratio of their speeds $= \dfrac{x}{t} : \dfrac{x}{2 \times 2t} = 1 : \dfrac{1}{4}$

$= 4 : 1$

10. Let speeds of A and B are x_1 and x_2 km/hr and times taken by them are t_1 and t_2 hrs, then

$$x_1 + x_2 = 7 \text{ km/hr} \qquad \text{...(i)}$$
$$t_1 + t_2 = 14 \text{ hrs} \qquad \text{...(ii)}$$

Now, $\dfrac{24}{x_1} + \dfrac{24}{x_2} = 14 \ \Rightarrow \ \dfrac{24(x_1 + x_2)}{x_1 x_2} = 14$

$$\therefore \ x_1 x_2 = \frac{24 \times 7}{14} = 12$$

Then, $x_1 - x_2 = \sqrt{(x_1 + x_2)^2 - 4x_1 x_2}$

$$= \sqrt{(7)^2 - 4 \times 12} = 1 \quad \text{...(iii)}$$

Solving *(i)* and *(iii)* we get $x_1 = 4$ km/hr

TIME AND WORK

1. A and B working together complete a work in 35 days. If A takes 60 days to complete it, how long would B alone take to complete it?
   A. 64 days
   B. 72 days
   C. 81 days
   D. 84 days

2. A few children working together can do a piece of work in 18 days. If the number of children employed on the work is made double, how long would they take to complete half of the work?

   A. $4\dfrac{1}{2}$ days
   B. $2\dfrac{1}{3}$ days

   C. $8\dfrac{3}{4}$ days
   D. $6\dfrac{1}{2}$ days

3. 10 men or 18 boys can do a piece of work in 15 days. In how many days would 25 men and 15 boys complete the same work working together?

   A. $5\dfrac{1}{2}$ days
   B. $4\dfrac{1}{2}$ days

   C. $6\dfrac{2}{3}$ days
   D. $2\dfrac{1}{3}$ days

4. A cistern is filled by a tap in $3\dfrac{1}{2}$ hours. Due to a leak in the bottom of the cistern, it takes half an hour longer to fill the cistern. If the cistern is full, how long will it take the leak to empty it?
   A. 28 hours
   B. 29 hours

   C. $31\dfrac{1}{3}$ hours
   D. 38 hours

5. A is twice as good a workman as B and thrice as good a workman as C. If C alone can do a piece of work in 24 days, how long would the

three persons take to finish the work working together?

   A. $3\dfrac{3}{11}$ days
   B. $4\dfrac{4}{7}$ days

   C. $4\dfrac{4}{11}$ days
   D. $3\dfrac{4}{11}$ days

6. If 3 men and 5 women can do a piece of work in 8 days and 2 men and 7 boys can do the same work in 12 days. Find the number of boys, the work done by whom can equate the work done by 10 women.
   A. 19 boys
   B. 21 boys
   C. 23 boys
   D. 15 boys

7. 8 men alone can complete a piece of work in 12 days. 4 women alone can complete the same piece of work in 48 days and 10 children alone can complete the piece of work in 24 days. In how many days can 10 men, 4 women and 10 children together complete the piece of work?
   A. 6
   B. 8
   C. 10
   D. 15

8. A works twice as fast as B. If B can complete a piece of work independently in 12 days. Find in how many days A and B together can complete the work?
   A. 8 days
   B. 6 days
   C. 4 days
   D. 18 days

9. A contractor undertook to complete a project in 90 days and employed 60 men on it. After 60 days, he found that $\dfrac{3}{4}$ of the work has already been completed. How many men can he discharge so that the project may be completed exactly on time?

A. 15	B. 20
C. 30	D. 40

10. A can do a piece of work in 25 days and B can do it in 20 days. They work together for 5 days and then A goes away. In how many days will B finish the remaining work?

A. 33 days	B. 20 days
C. 11 days	D. 10 days

ANSWERS

1	2	3	4	5	6	7	8	9	10
D	A	B	A	C	B	A	C	B	C

SOME SELECTED EXPLANATORY ANSWERS

1. (A + B)'s 1 day's work = $\dfrac{1}{35}$

and also, A's 1 day's work = $\dfrac{1}{60}$

Hence, B's 1 day's work = $\dfrac{1}{35} - \dfrac{1}{60} = \dfrac{5}{420} = \dfrac{1}{84}$

So, B will do the whole work in 84 days.

3. 10 men $\equiv$ 18 boys

25 men $\equiv \dfrac{18}{10} \times 25 = 45$ boys

Hence, 25 men + 15 boys = 45 + 15 = 60 boys

Now, 18 boys can do a piece of work in 15 days.

Hence, 60 boys will do a piece of work in

$\dfrac{15 \times 18}{60} = \dfrac{9}{2}$ days $= 4\dfrac{1}{2}$ days.

4. In 1 hour $\dfrac{2}{7}$ cistern is filled by the tap.

Hence, in $\dfrac{1}{2}$ hour $\dfrac{2}{14} = \dfrac{1}{7}$ cistern is filled by the tap.

So, $\dfrac{1}{7}$ cistern is emptied by the leakage in 4 hours.

So, 1 cistern will be emptied by the leakage in 28 hours.

6. Here, (3 men + 5 women) × 8

$\equiv$ (2 men + 7 boys) × 12

$\Rightarrow$ 40 women $\equiv$ 84 boys

$\therefore$ 10 women $\equiv \dfrac{84}{40} \times 10 = 21$ boys

Hence, work done by 10 women
= work done of 21 boys.

7. B's 1 day's work = $\dfrac{1}{4} - \dfrac{1}{12} = \dfrac{2}{12} = \dfrac{1}{6}$

Hence, B alone will complete the work in 6 days.

8. Ratio of efficiency of A and B = 2 : 1
Then, ratio of their time taking = 1 : 2
Hence, if B can complete the work in 12 days, then A in 6 days.

Now, (A + B)'s 1 day's work = $\dfrac{1}{6} + \dfrac{1}{12} = \dfrac{3}{12} = \dfrac{1}{4}$

So, A and B together can complete the work in 4 days.

9. After 60 days remaining work = $1 - \dfrac{3}{4} = \dfrac{1}{4}$

In 60 days $\dfrac{3}{4}$ work has been done by 60 men

In 30 days $\dfrac{1}{4}$ work will be done by

$60 \times \dfrac{4}{3} \times \dfrac{1}{4} \times \dfrac{60}{30} = 40$ men.

Hence, required number of men = 60 – 40 = 20 (which are to be discharged).

BOATS AND STREAMS

1. A boat goes 6 km upstream and back to the starting point in 2 hours. If the current of the stream runs at the rate of 4 km/hr, find the speed of the boat in still water.
A. 6 km/hr
B. 8 km/hr
C. 10 km/hr
D. 12 km/hr

2. A boat covers 24 km upstream and 36 km downstream in 6 hours, while it covers 36 km upstream and 24 km downstream in 6½ horus. Find the speed of the current.
A. 2 km/hr
B. 4 km/hr
C. 6 km/hr
D. 8 km/hr

3. A man can row 5 km/hr in still water and the speed of the stream is 1.5 km/hr. He takes an hour when he travels upstream to a place and back again to the starting point. How far is the place from the starting point?
A. 2.275 km
B. 3.5 km
C. 1.5 km
D. None of these

4. The speed of a boat in still water is 6 km/hr and the speed of the stream is 1.5 km/hr. A man rows to a place at a distance of 22.5 km and comes back to the starting point. Find the total time taken by him.
A. 8 hours
B. 10 hours
C. 12 hours
D. 4 hours

5. A boat covers 20 km downstream and 6 km upstream in 3 hours, while it covers 30 km downstream and 12 km upstream in 5 hours. What is the speed of boat in still water?
A. 6 km/hr
B. 8 km/hr
C. 10 km/hr
D. 12 km/hr.

6. Samir can travel 12 miles downstream in a certain river in 6 hours less than it takes him to travel the same distance upstream. But when he could double his rowing rate for his 24-mile round trip, the downstream 12 miles would then take only one hour less than the upstream 12 miles. Find the speed of the current in miles/hour.

A. $2\frac{2}{3}$
B. $2\frac{1}{3}$
C. $1\frac{2}{3}$
D. $1\frac{1}{3}$

7. A boat takes 6 hours to travel from place M to N downstream and back from N to M upstream. If the speed of the boat in still water is 4 km/hr; what is the distance between two places?
A. 6 kms
B. 8 kms
C. 12 kms
D. Data inadequate

8. A man can row upstream at 8 km/hr and downstream at 13 km/hr. The speed of the stream is:
A. 2.5 km/hr
B. 4.2 km/hr
C. 5 km/hr
D. 10.5 km/hr

9. A man's speed with the current is 15 km/hr and the speed of the current is 2.5 km/hr. The man's speed against the current is:
A. 12.5 km/hr
B. 10 km/hr
C. 9 km/hr
D. 8.5 km/hr

10. A motorboat, whose speed is 15 km/hr in still water goes 30 km downstream and comes back in a total of 4 hours 30 minutes. What is the speed of the stream (in km/hr)?
A. 10
B. 6
C. 5
D. 4

ANSWERS

1	2	3	4	5	6	7	8	9	10
B	A	A	A	B	B	D	A	B	C

SOME SELECTED EXPLANATORY ANSWERS

1. Let the speed of a boat in still water = x km/hr; then

$$\frac{6}{x-4}+\frac{6}{x+4}=2 \quad \Rightarrow \quad \frac{2x}{x^2-16}=\frac{1}{3}$$

$$\Rightarrow x^2-6x-16=0$$
$$\Rightarrow (x-8)(x+2)=0$$

Hence, the speed of the boat = 8 km/hr.

2. Let x km/hr and y km/hr be the speeds of the boat in still water and the speed of the current respectively, then

$$\frac{24}{x-y}+\frac{36}{x+y}=6 \Rightarrow \frac{4}{x-y}+\frac{6}{x+y}=1 \quad \text{...(i)}$$

And, $\dfrac{36}{x-y}+\dfrac{24}{x+y}=\dfrac{13}{2}$ $\quad$ ...(ii)

Solving these two equations, we get
$$x+y=12; \ x-y=8$$

Hence, $y=\dfrac{1}{2}(12-8)=2$ km/hr.

3. Let required distance be x km, then

$$\frac{x}{5-1.5}+\frac{x}{5+1.5}=1 \Rightarrow \frac{x\times2}{7}+\frac{x\times2}{13}=1$$

$$\Rightarrow \quad 40x=91 \qquad \therefore \ x=91/40=2.275 \text{ km}$$

4. Required time period $=\dfrac{22.5}{6+1.5}+\dfrac{22.5}{6-1.5}$

$$=\frac{45}{15}+\frac{45}{9}=8 \text{ hours.}$$

5. Let x km/hr and y km/hr be the speed of boat in still water and speed of current respectively; then

$$\frac{20}{x+y}+\frac{6}{x-y}=3 \qquad \text{...(i)}$$

and also, $\dfrac{30}{x+y}+\dfrac{12}{x-y}=5$

$$\Rightarrow \frac{15}{x+y}+\frac{6}{x-y}=\frac{5}{2} \qquad \text{...(ii)}$$

Solving equations *(i)* & *(ii)*, we get $x+y=10$ and $x-y=6$

Since, $x=\dfrac{1}{2}(10+6)=8$ km/hr.

6. Let x km/hr and y km/hr be the speed of rowing in still water and speed of the current respectively; then

$$\frac{12}{x-y}-\frac{12}{x+y}=6 \quad \Rightarrow \quad \frac{24y}{x^2-y^2}=6$$

$$\Rightarrow \quad x^2=y^2+4y \qquad\qquad \text{...(i)}$$

Again, $\dfrac{12}{2x-y}-\dfrac{12}{2x+y}=1$

$$\Rightarrow \frac{24y}{4x^2-y^2}=1 \quad \Rightarrow x^2=\frac{y^2+24y}{4} \quad \text{...(ii)}$$

From equations (i) and (ii), we get

$$y^2+4y=\frac{y^2+24y}{4} \Rightarrow 3y^2=8y$$

$$\therefore \quad y=\frac{8}{3}=2\frac{1}{3} \text{ miles/hr.}$$

8. The speed of the stream $=\dfrac{1}{2}(13-8)=\dfrac{5}{2}$
$$=2.5 \text{ km/hr.}$$

9. The man's speed in still water
$$=15-2.5=12.5 \text{ km/hr}$$
Hence, the men's speed against the current
$$=12.5-2.5=10 \text{ km/hr}$$

10. Let speed of the stream be x km/hr, then

$$\frac{30}{15+x}+\frac{30}{15-x}=4\frac{1}{2} \quad \Rightarrow \quad \frac{30\times30}{225-x^2}=\frac{9}{2}$$

$$\Rightarrow \frac{200}{225-x^2}=1 \qquad \Rightarrow x^2=225-200$$
$$\Rightarrow x^2=25 \qquad \therefore \quad x=5 \text{ km/hr.}$$

ALLIGATION OR MIXTURE

1. A shopkeeper buys 26 kgs of milk @ Rs. 16 per kg. He also buys from another source an inferior quality of milk @ Rs. 10 per kg. How much quantity of the latter should he buy to mix it with the former so that he can sell the mixture @ Rs. 14 per kg without making any loss?
   A. 13 kgs
   B. 12 kgs
   C. 14 kgs
   D. 16 kgs

2. Two vessels A and B contain mixture of milk and water in the ratio 4 : 1 and 9 : 11 respectively. They are mixed in the ratio of 3 : 2. Find the ratio of milk : water in the resulting mixture.
   A. 34 : 16
   B. 33 : 17
   C. 16 : 34
   D. 17 : 33

3. A shopkeeper has 50 kgs of rice. He sells a part of it at 20% profit and the rest at 40% profit. If he gains 25% on the whole, find the quantity of each part.
   A. 12.5 kgs and 37.5 kgs
   B. 37.5 kgs and 12.5 kgs
   C. 23.5 kgs and 21.5 kgs
   D. 21.5 kgs and 23.5 kgs

4. A man bought a certain quantity of sugar for Rs. 8000. He sells one-fourth of it at 20% loss. At what per cent profit should he sell the remainder stock so as to make an overall profit of 20%?
   A. 20%
   B. 30%
   C. 35%
   D. 40%

5. Rs. 675 was divided among 75 boys and girls. Each boy gets Rs. 20 whereas a girl gets Rs. 5. Find the number of boys and girls.
   A. 20, 55
   B. 15, 60
   C. 25, 50
   D. 30, 45

6. A vessel contains mixture of liquids A and B in the ratio 3 : 2. When 20 litres of the mixture is taken out and replaced by 20 litres of liquid B, the ratio changes to 1 : 4. How many litres of liquid A was there initially present in the vessel?
   A. 12 litres
   B. 18 litres
   C. 24 litres
   D. 22 litres

7. A container is full of milk. One-third of milk is taken out of it and replaced by same quantity of water. Then again one-third of the mixture is taken out of it and replaced by the same quantity of water. The process is repeated 4 times. If 16 litres of milk is left in the container at the end of 4th operation, find the capacity of the container.
   A. 76 litres
   B. 81 litres
   C. 82 litres
   D. 85 litres

8. The cost of type-I rice is Rs. 15 per kg and type-II is Rs. 20 per kg. If both type I and type II are mixed in the ratio of 2 : 3, then find the price per kg of the mixed variety.
   A. Rs. 19.50
   B. Rs. 19
   C. Rs. 18.50
   D. Rs. 18

9. In what ratio must a grocer mix two varieties of tea worth Rs. 60 a kg and Rs. 65 a kg so that by selling the mixture at Rs. 68.20 a kg he may gain 10%?
   A. 4 : 5
   B. 3 : 5
   C. 3 : 4
   D. 3 : 2

10. A vessel contains 80 litres of milk. 16 litres of milk was taken out of the vessel and replaced by water. Then 16 litres of mixture was withdrawn and again replaced by water. The operation was repeated for third time. How much milk is now left in the vessel?

A. 96.40 litres   B. 50.36 litres
C. 40.96 litres   D. 32.76 litres

ANSWERS

1	2	3	4	5	6	7	8	9	10
A	B	B	B	A	B	B	D	D	C

SOME SELECTED EXPLANATORY ANSWERS

1. 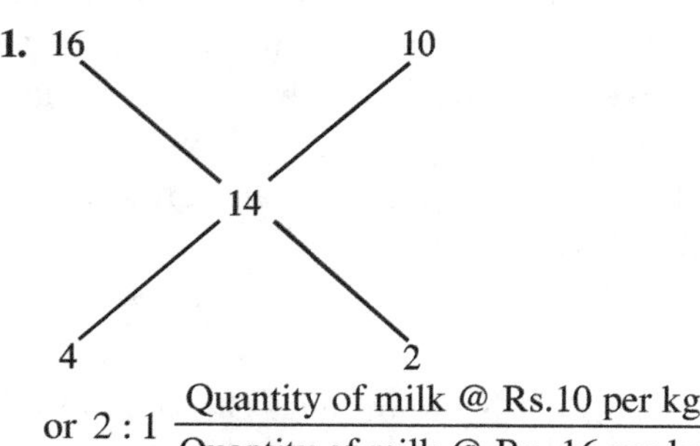

or 2 : 1 $\dfrac{\text{Quantity of milk @ Rs.10 per kg}}{\text{Quantity of milk @ Rs. 16 per kg}} = \dfrac{1}{2}$

So, quantity of milk @ Rs. 10 per kg. $= \dfrac{26}{2}$
$= 13$ kgs.

2. Fraction is

	Milk	Water
A :	$\dfrac{4}{5}$	$\dfrac{1}{5}$
B :	$\dfrac{9}{20}$	$\dfrac{11}{20}$

$(3A + 2B) = $ A and B : $\left(\dfrac{12}{5}+\dfrac{9}{10}\right)$ $\left(\dfrac{3}{5}+\dfrac{11}{10}\right)$

                   $\dfrac{33}{10}$ $\dfrac{17}{10}$

So, Ratio of milk : water in the resulting mixture
$= 33 : 17$.

3. 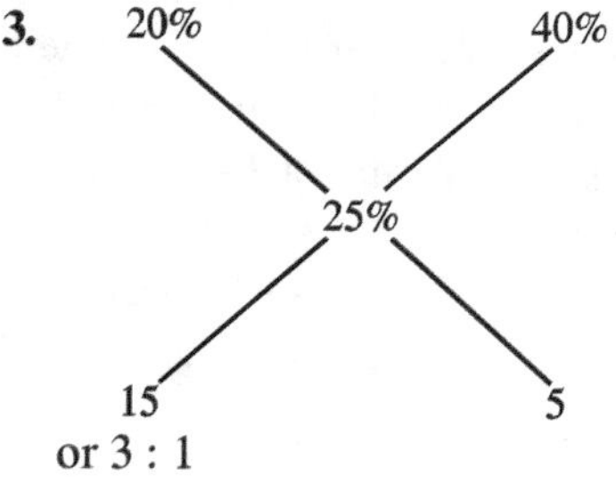

or 3 : 1

Quantity sold at 20% profit $= \dfrac{3}{3+1} \times 50$
$= 37.5$ kgs.
Quantity sold at 40% profit $= (50 - 37.5)$
$= 12.5$ kgs.

4. Let the remainder stock be sold at x% profit.

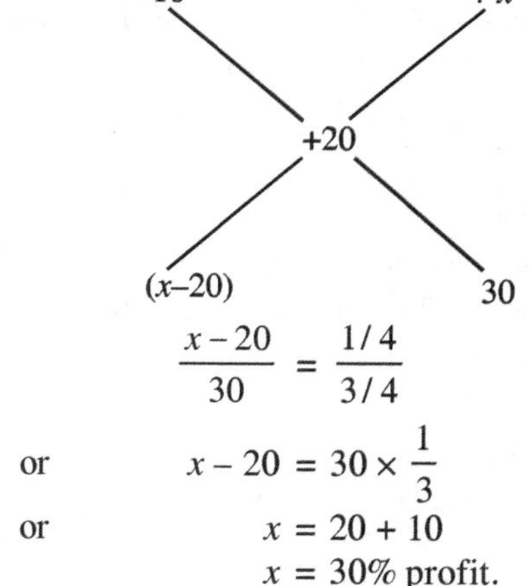

$\dfrac{x-20}{30} = \dfrac{1/4}{3/4}$

or $x - 20 = 30 \times \dfrac{1}{3}$
or $x = 20 + 10$
         $x = 30$% profit.

5. Average money per head (boy or girl)
$= $ Rs. $\dfrac{675}{75} = $ Rs. 9

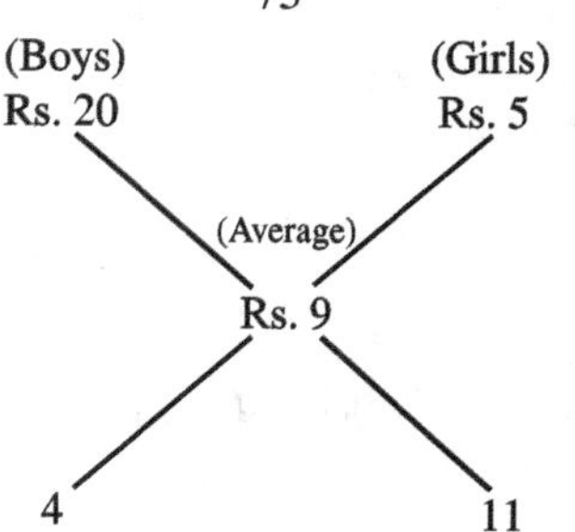

$$\text{Number of boys} = \frac{4}{4+11} \times 75 = 20$$

$$\text{Number of girls} = \frac{11}{4+11} \times 75 = 55.$$

6. % of liquid B initially present in the vessel

$$= \frac{2}{3+2} \times 100 = 40\%$$

% of liquid B finally present in the vessel

$$= \frac{4}{1+4} \times 100 = 80\%$$

The second solution is liquid B which is being mixed and it has 100% liquid B.

80% of liquid B present in the resultant mixture may be taken as average percentage. So, using rule of alligation on liquid B per cent, we can write,

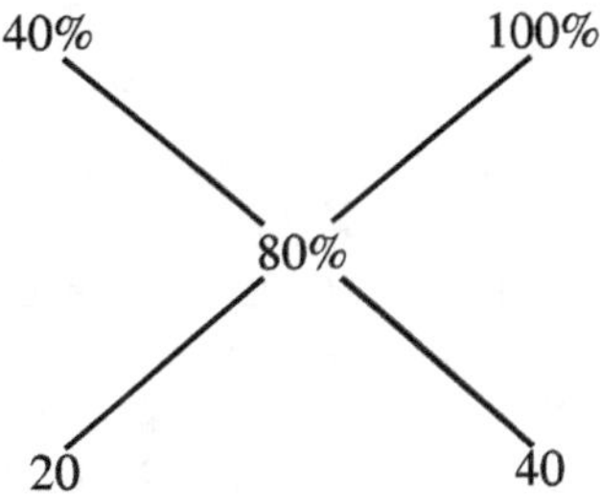

or   1 : 2

The ratio of liquid left in the vessel to liquid B being mixed = 1 : 2

Since the quantity of liquid B being mixed is 20 litres, the quantity of liquid left in the vessel is 10 litres.

Therefore, the total quantity of liquid initially present in the vessel

$$= 10 + 20 = 30 \text{ litres}$$

$$\text{Quantity of liquid A} = \frac{3}{2+3} \times 30$$

$$= 18 \text{ litres.}$$

7. Let capacity of the container be x litre; then

$$x(1 - 1/3)^4 = 16 \quad \Rightarrow \quad x\left(\frac{2}{3}\right)^4 = 16$$

$$\Rightarrow x \times \frac{16}{81} = 16 \qquad \therefore \quad x = 81 \text{ litres}$$

8. Let the price per kg of mixed variety be Rs. x; then

By the rule of alligation,

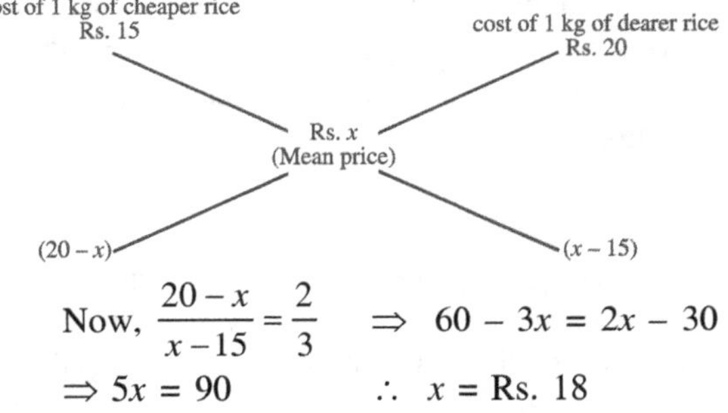

$$\text{Now, } \frac{20-x}{x-15} = \frac{2}{3} \quad \Rightarrow \quad 60 - 3x = 2x - 30$$

$$\Rightarrow 5x = 90 \qquad \therefore \quad x = \text{Rs. } 18$$

9. S.P. of 1 kg mixture = Rs. 68.20, Gain % = 10%

$$\text{Hence, C.P. of 1 kg mixture} = \frac{100}{110} \times \text{Rs. } 68.20$$

$$= \text{Rs. } 62$$

By the rule of alligation

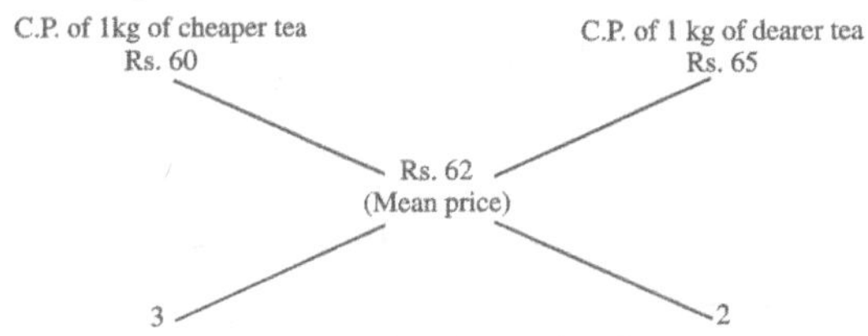

Hence, required ratio = 3 : 2

10. Amount of milk left $= 80 \left(1 - \dfrac{16}{80}\right)^3$

$$= 80 \left(\frac{4}{5}\right)^3$$

$$80 \times \frac{64}{125} = 40.96 \text{ litres.}$$

PERCENTAGE

1. A student who secures 20% marks in an examination fails by 30 marks. Another student who secures 32% gets 42 marks more than those required to pass. The percentage of marks required to pass is:
   A. 20
   B. 25
   C. 28
   D. 30

2. In a college election, a candidate secured 62% of the votes and is elected by a majority of 144 votes. The total number of votes polled is:
   A. 600
   B. 800
   C. 925
   D. 1200

3. In an organisation, 40% of the employees are matriculates, 50% of the remaining are graduates and the remaining 180 are postgraduates. How many employees are graduates?
   A. 360
   B. 240
   C. 300
   D. 180

4. The population of a village is 4500. $\frac{5}{9}$th of them are males and rest females. If 40% of the males are married, then the percentage of married female is :
   A. 35
   B. 40
   C. 50
   D. 60

5. A's income is 10% more than B's. How much per cent is B's income is less than A's?
   A. 10%
   B. 7%
   C. $9\frac{1}{11}\%$
   D. $6\frac{1}{2}\%$

6. If the price of a television set is increased by 25%, then by what percentage should the new price be reduced to bring the price back to original level?
   A. 15%
   B. 20%
   C. 25%
   D. 30%

7. In an election one of the two candidates gets 40% votes and loses by 100 votes. Total number of votes is :
   A. 500
   B. 400
   C. 600
   D. 1000

8. The gross income of a person is Rs. 20000. 10% of his income is exempted from income tax and his net income is Rs. 19100. The rate of income tax is :
   A. 3%
   B. 2%
   C. 4%
   D. 5%

9. The owner of a cell phone shop charges his customer 32% more than the cost price. If a customer paid Rs. 6600 for the cell phone, then what was the cost price of the cell phone?
   A. Rs. 5000
   B. Rs. 5500
   C. Rs. 5800
   D. Rs. 6100

10. If the cost of pins reduced by Rs. 4 per dozen, 12 more pins can be purchased for Rs. 48. The cost of pins per dozen after reduction is:
    A. Rs. 8
    B. Rs. 12
    C. Rs. 16
    D. Rs. 20

11. In an examination 80% of the students passed in Mathematics and 70% passed in English, while 10% students failed in both the subjects. If 360 students passed in both the subjects, find the total number of students who appeared in the examination.
    A. 400
    B. 600
    C. 630
    D. 640

12. Electric tax is increased by 20% and its consumption is decreased by 20%. The change in the expenditure is:
    A. 4% decrease
    B. 4% increase
    C. 5% decrease
    D. 5% increase

13. The selling price of certain commodity was reduced by 25%. As a result of it, the sales increased by 30%. What was the effect of it on cash collected by daily sales?
  A. 2.5% decrease
  B. 2.5% increase
  C. 5% decrease
  D. 5% increase

14. The wheat sold by a grocer contained 10% low quality wheat. What quantity of good quality wheat should be added to 150 kgs of wheat so that the percentage of low quality wheat becomes 5%?
  A. 50 kgs
  B. 85 kgs
  C. 135 kgs
  D. 150 kgs

15. Nilam spends 15% of her monthly income on household expenses. She spends 17% of the monthly income in travelling and 6% on medical expenses and saves the rest Rs. 15,500. What is her monthly income?
  A. Rs. 20,000
  B. Rs. 25,000
  C. Rs. 30,000
  D. Rs. 35,000

ANSWERS

1	2	3	4	5	6	7	8	9	10
B	A	D	C	C	B	A	D	A	B

11	12	13	14	15
B	A	A	D	B

SOME SELECTED EXPLANATORY ANSWERS

1. 20% of $x + 30 = $ 32% of $x - 42$

$\Rightarrow$ 12% of $x = 72$

$\Rightarrow$ $x = \dfrac{72 \times 100}{12} = 600$

Pass Mark = 20% of $600 + 30 = 150$

Pass percentage $= \left(\dfrac{150}{600} \times 100\right)\% = 25\%$

2. (62% of $x - $ 38% of x) = 144

$\Rightarrow$ 24% of $x = 144$ $\Rightarrow$ $x = \dfrac{144 \times 100}{24} = 600$

3. Matriculates $= \dfrac{40}{100} x = \dfrac{2x}{5}$

Remaining $= \left(x - \dfrac{2x}{5}\right) = \dfrac{3x}{5}$

Graduates $= \dfrac{50}{100} \times \dfrac{3x}{5} = \dfrac{3x}{10}$

Remaining $= \dfrac{3x}{5} - \dfrac{3x}{10} = \dfrac{3x}{10}$

Now, $\dfrac{3x}{10} = 180$

$\therefore$ $x = \dfrac{10 \times 180}{3} = 600$

$\therefore$ Graduates $= \dfrac{3 \times 600}{10} = 180$.

4. Males $= \left(\dfrac{5}{9} \times 4500\right) = 2500$

Females = 2000

$\therefore$ Married males $= \dfrac{40}{100} \times 2500 = 1000$

and married females = 1000

$\therefore$ Percentage of married females

$= \left(\dfrac{1000}{2000} \times 100\right)\% = 50\%$.

5. Required percentage $= \left[\dfrac{10}{(100 + 10)} \times 100\right]\%$

$= 9\dfrac{1}{11}\%$.

6. Required reduction $= \dfrac{25}{100 + 25} \times 100 = 20\%$.

7. Out of 100, difference in votes $= (60 - 40) = 20$
20% of $x = 100$

$$\therefore x = \frac{100 \times 100}{20} = 500 .$$

8. Gross income = Rs. 20000
Income exempted from income tax = 10% of gross income
$\therefore$ Income on which income tax is chargeable
$= (100 - 10\%) = 90\%$ of gross income

$$= 20000 \times \frac{90}{100} = \text{Rs. } 18000$$

$\therefore$ Total income tax paid on
$= $ Rs. 20000 $-$ Rs. 19100
$= $ Rs. 900

$$\therefore \text{ Rate per cent of income tax} = \frac{900}{18000} \times 100$$
$$= 5\%$$

9. Let cost price of the cell phone be Rs. x; then

$$x + \frac{32}{100} \times x = 6600 \quad \Rightarrow \quad \frac{132x}{100} = 6600$$

$$\therefore \quad x = \frac{100 \times 6600}{132} = \text{Rs. } 5000.$$

10. Let reduced price by Rs. x per dozen, then

$$\frac{48}{x} - \frac{48}{x+4} = 1 \quad \Rightarrow \quad \frac{48 \times 4}{x^2 + 4x} = 1$$
$$\Rightarrow \quad x^2 + 4x - 192 = 0$$
$$\Rightarrow \quad (x + 16)(x - 12) = 0$$
$$\therefore \qquad \qquad x = \text{Rs. } 12.$$

11. Here, percentage of students failed in Mathematics and English be 30% and 20% respectively.

Percentage of students failed either one or both
subjects $= 30 + 20 - 10 = 40\%$
Hence, percentage of pass students $= 100 - 40$
$$= 60\%$$

Now, $60\% = 360$

$$\therefore 100\% = \frac{360}{60} \times 100 = 600.$$

12. Let initially electric tax is Rs. 100 and consumption = 100 units
Decrease in consumption
$$= 100 \times 100 - 120 \times 80 = \text{Rs. } 400$$

$$\text{Hence, decrease percentage} = \frac{400 \times 100}{100 \times 100} = 4\% .$$

13. Let the selling price of a commodity be Rs. 100 and number of sales = 100 units
Decrease in daily cash $= 100 \times 100 - 75 \times 130$
$$= \text{Rs. } 250$$
Hence, decrease percentage

$$= \frac{250 \times 100}{100 \times 100} = 2.5 \% .$$

14. Let x kg of good wheat be added; then
$$\frac{10}{100} \times 150 = \frac{5}{100}(150 + x)$$
$$\Rightarrow 150 + x = 300 \quad \therefore \quad x = 150 \text{ kg.}$$

15. Let her monthly income be Rs. x; then

$$x - \left(\frac{15}{100} \times x + \frac{17}{100} \times x + \frac{6}{100} \times x \right) = 15{,}500$$

$$\Rightarrow x - \frac{38x}{100} = 15500 \quad \Rightarrow \quad \frac{62x}{100} = 15500$$

$$\therefore \quad x = \frac{15500 \times 100}{62} = \text{Rs. } 25000.$$

PROFIT AND LOSS

1. Ashok bought 25 kg of rice at the rate of Rs. 6 per kg and 35 kg of rice at the rate of Rs. 7 per kg. He mixed the two and sold the mixture at the rate of Rs. 6.75 per kg. What was his gain or loss in the transaction?
   A. Rs. 16 gain
   B. Rs. 16 loss
   C. Rs. 10 gain
   D. None of these

2. Profit after selling a commodity for Rs. 425 is same as loss after selling it for Rs. 355. The cost of the commodity is :
   A. Rs. 285
   B. Rs. 390
   C. Rs. 295
   D. Rs. 400

3. Ram bought 4 dozen apples at Rs. 12 per dozen and 2 dozen at Rs. 16 per dozen. He sold all of them to earn 20%. At what price per dozen did he sell the apples?
   A. Rs. 14.40
   B. Rs. 16.00
   C. Rs. 16.80
   D. Rs. 16.20

4. At what price must Kantilal sell a mixture of 80 kg sugar at Rs. 6.75 per kg with 120 kg at Rs. 8 per kg to gain 20%?
   A. Rs. 7.50 per kg
   B. Rs. 8.20 per kg
   C. Rs. 8.35 per kg
   D. Rs. 9 per kg

5. A person bought an article and sold it at a loss of 10%. If he had bought it for 20% less and sold it for Rs. 55 more, he would have had a profit of 40%. The C.P. of the article is :
   A. Rs. 200
   B. Rs. 225
   C. Rs. 250
   D. None of these

6. A dealer sold a machine to a shopkeeper at 20% profit. The shopkeeper sold the machine to a customer so as to get 25% profit for himself. The difference between the selling price of the dealer and that of the shopkeeper was found to be Rs. 129. What is the initial price of the machine?
   A. Rs. 410
   B. Rs. 420
   C. Rs. 430
   D. Rs. 440

7. A man bought a horse and cart. If he sold the horse at 10% loss and the cart at 20% gain he would not loss anything. If he sold the horse at 5% loss and the cart at 5% gain he would lose Rs. 10 in the bargain. What did he pay for each?
   A. Rs. 400, Rs. 200
   B. Rs. 300, Rs. 300
   C. Rs. 250, Rs. 350
   D. Rs. 350, Rs. 250

8. The marked price of a radio is 20% more than its cost price. If a discount of 10% is given on the marked price, the gain percentage is:
   A. 8
   B. 10
   C. 12
   D. 15

9. A dishonest dealer sells his goods at the cost price and still earns a profit of 60% by underweight. What weight does he use for a kg?
   A. 625 gms
   B. 750 gms
   C. 800 gms
   D. 850 gms

10. A man sells two horses for Rs. 990 each. On one he gains 10% and the other he loses 10%. What is his total percentage of gain or loss in the transaction?
    A. 1% gain
    B. 1% loss
    C. 2% gain
    D. 2% loss

ANSWERS

1	2	3	4	5	6	7	8	9	10
C	B	B	D	C	C	A	A	A	B

SOME SELECTED EXPLANATORY ANSWERS

1. C.P. of 60 kg mixture = Rs. $(25 \times 6 + 35 \times 7)$
$\qquad\qquad\qquad\quad$ = Rs. 395
$\quad$ S.P. of 60 kg mixtire = Rs. (60×6.75)
$\qquad\qquad\qquad\quad$ = Rs. 405
$\therefore \qquad\qquad$ Gain = Rs. $(405 - 395)$
$\qquad\qquad\qquad\quad$ = Rs. 10

2. Let $\qquad\qquad$ C.P. = Rs. x
$\quad$ Then, $\qquad 425 - x = x - 355 \Rightarrow 2x = 780$
$\therefore \qquad\qquad\qquad x =$ Rs. 390

3. C.P. of 6 dozen apples = Rs. $(12 \times 4 + 16 \times 2)$
$\qquad\qquad\qquad\qquad$ = Rs. 80

$\therefore \qquad\qquad$ S.P. = Rs. $\left(\dfrac{120}{100} \times 80 \right)$
$\qquad\qquad\qquad\quad$ = Rs. 96

$\therefore \qquad$ S.P. per dozen = Rs. $\left(\dfrac{96}{6} \right)$ = Rs. 16

4. $\qquad$ C.P. of 1 kg sugar = $\dfrac{80 \times 6.75 + 120 \times 8}{200}$
$\qquad\qquad\qquad\qquad$ = Rs. 7.50

$\therefore \qquad$ S.P. of 1 kg = Rs. $\left(\dfrac{120}{100} \times 7.50 \right)$
$\qquad\qquad\qquad\qquad$ = Rs. 9 per kg

5. Let $\qquad$ C.P. = Rs. x,

$\quad$ then $\qquad$ S.P. = $\dfrac{90}{100} \times x =$ Rs. $\dfrac{9x}{10}$

$\quad$ Now, when C.P. = Rs. $\dfrac{80x}{100} =$ Rs. $\dfrac{4x}{5}$;

$\quad$ then S.P. = $\dfrac{140}{100} \times \dfrac{4x}{5} =$ Rs. $\dfrac{28x}{25}$

$\quad$ But, $\dfrac{28x}{25} - \dfrac{9x}{10} = 55 \Rightarrow \dfrac{11x}{50} = 55$
$\therefore \qquad\qquad x =$ Rs. 250

6. Let the initial price = Rs. x; then C.P. for dealer

$$= \dfrac{120}{100} \times x = \text{Rs. } \dfrac{6x}{5}$$

Again, C.P. for shopkeeper = $\dfrac{125}{100} \times \dfrac{6x}{5}$

$$= \text{Rs. } \dfrac{3x}{2}$$

Now, $\dfrac{3x}{2} - \dfrac{6x}{5} = 129 \Rightarrow \dfrac{3x}{10} = 129$

$\therefore \ x = \dfrac{10 \times 129}{3} =$ Rs. 430

7. Here, 10% C.P. of horse = 20% C.P. of cart;
Hence, C.P. of horse = $2 \times$ C.P. of cart;
Let C.P. of cart and horse be Rs. x and Rs. $2x$
respectively; then,

$$\dfrac{5}{100} \times 2x - \dfrac{5}{100} \times x = 10 \Rightarrow \dfrac{1}{20} x = 10$$

$\therefore x = 200$
Hence, C.P. of a cart = Rs. 200 and C.P. of a
horse = $2 \times 200 =$ Rs. 400

8. Let C.P. be Rs. 100; then marked price
$\qquad\qquad\qquad$ = Rs. 120

Since, S.P. = $\dfrac{90}{100} \times 120 =$ Rs. 108

$\therefore$ Profit = $108 - 100 =$ Rs. 8, Hence, gain = 8%.

9. Required weight = $\dfrac{100}{160} \times 1000 = 625$ gms.

10. Here, loss % = $\left(\dfrac{10}{10} \right)^2 = 1\%$.

SIMPLE INTEREST

1. A lent a sum of Rs. 1250 to B at a certain rate of interest for 3 years and a sum of Rs. 1500 to C at the same rate of interest for 2 years. If he was paid total Rs. 258.75 as interest in both cases, find the rate of interest at which money was lent by him.

   A. $4\dfrac{1}{6}\%$ B. $6\dfrac{1}{4}\%$

   C. $2\dfrac{1}{7}\%$ D. $3\dfrac{5}{6}\%$

2. A invested Rs. 5000 at a certain rate of simple interest and Rs. 4000 for the same period at 1% higher rate of interest. If the interest in both cases is same, the former rate of interest is :
   A. 3%   B. 4%
   C. 6%   D. 5%

3. If a certain sum of money at simple interest amounts to Rs. 1900 in 3 years and to Rs. 2050 in 5 years, the rate per cent per annum is :
   A. 4½%   B. 3½%
   C. 2½%   D. 5¼%

4. A certain sum of money lent out on simple interest amounts to Rs. 1760 in 2 years and to Rs. 2000 in 5 years. Find the sum.
   A. Rs. 1650   B. Rs. 1500
   C. Rs. 1580   D. Rs. 1600

5. Out of the sum of Rs. 1550, a part was lent out at 5% p.a. simple interest and the remaining at 8% p.a. simple interest. If the total interest in both cases after 3 years is Rs. 300, the sum of money lent out at 8% p.a. simple interest was:
   A. Rs. 760   B. Rs. 775
   C. Rs. 750   D. Rs. 780

6. If simple interest on a certain sum of money for 4 years at 5% p.a. is same as the simple interest on Rs. 840 for 10 years at the rate of 4% p.a., the sum of money is:
   A. Rs. 1780   B. Rs. 1660
   C. Rs. 1680   D. Rs. 1620

7. What equal instalment of annual payment will discharge a debt which is due as Rs. 848 at the end of 4 years at 4% per annum simple interest?
   A. Rs. 200   B. Rs. 212
   C. Rs. 225   D. Rs. 250

8. Madhavi lent Rs. 5000 to Kamla for 5 years and Rs. 3000 to Vimla for 4 years. Find the rate of interest, if Madhavi gets an interest of Rs. 600 in the end.
   A. 1.62%   B. 2.5%
   C. 3%   D. 4%

9. A sum of money doubles itself in 7 years at simple interest. In how many years it will become four fold?
   A. 10 years   B. 14 years
   C. 21 years   D. 35 years

10. An amount doubles itself at the end of 8 years with a certain rate of simple interest. What will be the total simple interest on Rs. 8000 at that rate at the end of 4 years?
    A. Rs. 2000   B. Rs. 4000
    C. Rs. 6000   D. None of these

ANSWERS

1	2	3	4	5	6	7	8	9	10
D	B	A	D	C	C	A	A	C	B

SOME SELECTED EXPLANATORY ANSWERS

1. $\dfrac{1250 \times R \times 3}{100} + \dfrac{1500 \times R \times 2}{100} = 258.75$

$\Rightarrow 6750\ R = 25875$

$\therefore\quad R = \dfrac{25875}{6750} = \dfrac{23}{6} = 3\dfrac{5}{6}\%$

2. Here, $\dfrac{5000 \times R \times T}{100} = \dfrac{4000 \times (R+1) \times T}{100}$

$\Rightarrow 5R = 4R + 4 \quad \therefore\ R = 4\%$

3. Simple interest for 2 years
$\quad$ = Rs. 2050 – Rs. 1900 = Rs. 150

$\therefore$ Simple interest for 1 year = Rs. $\dfrac{150}{2}$

$\qquad\qquad\qquad\qquad = $ Rs. 75

Since simple interest for 3 years = Rs. 75 × 3
$\qquad\qquad\qquad\qquad\qquad = $ Rs. 225

$\therefore\quad$ Principal = Rs. 1900 – Rs. 225
$\qquad\qquad\quad = $ Rs. 1675

Hence, $\quad$ Rate = $\dfrac{75 \times 100}{1675 \times 1} = 4\frac{1}{2}\%$

4. Interest for 3 years = Rs. 2000 – Rs. 1760
$\qquad\qquad\qquad = $ Rs. 240

$\therefore$ Interest for 1 year = Rs. $\dfrac{240}{3}$ = Rs. 80

And interest for 2 years = Rs. 80 × 2 = Rs. 160

$\therefore$ Principal = Rs. 1760 – Rs. 160 = Rs. 1600

5. Let Rs. x and Rs $(1550 - x)$ were lent out at 8% and 5% respectively; then

$\dfrac{x \times 8 \times 3}{100} + \dfrac{(1550 - x) \times 5 \times 3}{100} = 300$

$\Rightarrow 24x + 23250 - 15x = 30000$

$\Rightarrow 9x = 6750 \quad \therefore\ x = \dfrac{6750}{9} = $ Rs. 750

6. Here, $\dfrac{P \times 5 \times 4}{100} = \dfrac{840 \times 4 \times 10}{100} \Rightarrow 5P = 8400$

$\therefore\ P = \dfrac{8400}{5} = $ Rs. 1680

7. Let equal instalment be Rs. x; then

$x + \dfrac{x \times 4 \times 3}{100} + x + \dfrac{x \times 4 \times 2}{100} + x$

$\qquad\qquad\qquad + \dfrac{x \times 4 \times 1}{100} + x = 848$

$\Rightarrow 4x + \dfrac{24x}{100} = 848 \quad \Rightarrow \dfrac{106x}{25} = 848$

$\therefore\ x = \dfrac{848 \times 25}{106} = $ Rs. 200

8. $\dfrac{5000 \times R \times 5}{100} + \dfrac{3000 \times R \times 4}{100} = 600$

$\Rightarrow\quad 250\ R + 120\ R = 600$

$\Rightarrow\qquad\qquad 370R = 600$

$\therefore\qquad\qquad R = \dfrac{600}{370} = 1.62\%$

9. Let principal be Rs. x; then amount = Rs. $2x$,
Hence, I = $2x - x$ = Rs. x.

$R = \dfrac{x \times 100}{x \times 7} = \dfrac{100}{7}\%$ p.a.

Now, amount = Rs. $4x$; then I = $4x - x$
$\qquad\qquad\qquad\qquad = $ Rs. $3x$

Hence, T = $\dfrac{3x \times 100}{x \times \dfrac{100}{7}} = \dfrac{3 \times 100 \times 7}{100} = 21$ years

10. Let principal = Rs. x; then amount = Rs. $2x$;
I = $2x - x$ = Rs. x

$R = \dfrac{x \times 100}{x \times 8} = \dfrac{25}{2}\%$

Again, $\quad$ I = $\dfrac{8000 \times 25 \times 4}{100 \times 2} = $ Rs. 4000

COMPOUND INTEREST

1. The compound interest on a certain sum of money invested for 3 years at 5% per annum is Rs. 1891.50. What will be the simple interest on the same sum at the same rate for 2 years?
   A. Rs. 1700
   B. Rs. 1200
   C. Rs. 1500
   D. Rs. 2100

2. A sum of money lent out at a certain rate of simple interest amounts to Rs. 6600 in 2 years and to Rs. 6900 in 3 years. What will be the compound interest on the same sum of money if lent out at the same rate for 2 years?
   A. Rs. 605
   B. Rs. 715
   C. Rs. 615
   D. Rs. 595

3. A man deposits Rs. 1200 in a bank on the 1st day of each year. If the bank pays 5% per annum compound interest on deposited sum of money, what will be the amount to his credit on the 10th day of the second year?
   A. Rs. 2560
   B. Rs. 2460
   C. Rs. 2370
   D. Rs. 2860

4. If the difference between compound and simple interest on a certain sum of money for 3 years at 5% per annum is Rs. 244, the sum is :
   A. Rs. 40000
   B. Rs. 25000
   C. Rs. 30000
   D. Rs. 32000

5. A man purchased a sewing machine for Rs. 5000. If due to sustained use value of this sewing machine depreciates by 6% annually, find its value after 3 years.
   A. Rs. 3775.67
   B. Rs. 4152.92
   C. Rs. 4250.25
   D. Rs. 4356.25

6. Find the sum on which the difference between compound and simple interest for 3 years at 10% per annum will be Rs. 868.
   A. Rs. 29500
   B. Rs. 27625
   C. Rs. 28500
   D. Rs. 28000

7. Samir invested Rs. 15000 at the rate of interest 10% p.a. for 1 year. If the interest compound six months. What amount will Samir get at the end of the year?
   A. Rs. 16,500
   B. Rs. 16525.50
   C. Rs. 16537.50
   D. Rs. 18,150

8. The compound interest on a certain sum for 2 years at 10% per annum is Rs. 525. The simple interest on the same sum for double the time at half the rate per cent per annum is:
   A. Rs. 800
   B. Rs. 600
   C. Rs. 500
   D. Rs. 400

9. The least number of complete years in which a sum of money put at 20% compound interest will be more than doubled is:
   A. 6
   B. 5
   C. 4
   D. 3

10. On a sum of money, the simple interest for 2 years is Rs. 660, while the compound interest is Rs. 696.30, the rate of interest being the same in both cases. Find the rate of interest.
    A. Rs. 12%
    B. 11%
    C. 10%
    D. 9%

ANSWERS

1	2	3	4	5	6	7	8	9	10
B	C	B	D	B	D	C	C	C	B

SOME SELECTED EXPLANATORY ANSWERS

1. Here, $1891.50 = P\left[\left(1+\dfrac{5}{100}\right)^3 - 1\right]$

$\Rightarrow \quad 1891.50 = P\left[\left(\dfrac{21}{20}\right)^3 - 1\right]$

$\Rightarrow \quad 1891.50 = P\left(\dfrac{1261}{8000}\right)$

$\therefore P = \dfrac{1891.50 \times 8000}{1261} = $ Rs. 12000

Now, S.I. $= \dfrac{12000 \times 5 \times 2}{100} = $ Rs. 1200

2. Here, 1 year's S.I. = Rs. 6900 – Rs. 6600
$\qquad\qquad\qquad = $ Rs. 300
$\therefore \quad$ 2 year's S.I. $= 300 \times 2 = $ Rs. 600
$\therefore \quad$ Principal = Rs. 6600 – Rs. 600
$\qquad\qquad\qquad = $ Rs. 6000

Hence, $\quad$ Rate $= \dfrac{600 \times 100}{6000 \times 2} = 5\%$

$\therefore \qquad$ C.I. $= 6000\left[\left(1+\dfrac{5}{100}\right)^2 - 1\right]$

$= 6000\left[\left(\dfrac{21}{20}\right)^2 - 1\right] = \dfrac{6000 \times 41}{400} = $ Rs. 615

3. Required amount $= 1200\left(1+\dfrac{5}{100}\right) + 1200$

$= 1200 \times \dfrac{21}{20} + 1200 = 1260 + 1200 = $ Rs. 2460

4. Here, $P\left[\left(1+\dfrac{5}{100}\right)^3 - 1\right] - \dfrac{P \times 5 \times 3}{100} = 244$

$\Rightarrow P \times \dfrac{1261}{8000} - \dfrac{3P}{20} = 244 \Rightarrow P \times \dfrac{61}{8000} = 244$

$\therefore \quad P = \dfrac{244 \times 8000}{61} = $ Rs. 32000

5. Here, value of the machine after 3 years

$= 5000\left(1-\dfrac{6}{100}\right)^3 = 5000 \times \dfrac{47}{50} \times \dfrac{47}{50} \times \dfrac{47}{50}$

$= $ Rs. 4152.92.

6. Here, $P\left[\left(1+\dfrac{10}{100}\right)^3 - 1\right] - \dfrac{P \times 10 \times 3}{100} = 868$

$\Rightarrow P \times \dfrac{331}{1000} - \dfrac{3P}{10} = 868$

$\Rightarrow P \times \dfrac{31}{1000} = 868 \quad \therefore \quad P = \dfrac{868 \times 1000}{31}$
$\qquad\qquad\qquad\qquad\qquad\qquad = $ Rs. 28000

7. $A = 15000\left(1+\dfrac{5}{100}\right)^2 = 15000 \times \dfrac{441}{400}$

$\qquad = $ Rs. 16537.50

8. Here, $P\left[\left(1+\dfrac{10}{100}\right)^2 - 1\right] = 525$

$\Rightarrow P\left[\dfrac{121}{100} - 1\right] = 525 \Rightarrow P \times \dfrac{21}{100} = 525$

$\therefore \quad P = \dfrac{525 \times 100}{21} = $ Rs. 2500

Hence, required S.I. $= \dfrac{2500 \times 5 \times 4}{100} = $ Rs. 500

9. Here, $P\left(1+\dfrac{20}{100}\right)^n > 2P \Rightarrow \left(\dfrac{6}{5}\right)^n > 2$

Hence, if $n = 4$ then, $\left(\dfrac{6}{5}\right)^4 = \dfrac{1296}{625} > 2$

So, $n = 4$ years

10. Here, S.I. for 1 year = Rs. 330
Since, simple interest of Rs. 330 for 1 year
$= 696.30 - 660 = $ Rs. 36.30

Hence, required rate $= \dfrac{36.30 \times 100}{330 \times 1} = \dfrac{3630}{330}$
$\qquad\qquad\qquad\qquad = 11\%$

AREA AND PERIMETER

1. If side of a square is reduced by 50%, its area will be reduced by
   A. 50%
   B. 75%
   C. 80%
   D. 60%

2. If each side of a square is doubled, its area will become
   A. double
   B. four times
   C. three times
   D. eight times

3. Three sides of a triangle are in the ratio of 17 : 15 : 8. If the perimeter of this triangle is 40 m, find its area
   A. 50 sq. m.
   B. 49 sq. m.
   C. 60 sq. m.
   D. 69 sq. m.

4. If the length of a rectangle is increased by 20% and width is decreased by 15%, then its area
   A. decreases by 4%
   B. increases by 2%
   C. decreases by 2%
   D. increases by 3%

5. If the length of a rectangle is increased by 20%, then by how much per cent its breadth must be decreased so as to keep its area unaltered?
   A. 25%
   B. $8\frac{1}{3}\%$
   C. $16\frac{2}{3}\%$
   D. 20%

6. The ratio of length and breadth of a rectangular plot is 71 : 61 respectively. The area of the plot is 17324 m². What is perimeter of the plot?
   A. 264 m
   B. 284 m
   C. 528 m
   D. 614 m

7. If the length and breadth of a rectangular field are increased, the area increases by 50%. If the increase in length was 20%, by what percentage was the breadth increased?
   A. 20%
   B. 25%
   C. 30%
   D. 40%

8. The length and breadth of a varandah is 40 m and 15 m respectively. How many stone slabs of size 6 decimetre × 5 decimetre each are needed in flooring it:
   A. 1000
   B. 2000
   C. 3000
   D. 4000

9. The circumference of a circular plot is 396 m. What is the area of the circular plot?
   A. 9,446 m²
   B. 9,856 m²
   C. 12,474 m²
   D. 18,634 m²

10. If the sides of an equilateral triangle are increased by 20%, 30% and 50% respectively to form a new triangle, the increase in the perimeter of the equilateral triangle is:
    A. 25%
    B. $33\frac{1}{3}\%$
    C. 50%
    D. 100%

ANSWERS

1	2	3	4	5	6	7	8	9	10
B	B	C	B	C	C	B	B	C	B

SOME SELECTED EXPLANATORY ANSWERS

1. Area of the square $= x^2$ sq. m.

Side of the new square $= x - 50\%$ of $x = \dfrac{x}{2}$ m

$\therefore$ Area of the new square $= \left(\dfrac{x}{2}\right)^2 = \dfrac{x^2}{4}$ sq. m.

$\therefore$ Reduction in area of the square $= x^2 - \dfrac{x^2}{4}$

$$= \dfrac{3x^2}{4} \text{ sq. m.}$$

$\therefore$ Percentage reduction $= \dfrac{3x^2/4}{x^2} \times 100 = 75\%$

2. Area of the square $= x^2$ sq. m

Now, area of the new square $= (2x)^2 = 4x^2$ sq. m

Hence, it is clear that if side of a square is doubled, its area becomes four times.

3. Suppose sides of the triangle are $17x$ m, $15x$ m and $8x$ metres

$\therefore$ Perimeter $= 17x + 15x + 8x = 40x$

Now, $\quad 40x = 40$

$\Rightarrow \quad\quad\quad x = 1$ m

Therefore, the sides are $17 \times 1 = 17$ m, $15 \times 1 = 15$ m and $8 \times 1 = 8$ m

$\because \quad\quad (17)^2 = (15)^2 + (8)^2,$

i.e., it is a right angled triangle

$\therefore$ Area of the right angled triangle

$$= \dfrac{1}{2} \times 8 \times 15 = 60 \text{ sq.m.}$$

4. Area of the rectangle $= xy$ sq. metre

Area of the new rectangle $= \dfrac{120}{100} x \times \dfrac{85}{100} y$

$$= 1.020 \, xy \text{ sq. metre}$$

$\therefore$ Increase in the area $= 1.02 \, xy - xy$

$$= .02 \, xy \text{ sq. m.}$$

$\therefore$ Percentage increase $= \dfrac{.02xy}{xy} \times 100 = 2\%$

5. Area of the rectangle $= xy$

On reducing the breadth by $A\%$ and increasing the length by 20%

Length of the new rectangle $= \dfrac{120x}{100} x = 1.2x$

Breadth of the new rectangle $= y - A\%$ of y

$$= y\left(1 - \dfrac{A}{100}\right)$$

$\therefore$ Area of the new rectangle $= 1.2x \times y\left(1 - \dfrac{A}{100}\right)$

Now, $xy = 1.2 \, xy\left(1 - \dfrac{A}{100}\right) \Rightarrow 1 = 1.2\dfrac{(100-A)}{100}$

$\Rightarrow \quad\quad\quad 1.2 \, A = 120 - 100$

$\therefore \quad\quad\quad A = \dfrac{20}{1.2} = 16\dfrac{2}{3}\%$

6. Let length and breadth of a rectangle be $71x$ and $61x$ m; then

$71x \times 61x = 17324 \Rightarrow x^2 = \dfrac{17324}{71 \times 61} = 4$

$\therefore \quad\quad x = 2$

Hence, length $= 71 \times 2 = 142$ m; breadth

$$= 61 \times 2 = 122 \text{ m}$$

Since, perimeter $= 2(142 + 122) = 2 \times 264$

$$= 528 \text{ m}$$

7. Here, $20 + x + \dfrac{20 \times x}{100} = 50 \Rightarrow x + \dfrac{x}{5} = 30$

$\Rightarrow \dfrac{6x}{5} = 30 \quad\quad\quad \therefore \ x = \dfrac{5 \times 30}{6} = 25$

Hence, breadth was increased by 25%

8. Required number of stone slabs $= \dfrac{40 \times 15}{\dfrac{6}{10} \times \dfrac{5}{10}}$

$$= \dfrac{40 \times 15 \times 100}{6 \times 5} = 2000$$

9. Radius of circular plot $= \dfrac{396 \times 7}{2 \times 22} = 63$ m

Area of the circular plot $= \dfrac{22}{7} \times 63 \times 63$

$$= 12,474 \text{ m}^2$$

VOLUME AND SURFACE AREA

1. If a solid sphere of 3 cm radius is melted and recast into a right circular cone whose base radius is same as that of the sphere, the height of the cone will be
   A. 8 cm
   B. 12 cm
   C. 6 cm
   D. 5 cm

2. Diameter of a roller is 2.4 m and it is 1.68 m long. If it takes 1000 complete revolutions once over to level a field, the area of the field is
   A. 12672 sq. m
   B. 12671 sq. m
   C. 12762 sq. m
   D. 11768 sq. m

3. If each edge of a cube is increased by 10%, then by how much per cent will the surface area of this cube be increased?
   A. 21%
   B. 18%
   C. 15%
   D. 20%

4. Height and base radius of a solid cylinder are 14 m and 4 m respectively. It is melted and recast into a solid cone of the same base radius as that of the cylinder, what will be the height of the cone?
   A. 21 m
   B. 42 m
   C. 48 m
   D. 54 m

5. A room is in the form of a cube of side 10 m. How many bales of cotton can be kept in it if each bale covers 5 cu m space?
   A. 100
   B. 175
   C. 200
   D. 225

6. Three cubes having side 2 cm, 3 cm and 4 cm respectively are melted together to form a new cube. The side of the new cube will be
   A. 3.526 cm
   B. 4.628 cm
   C. 4.626 cm
   D. 4.528 cm

7. If base diameter of a cylinder is increased by 50%, then by how much per cent its height must be decreased so as to keep its volume unaltered?
   A. 45.56%
   B. 55.56%
   C. 50.16%
   D. 62.33%

8. The surface area of a cube is 600 sq. m. Its diagonal is
   A. $10\sqrt{3}$ cm
   B. $5\sqrt{3}$ cm
   C. $4\sqrt{2}$ cm
   D. $10\sqrt{2}$ cm

9. The base diameter of a conical tomb is 28 m and its slant height is 50 m. Find the cost of white washing its curved surface at the rate of 80 paise per sq. m?
   A. Rs. 1860
   B. Rs. 1760
   C. Rs. 1950
   D. Rs. 1875

10. The volume of a cuboid is 1120 cu cm and its height is 5 cm while the length and the breadth of the cuboid are in the ratio 8 : 7. The length of this cylinder exceeds the breadth by
   A. 4 cm
   B. 2 cm
   C. 7 cm
   D. 5 cm

ANSWERS

1	2	3	4	5	6	7	8	9	10
B	A	A	B	C	C	B	A	B	B

SOME SELECTED EXPLANATORY ANSWERS

1. Volume of the cone = Volume of the sphere

$$\therefore \ \frac{1}{3}\pi(3)^2 \times h = \frac{4}{3}\pi \times 3^3 \Rightarrow h = 12 \text{ cm}$$

Hence, height of the cone = 12 cm.

2. Surface area of the roller = $2\pi rh$

$$= 2 \times \frac{22}{7} \times 1.2 \times 1.68 = 12.672 \text{ sq. m}$$

In one complete revolution, the roller covers 12.672 sq. m.

∴ It will cover in 1000 revolutions
    = 12.672 × 1000 = 12672 sq. m

Hence, area of the field = 12672 sq. m.

3. Percentage increase in the surface area of the

$$\text{cube} = \left(x + y + \frac{xy}{100}\right)\%$$

$$= \left(10 + 10 + \frac{10 \times 10}{100}\right)\% = 21\%.$$

4. Here,

volume of the cone = Volume of the cylinder

$$\Rightarrow \quad \frac{1}{3}\pi r^2 \times \text{height} = \pi r^2 \times 14$$

$$\therefore \qquad \text{Height} = 14 \times 3 = 42 \text{ m}$$

Thus, height of the cone = 42 m.

5. Volume of the cubical room = $(10)^3$
    = 1000 cu m

Number of cotton bales which can be placed in the room

$$= \frac{\text{Volume of the room}}{\text{Volume of each cotton bale}} = \frac{1000}{5} = 200.$$

6. Volume of the new cube = $2^3 + 3^3 + 4^3$
    = 8 + 27 + 64 = 99 cu cm

$$\therefore \text{ Side of the new cube} = \sqrt[3]{99} = 4.626 \text{ cm.}$$

7. Change in the volume of the cylinder

$$= \left(x + y + (-z) + \frac{xy + y(-z) + (-zx)}{100} + \frac{xy(-z)}{100^2}\right)\%$$

Since volume of the cylinder remains unchanged.

$$\therefore \qquad \text{Change} = 0\%$$

$$\text{Now,} \ \left(50 + 50 + (-z) + \frac{50 \times 50 - 50z - 50z}{100} + \frac{50 \times 50 \times (-z)}{100^2}\right) = 0$$

$$\therefore \quad 100 - z + 25 - z - .25z = 0$$

$$\Rightarrow 2.25z = 125 \Rightarrow z = \frac{125}{2.25} = 55.56$$

∴ Height of the cylinder should be decreased by 55.56%.

8. Here, $\qquad 6 \times (\text{side})^2 = 600$

$$\Rightarrow \qquad \qquad \text{side}^2 = 100$$

$$\Rightarrow \qquad \qquad \text{side} = \sqrt{100} = 10 \text{ cm}$$

$$\therefore \text{ Diagonal of the cube} = \sqrt{3} \times \text{side}$$

$$= \sqrt{3} \times 10$$

$$= 10\sqrt{3} \text{ cm.}$$

9. Area of the curved surface of the cone

$$= \frac{22}{7} \times \frac{28}{2} \times 50 = 2200 \text{ sq. m.}$$

∴ Cost of white washing at 80 paise per sq. m

$$= 2200 \times \frac{80}{100} = \text{Rs. } 1760.$$

10. Suppose the length and the breadth of the cuboid are $8x$ cm and $7x$ cm

$$\therefore \text{ Here,} \quad 8x \times 7x \times 5 = 1120$$

$$\Rightarrow x^2 = \frac{1120}{280} = 4 = (2)^2 \quad \Rightarrow \quad x = 2$$

∴ Length of the cuboid = 8 × 2 = 16 cm
    Breadth of the cuboid = 7 × 2 = 14 cm

Hence, it is clear that length of the cuboid exceeds the breadth by 2 cm.

ENGLISH LANGUAGE

1. Comprehension Passages

The objective of language comprehension test is to ascertain the ability of the candidates to understand the passage properly. Therefore candidates are required to take notice of the following points:

1. Read the full passage very attentively and intelligently.
2. Try to comprehend the gist of it.
3. Make a mental note of all the important details and points given in the passage.
4. Read the passage for the second time in case you have not been able to understand it satisfactorily.
5. Divide the time proportionately for all the passages.
6. Answer the questions on the basis of facts, as given in the paragraph.
7. Don't waste much time in answering the questions of any one passage.
8. Check all the answers once again, very carefully, to see whether any question is left unanswered by mistake.

MODEL QUESTIONS (FOR PRACTICE)

Directions: *Each of the following passages is followed by five questions. Read the passage carefully and then answer the questions that follow each. For each question, four probable answers A, B, C and D are given. Only one out of these is correct. Choose the correct answer.*

PASSAGE-1

The use of words like 'welcome', 'thank you', 'please', etc., at the right moment reflects a polite nature. The civic sense also lies within the scope of good manners. We should not shout or talk loudly in public places like hospitals and libraries and create disturbance. We should not cheat people or make fun of them. Cleanliness is also necessary. We must not throw the waste on roads and make use of dustbins. We should not harm the public property as it belongs to all of us. While in a queue, discipline should be maintained. We must give fair chance to others.

1. Expressions like 'welcome' 'thank you' and 'please' reflect
   A. happiness   B. discipline
   C. civic sense   D. polite nature

2. While in a library, we should
   A. respect others   B. avoid arguments
   C. talk in low tone D. be courteous

3. A public property belongs to
   A. nobody
   B. all of us
   C. government
   D. one who maintains it

4. Discipline is
A. the rule of proper conduct or action
B. the rule of road sense
C. making use of dustbins
D. forming a queue

5. The most appropriate title for this passage would be
A. Polite Nature
B. Courtesy
C. Good Manners
D. Civic Sense

PASSAGE-2

There is an old proverb 'Early to bed and early to rise makes a man healthy and wise.' I am in the habit of getting up early in the morning and have formed the habit of taking long morning walks in the past two years. It is a light exercise and best for physical fitness. The morning air which is fresh and pure is beneficial for the lungs. The early rays of the rising sun are good for healthy skin. 'Health is wealth' and doctors also recommend morning walk to their patients for gaining sound health and freshness of energy.

1. What is good for lungs?
A. Sunrays
B. Fresh air
C. Sound sleep
D. Light exercise

2. What is a light exercise?
A. Early to bed
B. Early to rise
C. Morning walk
D. Gaining sound health

3. What is good for skin?
A. Fresh air
B. Morning air
C. Morning walk
D. Rising sun's rays

4. What is best for physical fitness?
A. Light exercise
B. Long morning walk
C. Early to rise
D. Fresh and pure air

5. Long morning walk
A. bring sound sleep
B. ensures physical fitness
C. ensures healthy skin
D. keeps healthy, wealthy and wise

PASSAGE-3

Mahatma Gandhi lived a splendid long life and has set great moral standards before us. He showed to the world the true way to peace. He wished to see India prosper but he became a martyr for the noble cause of Hindu-Muslim unity at the time of partition when a religious fanatic, Nathuram Godse, shot him dead on January 30, 1948. His last words were 'Hey Ram'. He lived and died for his country and countryman.

1. Mahatma Gandhi showed the world the true way to
A. prosperity
B. love
C. truth
D. peace

2. Mahatma Gandhi became a martyr for the noble cause of
A. truth
B. non-violence
C. freedom of India
D. Hindu-Muslim unity

3. Mahatma Gandhi was shot dead
A. before India achieved independence
B. by a mad man
C. by an intolerant religious person
D. by a non-religious person

4. Mahatma Gandhi set great moral standards. It means
A. he was a great religious teacher
B. he was a great moralist
C. he made India morally stronger
D. moral was everything to him

5. Gandhiji lived and died for his country and countryman. It means
A. he was born in India and died in India
B. he was a patriot
C. he was a great moralist
D. he sacrified his life for India and her people

PASSAGE-4

On one hot day a crow felt very thirsty. He flew from one place to another in search of water. After long hours of labour he found a pitcher. Eagerly, he perched on the mouth of the pitcher. He found that the water was at the bottom of the vessel. He tried his best to dip his beak but did not succeed. He did not know what to do. Suddenly some pebbles lying nearby gave him an idea. One by one he dropped the pebbles with his beak into the pitcher. The level of water slowly came up to the mouth of the pitcher. The crow then drank the water and quenched his thirst.

1. The crow found a pitcher
   A. as it flew
   B. after many hours of labour
   C. full of water
   D. which was empty

2. What is the moral of the passage?
   A. No pains, no gains
   B. God helps those who help themselves
   C. Necessity is the mother of invention
   D. Try and try again, you will succeed at last

3. The crow flew from place to place
   A. in search of pitcher
   B. in search of pebbles
   C. in search of water
   D. in search of a vessel

4. The pitcher, the crow found
   A. was full of water
   B. was dry
   C. had little water in the bottom
   D. had water up to its mouth

5. As the crow dropped pebbles into the pitcher, what happend?
   A. The pitcher broke down
   B. The water leaked one of the pitcher
   C. The level of water into the pitcher rose up slowly
   D. Water level immediately rose to the mouth of the pitcher

PASSAGE-5

Once upon a time a crane and a fox lived in a forest. They were good friend. One day the fox invited the crane to a feast. He made a tasty food and served it before the crane on a plate. The crane could not eat anything because of the long beak. But the fox licked all his food. The crane felt insulted. He decided to teach the fox a lesson.

Next day he invited the fox. He prepared the same tasty food and placed it in front of the fox inside a narrow glass. The crane ate easily while the fox looked on. Now, it was the fox's turn to remain hungry.

1. What is the moral of the passage?
   A. Beware of the wicked
   B. One good turn deserves another
   C. Be contented with what you have
   D. Tit for tat

2. The crane could not eat tasty food because the
   A. food was served in a shallow plate
   B. food was very hot
   C. food was served in a long jar
   D. crane was not hungry

3. The fox had to remain hungry because
   A. the food served was not enough in quantity
   B. the food was served inside a narrow glass
   C. the food served was not tasty
   D. the food was all liquid

4. Why did the crane feel insulted?
   A. Because he was invited to feast but he could not eat anything
   B. Because the food was served in a shallow plate and he could not eat
   C. Because the food was too hot
   D. Because the fox gulped all the food quickly

5. The crane successfully taught a lesson to the fox when he invited the fox to a feast and served the food
   A. in a narrow glass
   B. in a large plate
   C. in a broken plate
   D. in a long jar

PASSAGE-6

The family set down at the table and began to talk about the summer holidays. They had to decide a place to visit during the vacation. Should they go to their village or to a hill station? The parents preferred the village while the children wished to go the hill station. After few moments of discussion the elders decided to visit both the places. First they shall go to the village for a week and then stay at the hill station for the remaining days. For the first time the family shall be together during the holidays. The children were happy with the holiday plan.

1. The purpose for which the family set down at the table was
   A. to decide a place to visit during the vacation
   B. to educate the children how to carry articles during a visit to a hill station
   C. to decide the date when they should start their journey
   D. to tell the children that they will visit a hill station during this vacation

2. The final plan was to visit
   A. their village
   B. a hill station
   C. their village as well as a hill station
   D. their home town

3. The final decision was made by
   A. the boys   B. the girls
   C. the women   D. the elders

4. They decided first to go to their village and stay there for
   A. a day   B. a week
   C. ten days   D. a fortnight

5. Why were children happy?
   A. Because a hill station was included in their holiday plan
   B. Because a visit to their village was excluded from their holiday plan
   C. Because their choice prevailed
   D. Because they were going all alone to the hill station

PASSAGE-7

Once Govind intended to go on pilgrimage with his family. He asked Mirind to accompany. But for his trade's reason, he did not go with him. So Govind thought it safe to leave the box of his jewellery with him, as it was dangerous to leave it in a lone house or take it on the journey. So he went to him with the box. He took him to a lonely place under a tree and handed it over to him. He told Mirind, "Keep it safe with you. I shall return from the journey after six month then I shall take it back from you." Mirind said, "Don't worry, I shall keep it as safe as own."

1. Govind intended to go
   A. for a business trip
   B. to a hill station
   C. on a long journey to a sacred place
   D. to his home town for a long period

2. Why did Govind leave his box of jewellery with Mirind?
   A. Because it was not safe to take the box with him on a long journey
   B. Because Mirind was his fast friend
   C. Because the box was very heavy
   D. Because his house was unsafe

3. Why did Govind take Mirind to a lonely place?
   A. To tell him that the box contained valuable jewellery
   B. So that no third person could see box
   C. To show him what was within the box
   D. To tell him that the box will remain with him

4. Where did Govind hand over the box of jewellery to Mirind?
   A. At Mirind's house
   B. At his own house
   C. In a lonely place
   D. In a lonely place under a tree

5. It was not safe to leave the box in a lone house. Here the word 'lone house' means
   A. a house in a deserted place
   B. a house where none lives
   C. a house without door and lock
   D. a house near the forest

PASSAGE-8

Zahir-ud-din Babar was the first Mughal emperor of India. A descendent of Timur on father's side and Changez Khan on his mother's side, Babar was a brave warrior. After defeating Ibrahim Lodhi in the First Battle of Panipat in 1526 he entered Delhi and soon gained control over Agra. After many more battles with Rajputs he extended his empire over Punjab, Uttar Pradesh and north Bihar. He died at a young age of 48 years in 1530 at his capital Agra without getting much time to consolidate his victories.

1. Zahir-ud-din Babar was the first
   A. Muslim ruler of India
   B. Mughal ruler of India
   C. Afghan ruler of India
   D. Turk ruler of India

2. Babar was born in the years
   A. 1480 B. 1482
   C. 1492 D. 1962

3. Babar first occupied
   A. Punjab B. Agra
   C. Delhi D. Panipat

4. Babar was a brave warrior. Here brave warrior means
   A. courageous soldier
   B. a kind hearted soldier
   C. a clever fighter
   D. a victorious general

5. Babar extended his empire over Punjab and Uttar Pradesh after many more battles with the
   A. Afghans B. Rajputs
   C. Mughals D. Lodhies

PASSAGE-9

Our National Flag is tricolour. It has three equal horizontal strips. The strip at the top is saffron, in the middle is white and at the bottom is green. The ratio of width to length of the flag is 2 : 3. In the centre of the white strip is a wheel in navy blue. The wheel represents the *chakra*. Its design is similar to the wheel which appears on the abacus of the Sarnath Lion Capital of Ashoka. Its diameter approximates to the width of the white strip. The wheel has 24 spokes. It was adopted by Constituent Assembly on July 22, 1947. We love our national flag. We respect it. We are ready to sacrifice our life to protect its honour. It represents the nation. So it is a symbol of national honour.

1. In our national flag the wheel is located in the centre of
   A. saffron strip B. white strip
   C. green strip D. blue strip

2. In our national flag which of the strips is at the bottom in our national flag
   A. blue C. saffron
   B. white D. green

3. Why do we love our national flag?
   A. Because it is tricolour
   B. Because it has three strips
   C. Because it has a wheel at the centre
   D. Because it is a symbol of national honour

4. Our national flag was approved by
   A. President
   B. Lok Sabha
   C. Parliament
   D. Constituent Assembly

5. The diameter approximates to the width of the white strip. Here the word 'approximates' means
   A. is more or less equal
   B. is exactly equal
   C. is not equal
   D. is related

PASSAGE-10

Distance in large cities are long. All the people do not have their own means of transport. They have to depend upon the state or private buses. The number of bus users is very large. Every bus stop is, therefore, crowded. The number of buses is not adequate. Thus people suffer the torture of long wait at the bus stop. Some bus stops are quite orderly. People form queues and get into the buses turn by turn. However, often this order is forgotten and confusion spreads when the bus comes and the law of jungle prevails.

1. Why are the bus stops crowded?
   A. Because they are small is size
   B. Because the number of passengers is very large
   C. Because they are situated at some busy centre
   D. Because people do not form queues

2. Long wait at the bus stop is the result of
   A. over-crowding in the buses
   B. late running of buses
   C. shortage of buses
   D. slow speed of buses

3. Some bus stops are quite orderly where
   A. there is no crowd
   B. the number of buses is adequate

C. people do not have to wait for long
D. people form queues and enter the buses one by one

4. Most of the people who travel by buses are
A. non-working
B. do not have their own vehicles
C. have to go a long distance
D. live in large cities

5. What happens when people do not have their own transport?
A. They have to wait for a bus at a bus stop
B. They have to depend upon the state or private buses
C. They have to travel long distances
D. They form queues and get into buses one by one

PASSAGE-11

A certain king once fell ill and doctors said that only a sudden fright would restore his health but the king was not a man for anyone to play tricks on, except his fool. One day, when the fool was with him in his boat he cleverly pushed the king into water but he was rescued and put to bed. The fright, the bath and bed cured the diseased king, but he was so angry with the fool that he turned him out of the country.

1. What did the doctor say about the king?
A. Only a sudden fright would restore the king's health
B. Only fool would cure the king
C. Only a boat trick could cure the king
D. The king had suffered a sudden fright

2. He cleverly pushed the king into water but *he* was rescued and put to bed. In this sentence *he* refers to
A. the king   B. the fool
C. the doctor   D. the river

3. When the fool pushed the king into water they were
A. in the palace   B. in the bed
C. in the garden   D. in a boat

4. Who played the trick on the king?
A. The doctor   B. The boatman
C. The fool   D. The fright

5. The fool who cured the king was
A. rewarded
B. thrown into water
C. turned out of the country
D. put into jail

ANSWERS

Passage 1.	1	2	3	4	5
	D	C	B	A	C
Passage 2.	1	2	3	4	5
	B	C	D	B	B
Passage 3.	1	2	3	4	5
	D	D	C	B	D
Passage 4.	1	2	3	4	5
	B	C	C	C	C
Passage 5.	1	2	3	4	5
	D	A	B	B	A
Passage 6.	1	2	3	4	5
	A	C	D	B	A

Passage 7.	1	2	3	4	5
	C	A	B	D	B
Passage 8.	1	2	3	4	5
	B	B	C	A	B
Passage 9.	1	2	3	4	5
	B	D	D	D	A
Passage 10.	1	2	3	4	5
	B	C	D	B	B
Passage 11.	1	2	3	4	5
	A	A	D	C	C

2. English Grammar

Part of speech	Definition or Function	Examples
Noun	Name of a person, place, animal, quality or thing	Ram, boy, dog pen, sun, Delhi, truth, honesty
Pronoun	Used in place of a noun	I, you, he she, they
Articles & Determiners	Points out indefinite and definite nouns	a, an, the, few, some
Adjective	Describes a noun or pronoun	big, honest, wooden valuable, quiet, deep, soft, narrow
Adverb	Describes a verb, an adjective or another adverb	silently, widely, softly, quietly, very, carefully
Verb	Tells about action or state of something or someone	is, am, was, have, do, like, walk, work, make, throw, tell
Conjuction	Joins words, clauses or sentences	and, but, when, yet, while, else
Preposition	Links a noun or pronoun to another word	at, to, after, on for, under, over, with
Interjection	Expresses sudden feelings or emotions	Ah!, Alas!, oh!, ouch!, hi!, well!, Hurrah!

NOUNS

A word which denotes a person, a thing, an animal or a place is said to be a noun.

There are two noun numbers in English — the *Singular* and the *Plural*.

Singular Numbers : A noun that denotes one person or one thing, is said to be in the Singular number. For example — book, pencil, bird, dog, hen etc. are in singular number.

Plural Number : A noun that denotes more than one person or one thing is said to be in plural number. For example — boys, pens, lions, girls, men etc. are in plural number.

REMEMBER

Singular	*Plural*
Cat	Cats
Book	Books
Pen	Pens
Room	Rooms
Tree	Trees
Bus	Buses
Bush	Bushes
Box	Boxes
Glass	Glasses
Dish	Dishes
Judge	Judges
Tax	Taxes
Watch	Watches
Calf	Calves
Thief	Thieves
Knife	Knives

Singular	*Plural*
Scarf	Scarves
Wife	Wives
Leaf	Leaves
Wolf	Wolves
Half	Halves
Monarch	Monarchs
Roof	Roofs
Hoof	Hoofs
Gulf	Gulfs
Staff	Staffs
Radio	Radios
Bamboo	Bamboos
Folio	Folios
Hero	Heroes
Volcano	Volcanoes
Mango	Mangoes
Potato	Potatoes
Photo	Photos
Piano	Pianos
Baby	Babies
Fly	Flies
Country	Countries
Lady	Ladies
Boy	Boys
Monkey	Monkeys
Ox	Oxen
Child	Children
Man	Men
Woman	Women
Tooth	Teeth
Axis	Axes
Basis	Bases
Foot	Feet
Goose	Geese
Englishman	Englishmen
Radius	Radii
Vertex	Vertices
Stimulus	Stimuli

1. Note the plurals of the following nouns:

Singular	*Plural*	*Singular*	*Plural*
copy	copies	cry	cries
baby	babies	duty	duties
body	bodies	country	countries
family	families	diary	diaries
fly	flies	fairy	fairies

city	cities	spy	spies
army	armies	storey	storeys
bay	bays	monkey	monkeys

2. The following nouns do not undergo any change in plural form, in general.

Singular	*Plural*	*Singular*	*Plural*
deer	deer	sheep	sheep
thousand	thousand	pair	pair
hundred	hundred	score	score
dozen	dozen	gross	gross

Note: We can write—

(*a*) thousands of men; (*b*) two pairs of shoes; (*c*) dozens of mangoes; (*d*) scores of people etc.
But—
(*a*) two thousand rupees; (*b*) three hundred men; (*c*) five dozen eggs, etc.

3. The following nouns are usually used in plural forms. They take a plural verb after them—

eatables	fetters	surroundings
riches	alms	spectacles
trousers	pants	scissors
premises	thanks	annals
congratulations	goods	shorts
tongs	pains	arms
breeches	(for troubles)	

4. The following are the nouns which are plural in appearance but are usually used in singular number. They are followed by a singular verb—

news	politics	physics
mathematics	economics	ethics
politics	classics	gallows
statistics	athletics	innings
mechanics	summons	mumps

5. Collective nouns often used as plurals—

public	police	cattle
audience	clergy	folk
people	poultry	nation
elite	gentry	glitterati

6. The nouns that are usually used in singular forms—

advice	hair	rice
fuel	alphabet	machinery
offspring	issue	furniture
mischief	stationery	luggage
bedding	information	abuse

7. Material nouns are always used in singular number—

gold	copper	milk
water	silk	wool

Note: They may be used in plural with a different meaning.

copper coins (coppers), chains or fetters (irons), cans made of tin (tins).

GENDERS

The difference in sex is denoted by Gender in grammar. The various genders are as follows :

1. **Masculine Gender :** A noun that denotes a male is said to be of the masculine gender, as man, uncle, ox, boy etc.
2. **Feminine Gender :** A noun that denotes a female is said to be of feminine gender, as woman, aunt, princess, cow etc.
3. **Common Gender :** Nouns which denote both males and females are said to be of the common gender, as friend, cousin, person, parent, baby etc.
4. **Neuter Gender :** A noun that denotes the name of object without life is said to be of neuter gender, as file, table, pencil.

REMEMBER

Masculine	Feminine
Boy	Girl
Son	Daughter
Brother	Sister
Murderer	Murderess
Sorcerer	Sorceress
Son-in-law	Daughter-in-law
Father-in-law	Mother-in-law
Man-servant	Maid-servant
Land-lord	Land-lady
Bachelor	Maid
Gentleman	Lady
Monk	Nun
Earl	Countess
Lad	Lass
Sir	Madam
Duke	Dutchess
Emperor	Empress
Milk-man	Milk-maid
Pea-cock	Pea-hen

Masculine	Feminine
Step-father	Step-mother
Hero	Heroine
Viceroy	Vicerine
Mr.	Mrs.
Governor	Governess
Master	Mistress
Wizard	Witch
Heir	Heiress
Host	Hostess
Lion	Lioness
Mayor	Mayoress
Actor	Actress
Buck	Doe
Colt	Filly
Dog	Bitch
Horse	Mare
Count	Countess
Hunter	Huntress
Prince	Princess
Abbot	Abbess
God	Goddess
Author	Authoress
Ox	Cow
Widower	Widow
Grand-father	Grand-mother
He-goat	She-goat
Milk-man	Milk-woman
Bridegroom	Bride
Tiger	Tigress
Priest	Priestess
Poet	Poetess
Shepherd	Shepherdess
Nephew	Niece
Stag	Hind

PRONOUNS

The repetition of a noun in a sentence or a set of sentences is really boring. So, instead of repeating the noun, we can use a word (for that noun) called the pronoun.

"A pronoun is a word that we use instead of a noun".

Example:

This is *Sachin. He* plays cricket.

Note: *He* is the pronoun used in place of *Sachin.*

Kinds of Pronouns

1. **Personal pronouns :** A pronoun which is used instead of the name of a person is known as a 'Personal Pronoun'. A list of the 'Personal pronouns' is listed below :

   I, my, mine, me, we   (First Person)
   You, your, yours   (Second Person)
   He, his, him, she, her, hers, it,
   its, they, their, theirs, them   (Third Person)

2. **Demonstrative, Indefinite and Distributive Pronouns :**

   (a) **Demonstrative Pronouns :** Pronouns used to point out the objects to which they refer are called Demonstrative Pronouns.

   Examples :
   (i) *This* is a present from my uncle.
   (ii) *These* are merely excuses.
   (iii) Bembay mangoes are better than *those* of Bangaluru.

   (b) **Indefinite Pronouns :** All pronouns which refer to persons or things in a general way and do not refer to any particular person or thing are called Indefinite Pronouns.

   Examples :
   (i) *Somebody* has stolen my watch.
   (ii) *Few* escaped unhurt.
   (iii) Did you ask *anybody* to come?

   (c) **Distributive Pronouns :** Each, either, neither are called distributive pronouns because they refer to persons or things one at a time. For this reason they are always singular and followed by the verb in singular.

   Examples :
   (i) *Each* of the men received a reward.
   (ii) *These* men received *each* a reward.
   (iii) *Either* of you can go.

3. **Relative Pronouns :** A relative pronoun refers or relates to some noun going before, which is called its Antecedent.

Examples :
(i) I met Hari *who* used to live here.
(ii) I have found the pen *which* I had lost.
(iii) Here is the book *that* you lent me.

4. **Interrogative Pronouns :** These pronouns, are used for asking questions.

Examples :
(i) *Whose* book is this?
(ii) *What* will all the neighbours say?
(iii) *Which* do you prefer, tea or coffee?

Note : Interrogative pronouns can also be used in asking indirect questions. Consider the following examples :
(i) I asked *who* was speaking.
(ii) Tell me *what* you have done.
(iii) Say *which* you would like best.

Behaviour of the Pronouns

1. If three pronouns are used together in the same sentence they are arranged in the following order :

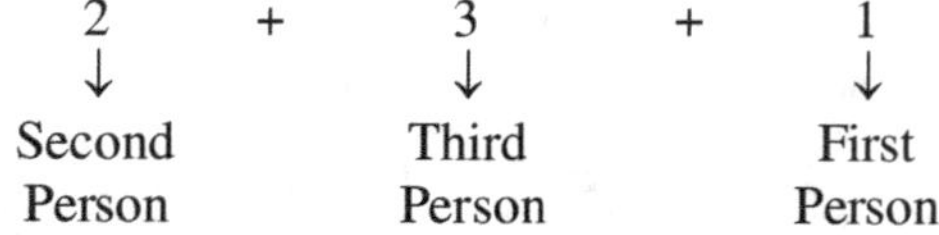

I, you and he must help *that* poor man.
          (Incorrect)
You, he and I must help *that* poor man.
          (Correct)

2. When two or more singular nouns are joined by and, the pronoun used for them should be plural.

Examples :
Mohan and Sohan are friends. *They* play football. *They* live at Lajpat Nagar.

3. But if these nouns joined by and refer to the same person or thing, the pronoun used should be singular.

Examples :
(i) Delhi, the beautiful city and the capital of India, is famous for *its* historical monuments.
(ii) The manager and owner of the firm expressed *his* views on the demands of the workers.

4. When two nouns are used with as well as, the pronoun agrees with the first subject.
   Examples :
   (a) Mohan as well as his friends is doing *his* work.
   (b) The students as well as their teachers are doing *their* work.

5. When two singular nouns joined by 'and' are preceded by *each* or *every,* the pronoun used must be singular and should agree in gender with the second noun.
   Examples :
   (a) Every man and every woman will do *her* best for the nation.
   (b) Each boy and each girl went to *her* house.

6. When two nouns are joined by using 'with', the pronoun agrees with the noun coming before 'with'.
   Examples :
   (a) The boy with *his* parents has gone to see a movie.
   (b) The children with *their* parents have gone to picnic.

7. When two different nouns are joined by either.......... or; neither .... nor, the pronoun is used according to the number and gender of the second noun.
   Examples :
   (a) Either your sister or you have done *your* work.
   (b) Neither the students nor the teacher was in *his* class.

8. The pronoun coming after '*than*' must be in the same case as that coming before '*than*'.
   Examples :
   (a) She plays better than *me.*　　(Incorrect)
       She plays better than *I.*　　(Correct)
   (b) His elder brother is more intelligent than *him.*　　(Incorrect)
       His elder brother is more intelligent than *he.*　　(Correct)

9. 'Many a' always takes a singular pronoun and singular verb.
   Example :
   Many a soldier has met *his* death in the battle field.

10. 'Who', 'Whose', 'Whom' are used only for persons.
    Examples :
    (a) *Who* is knocking at the door?
    (b) *Whose* pen is this?
    (c) *What* do you want?

11. 'Which' is used for things.
    Example :
    Which game do you like?

MULTIPLE CHOICE QUESTIONS

Directions: *In the following questions choose the correct options to fill the blanks.*

1. The place was so dirty that ..... wished to run away from there.
   A. everybody　　B. anybody
   C. few　　D. some

2. ..... was there to help me.
   A. Somebody　　B. Anything
   C. Anybody　　D. Nobody

3. Is there .... to eat?
   A. some　　B. something
   C. any　　D. few

4. ..... of the students were making a great noise.
   A. Anyone　　B. Somebody
   C. Many　　D. Nobody

5. ..... of the students can solve this sum.
   A. Someone　　B. Anybody
   C. Somebody　　D. None

6. ...... of us should try our best to make India a heaven.
   A. Any　　B. Somebody
   C. Anybody　　D. All

7. ...... of us do not know the real meaning of our lives.
   A. Any　　B. Something
   C. Several　　D. Many

8. My .... black.
   A. hairs are　　B. hair is
   C. hairs shall　　D. hair will

9. She saw two .... on the last Sunday.
    A. thiefs   B. theifs
    C. thieves   D. theives

10. My sister is a ....
    A. bacheloress   B. bachelor
    C. unmaried   D. spinster

11. One is supposed to do ....
    A. our duty   B. their duty
    C. one's duty   D. his duty

12. Take anything .... you want.
    A. that   B. which
    C. than   D. then

13. I cannot tolerate ....
    A. separated you
    B. your separation
    C. separation from you
    D. you separated

14. He is .... faithful partner.
    A. Yours   B. You
    C. Your   D. Your's

15. Ajay is more smart than ....
    A. her   B. hers
    C. herself   D. she

16. Vivek works harder than ....
    A. me   B. I
    C. her   D. his

17. They should help ....
    A. the poor people   B. the poor
    C. the poor persons   D. the poor peoples

18. .... are mad.
    A. All his sons   B. His all sons
    C. Sons all his   D. All sons his

19. The poor fellow .... to fate.
    A. resigned
    B. resigned himself
    C. resigned itself
    D. resigned themselves

20. Nobody will help you but ....
    A. I   B. me
    C. ours   D. his

21. It is a good chance, You must avail ....
    this opportunity.
    A. of   B. yourself of
    C. for   D. from

22. The person who is elected .... my relative.
    A. is   B. he is
    C. his   D. him

23. He made ....
    A. yours mention   B. mention of you
    C. mention for you   D. mention about you

24. .... I know, he is quite faithful.
    A. As far as   B. So far as
    C. So far this   D. So far so

25. It is a duty of a person to take .... for his
    family.
    A. pain   B. pains
    C. pain-killers   D. pained

26. She does not love .... husband.
    A. his   B. her
    C. its   D. their

27. Let .... work together.
    A. him and me   B. he and I
    C. he and him   D. I and me

28. Copper, Silver and Gold ....
    A. each will do   B. either will do
    C. any one will do   D. any will do

29. Jessica and Roma are very irregular ....
    habits.
    A. in her   B. in their
    C. in its   D. in every

30. One likes to enjoy .... who was a great
    poet.
    A. The sonnets of Shakespeare
    B. Shakespeare's sonnets
    C. Sonnets
    D. Shakespeare

31. That is the boy .... everybody loves.
    A. whom   B. who
    C. that   D. whose

32. That is the girl .... won the first prize.
    A. whom   B. who
    C. whose   D. which

33. That is the man .... purse was lost.
    A. who   B. whom
    C. whose   D. their

ANSWERS

1	2	3	4	5	6	7	8	9	10
A	D	B	C	D	D	D	B	C	D
11	**12**	**13**	**14**	**15**	**16**	**17**	**18**	**19**	**20**
C	A	C	C	D	B	B	A	B	B
21	**22**	**23**	**24**	**25**	**26**	**27**	**28**	**29**	**30**
B	A	B	A	B	B	A	C	B	A
31	**32**	**33**							
A	B	C							

ARTICLES

The family of the articles has only three members. They are : A, An and The. However, they fall under two groups :

(a) Definite Article *(b)* Indefinite Article

'The' is known as definite article whereas 'a' and 'an' are known as indefinite articles.

Use of the Definite Article 'The'

'The' is used before

1. The superlative degree :
   He is the ablest man of the town.
   (ablest is a superlative degree)

2. The name of states, countries etc. having a descriptive name :
   (i) The J & K is a small state. (J & K is a descriptive name)
   (ii) He lives in the U.S.A. (U.S.A. is a descriptive name)
   (But the Delhi and the America are wrong because neither Delhi nor America is a descriptive name)

3. The names of the scriptures :
   The Gita is a holy book. (Gita is a scripture)

4. Name of newspapers :
   The Tribune is published from Chandigarh.

5. Name of rivers, canals, seas, oceans, bays, gulfs, groups of islands etc. :
   (i) The Ganga is a holy river.
   (ii) The Indian Ocean is the deepest ocean.
   (iii) The Persian Gulf is a narrow gulf.

6. The name of famous buildings :
   The Taj is one of the best buildings in India.

7. The names of nationals, sects and communities:
   (i) The English defeated the Germans in the World War.
   (ii) The rich should help the poor.
   (iii) The Hindus believe in the caste system.

8. Proper nouns used as common nouns :
   (i) Kalidas is the Shakespeare of India.
   (ii) Delhi is the London of India.

9. Famous historical events :
   The Industrial Revolution changed the face of England.

10. The directions and the celestial bodies:
    The sun rises in the east.

11. Titles :
    Akbar, the Great was loved by his subjects.

Do not use 'the'

1. Before languages :
   The English is an international language. (Incorrect)
   English is an international language. (Correct)

2. Before the names of games :
   The hockey is a popular game. (Incorrect)
   Hockey is a popular game. (Correct)

Use of the Indefinite Articles 'A' and 'An'

'A' is used before :

1. All singular common nouns beginning with a consonant :
   (i) A boy sings a song.

(ii) A black and a white cow were grazing in the field.

2. If a word begins with a vowel but gives the sound of a consonant, 'a' should be used before it :
   (i) He was helped in his work by a European.
   (ii) He is a one-eyed man.
   (iii) It is a useful work.

'An' is used as follows :

1. All singular common nouns beginning with a vowel (*i.e.*, a, e, i, o, u) :
   (i) He is an artist.
   (ii) He is an old man.
   (iii) I intend to buy an umbrella.

2. If a word starts with a consonant but gives the sound of a vowel, "an" should be used before it :
   (i) Brutus is an honourable man.
   (ii) He is an honour to his profession.
   (iii) He is an L.L.B.

(iv) He is an M.A.
(v) You will reach there in an hour.

Demonstratives, that, these and those

1. The demonstrative adjectives and pronouns are for objects nearby the speaker:
   this (singular) those (plural)
   and for objects far away from the speaker.
   That (singular) those (plural)

2. Demonstratives are the only adjectives that agree in number with their nouns.
   That hat is nice.
   Those hats are nice.

3. When there is the idea of selection, the pronoun "one" (or "ones") often follows the demonstrative.
   I want a book. I'll get this (one).
   If the demonstrative is followed by an adjective, "one"(or "ones") must be used.
   I want a book. I'll get this big one.

MULTIPLE CHOICE QUESTIONS

Directions: *In the following questions choose the correct options to fill the blanks.*

1. .... will have to be paid for this material.
A. Half rupee
B. Half a rupee
C. A half rupee
D. An half rupee

2. .... is taking keen interest in India.
A. The USA
B. USA
C. An USA
D. A USA

3. Only .... can save our country.
A. the Hitler
B. a Hitler
C. Hitler
D. an Hitler

4. I can run for ....
A. hundred miles
B. the hundred miles
C. a hundred miles
D. an hundred miles.

5. .... man-eater has been killed.
A. The
B. A
C. An
D. Either A or B

6. What .... fine idea!
A. the
B. an
C. a
D. No article

7. .... earth is moving around the sun.
A. An
B. A

C. The
D. No article

8. This is .... first example while I got.
A. the
B. a
C. an
D. No article

9. This is .... house which was built during earthquake.
A. a
B. an
C. the
D. No article

10. .... America is a rich country.
A. The
B. An
C. A
D. No article

11. .... U.S.A. is a developed country.
A. A
B. An
C. The
D. No article

12. .... Bible is a holy book.
A. A
B. The
C. An
D. No article

13. .... rich should help the poor.
A. The
B. A
C. An
D. No article

14. .... Gold is a costly metal.
A. The
B. A
C. An
D. No article

15. Kalidas is .... Shakespeare of India.
A. a   B. an
C. the   D. No article

16. I cannot do .... difficult work.
A. a such   B. the such
C. such the   D. such a

17. How foolish .... plan it is!
A. a   B. an
C. the   D. No article

18. An ink is .... useful article.
A. an   B. a
C. the   D. No article

19. There are .... husband and wife.
A. a   B. an
C. the   D. No article

20. He is learning .... French
A. the   B. a
C. an   D. No article

ANSWERS

1	2	3	4	5	6	7	8	9	10
B	A	B	C	D	C	C	A	C	D

11	12	13	14	15	16	17	18	19	20
C	B	A	D	C	D	A	B	D	D

ADJECTIVES & ADVERBS

An Adjective is a word which adds something to the meaning of a noun or a pronoun.

Mridula is an *intelligent* girl.

He has a *black* goat.

He is a *brilliant* student.

She is a *clever* girl.

It is a *beautiful* picture.

In the sentences given above, the words in italics are adjectives.

An Adverb is a word which qualifies the meaning of a Verb, an Adjective or another Adverb.

(*i*) He talks *slowly*.

(*ii*) He is a *very* good student.

(*iii*) He talks *very* slowly.

In sentence (*i*), *slowly* qualifies the verb *talks*.

In sentence (*ii*), *very* qualifies the adjective *good*.

In sentence (*iii*), *very* qualifies the adverb *slowly*.

Adjectives have three degrees of comparison :

1. **Positive Degree :** It expresses the common form of an adjective.

   Example :

   Ram is a *tall* boy.

   In the above sentence *tall* is an adjective and expresses the common form.

2. **Comparative Degree :** It expresses the more of the same form.

Example :

Ram is *taller* than Mahesh.

In the above sentence *taller* is an adjective that expresses the more of the common form of the adjective *tall*.

"When and How to Use" Comparative Degree?

(a) Comparative Degree is used when two persons or two groups of persons or things are compared.

   Examples :

   (a) He is *wiser* than his younger brother.

   (b) This glass is *cleaner* than the other.

(b) When two different qualities in the same person are compared, more is used instead of 'er' to form the comparative. The formula used in this case should be :

   More + Positive Degree

   She is *fairer* than polite.   (Incorrect)

   She is *more fair* than polite.   (Correct)

(c) When selection of one out of two persons or things is meant, the degree of comparison is followed by of and *the* is used before it.

   Example :

   Zia is abler of *the* two sisters.

(d) If two comparatives are used in the same sentence to impress upon an idea, both should be preceded by the definite article.

Examples :
 (i) The higher you go, the cooler it is.
(ii) The more we get, the more we desire.

(e) When one person or thing is compared with another of the same kind, other is used after the comparative degree. In such sentences other is normally preceded by any or all.

Examples :
(i) Kalidas is greater than any dramatist. (Incorrect)
   Kalidas is greater than any other dramatist. (Correct)
(ii) Lead is heavier than all metals. (Incorrect)
   Lead is heavier than all other metals. (Correct)

(f) Senior, junior, superior, inferior, prior, anterior (earlier than) and posterior (later than) are always followed by 'to'.

Examples :
 (i) Ram is senior *to* Mohan by three years.
(ii) That pen is inferior *to* that.
(iii) He is junior *to* me in rank.
(iv) This event was posterior *to* that.
Note: Never use *than* after the above mentioned adjectives.

Important Information

(a) 'Preferable' is also used as an adjective of the comparative degree. As such, it is always followed by *to* and not *a*.
Death is preferable than dishonour. (Incorrect)
Death is preferable *to* dishonour. (Correct)

(b) To intensify the Degree of comparison, we use *far* or *much* before the comparative.
Examples :
(i) This book is *far* better than that.
(ii) His performance was *much* better than Mohan's.
Warning : Always avoid the use of double comparatives.
Don't say : Ram is more cleverer than his younger brother.
Say: Ram is cleverer than his younger brother.

3. **Superlative Degree :** It expresses the most of the common form of an adjective.
Example :
He is the ablest man of the town.

How and when to use the Superlative Degree?

(a) The Superlative Degree is used when more than two persons or things are compared.

(b) The Superlative Degree is generally preceded by 'the' and followed by 'of' in most of the cases or otherwise.

(c) When an adjective of the superlative degree is preceded by a Possessive Adjective or a Noun in the Possessive case, 'the' should not be used before it.
Example :
Which is Kalidas' best play?
It will be a blunder to use 'the' before the Superlative Degree in such cases.
Don't say : Which is Kalidas' the best play.

(d) To intensify the degree of comparison, *by far* is used before the superlative degree.
Example :
India is *by far* the most beautiful country of the world.
Note: Always avoid the use of double superlatives.
Don't say : He is the most strongest boy in the class.
Say : He is the strongest boy in the class.

Use of some Important Adjectives

1. (a) 'Some' is used as follows :
   (i) With countable nouns where it means— a little, a small quantity.
   (ii) In a question which shows some request.
   Examples :
   (i) There is some water in the bottle.
   (ii) Some of the students were absent yesterday.
   (iii) Will you have some milk?
   (iv) Will you buy some fruit for me?

(b) **'Any'** is used as follows :
   (i) In negative sentences.
   (ii) In interrogative sentences.

(iii) After 'Hardly', 'Scarcely' and 'Barely'.
(iv) After 'If'.
Examples :
(i)   There is not any sugar in the pot.
(ii) We haven't any rice in the house.
(iii) I have hardly any money.
(iv) There are scarcely any plants in this field.
(v) If there is any danger, blow the whistle.

2. (a) **Older :** Older (and oldest) are used for persons animals and things. But 'Older' and 'Oldest' refer to the persons who do not belong to the same family.
Examples :
(i)   Radha is older than Shyama.
(ii) John is the oldest member of the staff. 'Older' and 'Oldest' refer to the persons who do not belong to the same family.

(b) **Elder** (and **eldest**) are used in respect of the members of the same family like sons, daughters, brothers, sisters.
Examples :
(i)   My elder sister is a lecturer.
(ii) Meenakshi is the eldest of the three sisters.
Note :
(i)   'Elder' is not followed by 'than'.
(ii) 'Elder' and 'Eldest' cannot be used for things.

3. (a) **'Few'** is negative and is the opposite of 'Many'. It means 'not many'.
(b) **'A few'** is positive and means 'some at least'. It is the opposite of 'None'.
(c) **'The few'** means 'minority' and suggests 'whether there is'.
Examples :
(i)   We have few holidays in school.
(ii) Only a few boys will fail in the examination.
(iii) The few poems that he wrote are very popular.

4. (a) **Further** means 'something additional'.
(b) **Farther** means 'a greater distance'.
Examples :
(i)   Further discussion will be held in the office of the principal.
(ii) Amritsar is farther from Delhi than Ambala.

5. (a) **Little** is negative. It means, 'not much', or 'hardly any'.
(b) **A little** is positive. It means 'some quantity'.
(c) **The little** denotes quantity. It means, 'not much but all that is, or whatever quantity there is'.
Examples :
(i)   There is little hope of his success.
(ii) He knows a little of everything.
(iii) I have spent the little money I had.
(iv) The little knowledge of shoe-making proved very useful to me.

6. (a) **'Much'** expresses 'quantity'.
(b) **'Many'** expresses 'number'.
(c) **'Many a'**—'Singular noun' and 'Singular verb' are used with 'many a'.
Examples :
(i)   There is not *much* water in the jug.
(ii) *Many* boys are absent today.
(iii) *Many* a battle has been fought on the soil of India.

7. (a) **'Less'** denotes 'in a small degree'.
(b) **'Fewer'** denotes 'number'.
Examples :
(i)   He devotes less time to his studies.
(ii) There are no fewer than ten chairs in this room.

8. (a) **'Each'** is used for a single number of 'two persons' or 'things'.
(b) **'Every'** is used for a single number of 'many persons' or 'things'.
Examples :
(i)   Each boy must take part in games.
(ii) There are only two poets. Each poet recited his poem.
(iii) Every man dies in this world.
(iv) Every man is expected to do his duty.

9. (a) **'Either'** means one of the two or both.
(b) **'Neither'** is negative of the either.
Examples :
(i)   You may buy either of these two chairs.
(ii) Neither of them could speak on the stage.

10. (a) **'Later'** expresses 'late in time'.
   (b) **'Latter'** means 'second in position or order'.
   Examples :
   (i) My father reached later than I expected.
   (ii) The latter position was better than the former.

Use of some Important Adverbs

1. (a) Also, too, enough:
   (i) He taught English. Also, he edited the school magazine
   (ii) He is a writer and also he is a painter.
   (iii) He is too obstinate to listen to any reason.
   (iv) This is too difficult a piece for the junior students.
   (v) Sarla was kind enough to help the poor.
   (vi) He is brave enough to help the truth.
   Note: 'Too' is used in a negative sense, but enough is used in a positive sense.
   (b) Fairly and rather: Both suggest the meaning 'moderately'. But, mainly 'fairly' is used with the words that denote a positive meaning and rather is used with the words that denote a negative meaning:
   (i) Rita did fairly well in that competition, but her performance was rather poor in sports.
   (ii) Mona is fairly rich, but she is rather stingy.
   Note: 'Rather' can also be used in a positive sense.
   (i) This is a rather interesting job.
   (ii) That boy is rather smart.
   (c) Hardly, barely, scarcely: These words mostly convey the negative suggestions and are almost similar.
   (i) I have hardly any strength now.

(ii) There was barely any supply to the township,
(iii) There were scarcely a hundred guests present.
Note: With slight variance in the meaning, the words given above convey the idea of 'very little', 'not enough', 'lack of quantity and number'.
(d) Yet, Still: These adverbs can often be used to connect the sentence units:
   (i) He has been defeated many times in the contest; still he wants to be a competitor.
   (ii) Mona was sick; yet she went on doing her work.
(e) Alone:
   (i) He alone (none else) is capable of handling that fire,
   (ii) He hunted all alone in the forest. (not in any company)
Special Note:
(a) Apart from their conventional positions the adverbs might be used in different positions with different meanings and angles.
   (i) He had only four books.
   (ii) John only contacted his friend in need.
   (iii) He greeted me only.
   (iv) Only he greeted me there.
(b) Inversion: Some adverbs can be inverted *i.e.* placed in the beginning of the sentence and then be followed by an interrogative form. The most common of these adverb are: so, seldom, never, nowhere, under no circumstances, hardly, scarcely etc.
   (i) So big was the bus that it could not enter the narrow lane.
   (ii) Hardly had he reached the station when he received the message.

MULTIPLE CHOICE QUESTIONS

Directions: *In the following questions choose the correct options to fill the blanks.*

1. The girl whom you met is the .... sister of Ravi.

A. eldest
B. elder
C. older
D. oldest

2. The historical place is ....
A. seeing worth

B.   worthy of seeing
C.   worth seeing
D.   worthy seeing

3. These flowers smell ....
A.   sweet   B.   sweetly
C.   more sweetly   D.   sweetest

4. .... aspirant cannot pass the entrance examination.
A.   Each   B.   Every
C.   All   D.   No

5. Harivansh Rai .... second Shakespeare.
A.   is a   B.   is
C.   is the   D.   is an

6. .... student in the class got prizes.
A.   Each and every   B.   Every and each
C.   Every   D.   Never

7. It is .... picture than the one we saw last Monday.
A.   interesting   B.   much interesting
C.   more interesting D.   most interesting

8. She is clever ....
A.   that her mother is
B.   as her mother is
C.   to her mother is
D.   than her mother is

9. They will get ....
A.   Red, green and black paper
B.   Red, green black paper
C.   Red and green and black paper
D.   Red green black paper

10. Health is .... wealth.
A.   preferable to
B.   more preferable than
C.   more preferable to
D.   most preferable then

11. .... water that was in the jug evaporated.
A.   Little   B.   The little
C.   Small   D.   A small

12. He has not sung .... songs.
A.   much   B.   most
C.   more   D.   many

13. Srishti has searched .... office.
A.   whole the   B.   the whole
C.   a whole   D.   some whole

14. Premchand was .... best and .... famous writer.
A.   a, the most   B.   the, a most
C.   the, more   D.   the, the most

15. William Shakespeare is famous as ....
A.   a poet and a dramatist
B.   a poet and dramatist
C.   the poet and the dramatist
D.   a poet and the dramatist

16. What does .... leader suggest?
A.   other   B.   another
C.   others   D.   anothers

17. He .... money.
A.   has few   B.   have few
C.   has little   D.   have little

18. The .... boys are rewarded.
A.   first two   B.   two first
C.   firsts two   D.   two's first

19. He is .... brave.
A.   stronger than
B.   stronger then
C.   more strong then
D.   more strong than

20. No sooner said ....
A.   so done   B.   and done
C.   then done   D.   but done

21. She returned .... than I had thought.
A.   quickly   B.   more quicker
C.   more quickly   D.   quicker

22. He is .... foolish person.
A.   rather the   B.   a rather
C.   rather a   D.   rather

23. This pen .... rupees.
A.   costs twenty
B.   twenty costs only
C.   costs only twenty
D.   only costs twenty

24. It is .... pride.
A.   nothing else but
B.   nothing else than
C.   else nothing than
D.   but

25. This tea is .... to drink.
A.   too hot   B.   very hot
C.   enough hot   D.   much hot

ANSWERS

1	2	3	4	5	6	7	8	9	10
A	C	A	B	A	C	C	C	A	A

11	12	13	14	15	16	17	18	19	20
B	D	B	D	B	B	C	A	D	C

21	22	23	24	25
C	C	C	A	A

DETERMINERS

Determiners are actually Adjectives. They are always followed by nouns.

Determiners are of the following kinds:

1. Demonstrative Determiners
this, that, these, those

2. Possessive Determiners
my, our, your, his, her, its, their

3. Quantitative Determiners
some, any, much, enough, sufficient, whole, a little, the little, little, all, both

4. Numerical Determiners
a few, some, few, the few, any, several, many, no, etc.

One, two, three ...   (Cardinals)
First, second, third ...   (Ordinals)

5. Distributive Determiners
either, neither

6. Articles
Indefinite: a, an
Definite: the

MULTIPLE CHOICE QUESTIONS

Directions: *In the following questions choose the correct options to fill the blanks.*

1. Give me .... rice.
   A. some   B. few
   C. a few   D. any

2. .... sheep grazing on the slope of the hill had gone away.
   A. Any   B. The few
   C. This   D. Much

3. Have you got .... magazines to read?
   A. all   B. much
   C. some   D. little

4. I have .... money that I want to spend on shares.
   A. any   B. much
   C. less   D. some

5. There is .... owl on the branch of the tree.
   A. a   B. the
   C. an   D. some

6. My brother is .... MBA.
   A. a   B. an
   C. the   D. any

7. Have you got .... cheese?
   A. some   B. many
   C. a few   D. few

8. No, I have not got .... cheese.
   A. many   B. few
   C. any   D. some

9. There is only .... milk left in the bottle.
   A. enough   B. few
   C. much   D. a little

10. There is .... hope of his recovery.
   A. any   B. little
   C. many   D. few

11. .... dogs were barking at the strangers.
   A. Some   B. Any
   C. Much   D. Less

12. The girl bought her father .... juice.
  A. few   B. some
  C. any   D. many

13. You should take .... honey everyday.
  A. any   B. many
  C. a little   D. a few

14. .... boy was punished by the teacher.
  A. Either   B. All
  C. Any   D. Many

15. .... girl was asked to join the army.
  A. None   B. Neither
  C. All   D. Any

16. .... water in the jug has been drunk by Mohan.

  A. The little   B. The few
  C. A few   D. Few

17. I shall play .... piano at the party.
  A. some   B. any
  C. the   D. few

18. .... labourers were found dead in the mine.
  A. Any   B. Fewer
  C. Many   D. Less

19. Could I borrow .... umbrella?
  A. our   B. your
  C. yours   D. my

20. My brother is standing in the .... row.
  A. any   B. many
  C. some   D. first

ANSWERS

1	2	3	4	5	6	7	8	9	10
A	B	C	D	C	B	A	C	D	B

11	12	13	14	15	16	17	18	19	20
A	B	C	A	B	A	C	C	B	D

THE VERB

A Verb is a word that tells something about the action or state of or happenning to a person or thing.

A Verb tells the following:

1. What a person or thing does.
   Sachin goes to school daily.
   The bell *rang* loudly.
   Many birds fly in the sky.
   She *sang* a song.
2. What a person or thing is.
   India *is* the biggest democracy in the world.
   Ram Mehar *is* very rich.
   They *are* happy.
3. What is done to a person or thing.
   You *are liked* by all.
   Two thieves *were arrested.*
   Four students *were punished* by the teacher.
4. What happens to a person or thing.
   His maternal uncle *died* last week.
   Two ships *sank* yesterday.
   Leaves *turn* yellow in autumn.
5. What a person or thing has, had, and so on.
   I *have* a new car.
   He *had* a scooter last year.
   He *has* several cows and goats.

It goes without saying that a verb is the most important part of a sentence. No sentence is complete without a Verb.

Important Information

1. If two or more singular nouns are joined by 'and' the verb used will be plural.

   Example:
   (i) He and I were going to the market.
   (ii) Ram and Mohan are friends.

2. If two singular nouns joined by 'and' points out to the same thing or person, the verb used must be singular.
   Example:
   (i) Rice and curry is the favourite food of the Punjabis.
   (ii) The Collector and District Magistrate is away.

3. In case two subjects are joined by 'as well as' the verb agrees with the first subject.
   Example :
   (i) Kanta as well as her children is playing.
   (ii) Children as well as their mother are playing.

In the case of first sentence the verb (is) agrees with Kanta and in the case of second sentence the verb (are) agrees with the children.

4. 'Neither', 'Either', 'Every', 'Each', 'Everyone', and 'Many a' are followed by a singular verb.
   Example :
   (i) Either of the plans is to be adopted.
   (ii) Neither of the two brothers is sure to pass.
   (iii) Every student is expected to be obedient.
   (iv) Everyone of them desires this.
   (v) Many a person is drowned in the sea.

5. If two subjects are joined by 'Either .... or' / 'Neither .... nor', the verb agrees with the subject near to it.
   Example :
   (i) Either my brother or I am to do this work.
   (ii) Neither he nor they are prepared to do this work.

6. 'A great many' is always followed by a 'plural noun' and a 'plural verb'. For example :
   A great many students have been declared successful.

7. Similarly if two subjects are joined by 'with', 'together with', 'no less than', in addition to 'and not', etc. the verb agrees with the first subject.
   Example :
   (i) The boy with his parents has arrived.
   (ii) He, no less than I, is to blame.

8. Nouns, plural in form, but singular in meaning, take a singular verb.
   Example :
   This news was broadcast from television yesterday.

MULTIPLE CHOICE QUESTIONS

Directions: *In the following questions choose the correct options to fill the blanks.*

1. The bus with all its passengers .... lost.
   A. were   B. was
   C. are   D. would

2. You as well as I .... responsible for this work.
   A. am   B. are
   C. was   D. is

3. Raghava like all his companions .... a spoiled child.
   A. are   B. were
   C. is   D. will be

4. Pen and ink .... required for me.
   A. are   B. were
   C. is   D. has required

5. Every girl and every boy .... attended the seminar.
   A. have   B. has
   C. is   D. are

6. Not only she but all her sisters ...... been married.
   A. has   B. have
   C. is   D. are

7. There .... nothing but miseries in life.
   A. is   B. are
   C. were   D. will be

8. Neither prose nor poem .... given.
   A. were   B. was
   C. has   D. have

9. Either he or I .... wrong.
   A. is   B. are
   C. am   D. were

10. Either Sulekha or Rekha .... coming here.
    A. are   B. is
    C. were   D. have

11. .... the child or his parents to blame?
    A. Is   B. Are
    C. Were   D. Has

12. You and I .... neighbours.
    A. am   B. are
    C. was   D. has

13. The house with all its belongings ..... sold away.
    A. were   B. are
    C. was   D. must

14. Either water or juice .... required.
    A. is   B. are
    C. were   D. has

15. There were not as many tables as .... required.
    A. was   B. were
    C. is   D. are

16. They each .... a book.
  A. have   B. are
  C. has   D. is
17. He and I .... class friends.
  A. is   B. am
  C. was   D. are
18. She as well as I .... guilty.
  A. is   B. are
  C. am   D. must be
19. Purushottam .... not read more on this chapter.
  A. needs   B. has been need
  C. need   D. had been need
20. He came .... to his aunt.
  A. run   B. running
  C. to run   D. in run
21. She dislikes .... meat.
  A. eat to   B. to eat

  C. eating   D. to eating
22. He likes ....
  A. sing to   B. singing
  C. to sing   D. to singing
23. We are ready .... the match.
  A. play to   B. to playing
  C. playing   D. to play
24. .... is injurious to health.
  A. Smoking   B. To smoke
  C. To smoking   D. Smoke to
25. He loves .... raw vegetables.
  A. eaten   B. eating
  C. to eating   D. eat to
26. He seemed .... finished his homework.
  A. have to   B. to have
  C. having   D. to having

ANSWERS

1	2	3	4	5	6	7	8	9	10
B	B	C	C	B	B	A	B	C	B

11	12	13	14	15	16	17	18	19	20
A	B	C	A	B	A	D	A	C	B

21	22	23	24	25	26
C	B	D	A	B	B

CONJUNCTIONS

A conjunction is a word which connects words, clauses or sentences.

Look at the following sentences.

(i) He bought apples *and* mangoes.

(ii) God made the country *and* man made the town.

(iii) The door was open *but* there was no one in the house.

(iv) He knows that I am here *and* that I want to see him.

In the sentence (i), *and* connects two words—*apples* and *mangoes*.

In the sentence (ii), *and* connects two sentences—*God made the country* and *man made the town.*

In the sentence (iii), *but* connects two sentences—*The door was open* and *there was no one in the house.*

In the sentence (iv), *and* connects two clauses—*that I am here* and *that I want to see him.*

The main coordinating conjunctions are:

and, but, for, or, nor, also, either ..... or, neither ..... nor.

There are some conjunctions which are used in pairs. They are:

either .... or, ... neither .... nor, both .... and, though .... yet, whether .... or, not only .... but also.

Example: *Either* take it *or* leave it.

It is *neither* useful *nor* ornamental.

They *both* like *and* respect me.

Though he is suffering from high fever, *yet* he does not cry.

He does not care *whether* you go *or* stay.

He is *not only* doltish, *but also* obstinate.

The conjunctions which are used in pairs in this way, are called correlative conjunctions, or merely correlatives.

Use of Important Conjunctions

1. **As soon as :** As soon as denotes simultaneous time.

   Example : As soon as he saw his enemy, he took to his heels.

2. **No sooner .... than :**
   (a) 'No sooner' is always followed by 'than'.
   (b) Please remember that 'No sooner' is always followed by do/does/did. As such only first form of the verb should be used after the subject.

   Example :

   No sooner did he see his enemy than he took to his heels.

3. **Hardly :** Hardly is followed by when.

   Examples :
   (i) Hardly had I left the house when it started raining.
   (ii) We had hardly come into the room when his father began chastising him.

   Note :
   A. Hardly is never followed by than.
   B. 'Scarcely' can also be used in the sense and manner of 'Hardly'.

4. **Lest :** Lest is used in the sense of so that .... not. It is always followed by should. Lest is negative in sense. Hence 'not' should never be used with it.

   Example :

   Work hard lest you should fail.

   Note : 'Lest' is always followed by 'should' and not 'may'.

5. **Unless :** Unless expresses condition. It is also used in the negative sense. Use of 'not' is not allowed with unless because unless is already in the negative sense.

   Example :

   Unless you labour hard you will not pass.

6. **Until :** 'Until' expresses time. It means 'till not'.

   Example :

   Wait here until I return.

   Note : Until is in the negative sense. So 'not' should not be used with it. Example :
   Wait here until I do not return.　　(Incorrect)
   Wait here until I return.　　　　　(Correct)

7. **As well as :** When two subjects are joined by 'as well as', the verb always agrees with the first subject.

   Examples :
   (i) The teacher as well as students is playing.
   (ii) Students as well as the teacher are playing.

   Note : 'Both' and 'as well as' cannot be used together in the same sentence.

   Examples :

   Both Sita as well as Kanta are beautiful.
   　　　　　　　　　　　　　　　(Incorrect)
   Sita as well as Kanta is beautiful.　(Correct)
   Both Sita and Kanta are beautiful. (Correct)

8. **As if :** 'As if' is used in the sense of pretension. While using 'as if' in a sentence, we should see that even the third person singular subject gets 'were'.

   Example :

   He talks as if he were mad.

9. **Till :** Till expresses time. Till is always used in the affirmative.

   Example :

   We did not come back till sunset.

10. **Rather than :** 'Rather than' is used in the sense of 'preference'. 'Rather' is always followed by 'than'.

    Example :

    I would rather die than submit.

11. **As long as/so long as :** Both express time during which an action or event takes place.

    Example :

    As long as there is life, there is hope.

12. **However :** It is both a subordinate and co-ordinate clause.

    Examples :
    (a) Mala worked hard, she however, failed.
    (b) However hard he may work, he cannot pass.

13. **Such as :** 'Such as' gives us the sense of 'like'. Such is always followed by 'as'.

    Example :

    Life is such a puzzle as cannot be solved.

MULTIPLE CHOICE QUESTIONS

Directions: *In the following questions choose the correct options to fill the blanks.*

1. Neither he .... his friend is good.
   A. or B. and
   C. but D. nor

2. The officer asked the peon .... why he was late.
   A. that B. if
   C. but D. No word needed

3. Both Ajay .... Vijay are intelligent.
   A. or B. nor
   C. and D. No word needed

4. No Sooner did the thief see the public .... he ran away.
   A. then B. and
   C. but D. than

5. Abhinav .... his brothers was going to Mumbai.
   A. but B. yet
   C. No word needed D. together with

6. He behaves .... he were the captain of the team.
   A. as if B. as
   C. No word needed D. that

7. Either Rupali .... Sonali is going to attend the meeting.
   A. and B. but
   C. nor D. or

8. Neither Nirmal .... Ashwinee is going to listen the speech.
   A. and B. but
   C. nor D. or

9. Ravi .... Prakash are going to Kolkata.
   A. or B. nor
   C. but D. and

10. Rice .... curry is my usual breakfast.
    A. and B. but
    C. then D. than

11. Hardly had he left .... his brother came.
    A. then B. than
    C. when D. that

12. I would rather have a copy .... a book.
    A. then B. than
    C. when D. that

13. He is no other .... my friend.
    A. then B. than
    C. when D. but

14. He saw a snake ....he awoke.
    A. then B. when
    C. than D. No word needed

15. Ten years have passed .... my grandmother died.
    A. since B. when
    C. then D. than

16. She is .... good .... bad.
    A. either, not B. neither, or
    C. neither, nor D. neither, than

17. The cellphone is both cheap .... best.
    A. than B. and
    C. then D. or

18. No sooner did the rogue see the police .... he disappeared.
    A. then B. than
    C. so D. because

19. Srishti will go .... Sanju goes.
    A. if B. than
    C. then D. although

20. She is wise .... timid.
    A. and B. yet
    C. but D. however

21. Make hay .... the sun shines.
    A. though B. while
    C. after D. before

22. He is so weak .... he cannot walk.
    A. but B. that
    C. then D. so

23. Although he is rich, ... he is unhappy.
    A. but B. yet
    C. so D. still

24. Wait here .... I come back.
    A. till B. until
    C. before D. after

25. He is my friend .... I shall help him.
 A. so
 B. hence
 C. that is why
 D. therefore

26. He must go away .... he will be beaten.
 A. otherwise B. and
 C. or D. else

27. God loves good men .... good men love God.
 A. and B. or
 C. that D. those

28. He was late .... he was not punished.
 A. but B. yet
 C. still D. therefore

29. Walk slowly ...., you may fall.
 A. and B. or
 C. so D. otherwise

30. Work hard, ... you will fail.
 A. and B. or
 C. otherwise D. else

ANSWERS

1	2	3	4	5	6	7	8	9	10
D	D	C	D	D	A	D	C	D	A
11	**12**	**13**	**14**	**15**	**16**	**17**	**18**	**19**	**20**
C	B	B	B	A	C	B	B	A	C
21	**22**	**23**	**24**	**25**	**26**	**27**	**28**	**29**	**30**
B	B	B	A	B	C	A	C	D	D

PREPOSITIONS

A *Preposition* is a word which is placed before a noun or a pronoun to show its relation to some other word in the sentence.

 1. I saw a goat *in* the field.
 2. I am fond *of* hot coffee.

In sentence 1, the word *in* shows the relation between two things—*goat* and *field.*

In sentence 2, the word *of* shows the relation between the attribute expressed by the adjective *found* and *tea.*

The words *in* and *of* are here used as prepositions.

The noun or pronoun which is used with a preposition is called its object. The noun or pronoun is in the objective case. It is governed by the preposition. Now it is absolutely clear that in sentence 1, the noun *field* is in the objective case. The word *field* is governed by the preposition *in.*

A preposition may have two or more objects.

The road runs over *hill* and *plain.*

Here, the words *hill* and *plain* are used as objects.

Use of Important Prepositions

1. Among, Between

'Among' is used for more than two persons or things; '**Between**' is used only for two.

Examples :
(i) Distribute these sweets *among* the poor students of the class.
(ii) Distribute these books *between* Ram and Shyam.

2. Among, In

'Among' is used before collective plural nouns. '**In**' is used before collective singular nouns.

Examples :
(i) I found him standing *among* the crowd.
(ii) I saw him in the crowd.

3. Beside, Besides

'**Beside**' means 'by the side of'. '**Besides**' means 'in addition to'.

Examples :
(i) The daughter was sitting *beside* her mother.
(ii) *Besides* his relatives, he invited his friends also.

4. In, Within

'**In**' means at the expiry of a period of time in future, '**Within**' means before the expiry of a period of time in any tense.

Examples :
(i) She will return *in* a week.
(ii) I shall finish my work *within* a weak.

5. On, Upon
'**On**' is used for things at rest; '**Upon**' is used for things in motion.
Examples :
(i) He is sitting *on* the floor.
(ii) The dog sprang *upon* the table.

6. By, With
'**By**' denotes the agent or doer, '**With**' denotes the instrument with which anything is done.
Examples :
(i) The bird was killed *by* the hunter with an arrow.
(ii) He beat the dog *with* a stick.
(iii) I shall reach here *by* five o'clock.

7. After, In
'**After**' means at the end of a period of time in the past. '**In**' means at the end of a period of time in future.
Examples :
(i) I shall return your book *in* a week.
(ii) He returned the book *after* a week.

8. For, From, Since
'**For**' is used before a noun denoting a period of time with all the tenses. '**From**' is used before a noun or phrase denoting a point of time, it is used in all the tenses. '**Since**' is used before a noun or phrase denoting some point of time and is always produced by a verb in the perfect continuous tense or third form of a verb.
Examples :
(i) We have been playing cards *for* two hours.
(ii) She stayed with her uncle *from* the 15th of March to the 15th of May.
(iii) I have been reading this book *since* morning.

9. Above, Over
'**Above**' means 'higher from', **Over** is used in the following four senses :
(i) In the sense of 'above' :
At noon, the sun is *over* our heads.

(ii) In the sense of 'beyond' :
I cannot get *over* my disappointment.
(iii) In the sense of 'Superiority' :
God *over* all blesses for ever more.
(iv) In the sense of 'Conclusion' :
It is all *over* with me.

10. At, Towards
'**At**' denotes the idea of aim, '**Towards**' denotes the idea of destination.
Examples :
(i) He threw the stone *at* the cat.
(ii) He went *towards* the house.

11. At, In, On
'At' is used as follows :
(i) '**At**' is used with small towns and villages.
Examples :
(a) He was born *at* Sonepat.
(b) He lives *at* village Bangra. (Bangra is a village)
(ii) '**At**' is used before a noun denoting a definite point of time.
Example :
He called on me *at* 9 p.m. yesterday.
'In' is used as follows :
(iii) '**In**' is used with the names of big cities, provinces and countries.
Examples :
(a) His father lives *in* England.
(b) His younger brother lives *in* Calcutta.
(iv) '**In**' is used before the names of months and years.
Example :
His elder sister was born *in* 1972 *in* the month of May.
'**On**' is used with dates and names of days.
Examples :
(a) I joined college *on* the 26th April.
(b) He will leave for Kolkata *on* Wednesday next.

Important Information

1. '**In**' is also used in the following phrases :
In the morning; In the evening, In winter, In summer.

2. **'In'** also denotes a place inside anything.
   He travelled *in* a crowded bus.
3. **'At'** is used in the following phrases :
   At home, *At* the station, *At* work, *At* play.

12. Below, Beneath
Below means 'of lower level in position, dignity and expectation' etc. *Beneath* means 'under'.
Examples :
(i) It is *below* my dignity to talk to her.
(ii) They rested *beneath* the shade of a tree.

13. In, Into, To
'In' expresses Rest or Motion inside anything. **'Into'** expresses Motion towards the inside of anything or change from one medium to another. **'To'** denotes motion from one place to another.
Examples :
(i) The boys are *in* the room.
(ii) Translate this passage from English *into* Hindi.

(iii) Every morning he goes *to* the temple.

14. Till, By, Of, Off
- 'Till' means upto or not earlier than.
- 'By' means not later than.
- 'Of' shows cause, source, separation, quality, contents, possession, apposition, point of reference, space in time etc.
- 'Off' shows separation at a near distance, and detached condition.

Consider the following examples:
(i) I shall work *till* 5 a.m.
(ii) Madhu died *of* cancer.
(iii) The nib *of* the pen is made *of* gold.
(iv) He presented me a bottle *of* perfume.
(v) Our principal is a man *of* principle.
(vi) He lived in the house *of* his friend.
(vii) *By* this time tomorrow, I'll have finished my job.
(viii) My house is *off* the road.
(ix) The book fell *off* the table.

MULTIPLE CHOICE QUESTIONS

Directions: *Tick the correct preposition for the blank in each of the following sentences.*

1. He applied ...... the manager.
   A. for   B. to
   C. with   D. by
2. Trust ...... God and do the right.
   A. in   B. for
   C. to   D. with
3. She is worthy ...... a prize.
   A. with   B. for
   C. to   D. of
4. Mr. Gomes has no taste ...... music.
   A. of   B. for
   C. with   D. to
5. You are hard ...... hearing.
   A. at   B. of
   C. with   D. for
6. He is sure ...... his success
   A. for   B. with
   C. on   D. of

7. Preeti was warned ...... the danger ahead.
   A. for   B. at
   C. of   D. about
8. I am thankful ...... you for a good advice.
   A. for   B. with
   C. to   D. of
9. Deepak would not surrender ...... the police.
   A. with   B. to
   C. for   D. on
10. The small plant in your lawn is very sensitive ...... touch.
    A. on   B. with
    C. to   D. about
11. Divya was sure to succeed ...... the examination.
    A. for   B. in
    C. to   D. with
12. Geeta was jealous ...... Ravina's beauty.
    A. to   B. with
    C. for   D. of

13. He was ignorant ..... what was happening there.
   A. for   B. of
   C. to   D. with

14. Your pen is inferior ...... mine.
   A. than   B. with
   C. from   D. to

15. Reenu is no match ...... Meenu.
   A. to   B. for
   C. with   D. upon

16. It is necessary ...... you to apply for this job.
   A. on   B. with
   C. for   D. to

17. Be loyal ...... your country.
   A. for   B. to
   C. on   D. with

18. Mukesh is junior ...... me.
   A. than   B. to
   C. from   D. of

19. Deepika was innocent ...... the crime.
   A. of   B. with
   C. from   D. to

20. I am desirous.... joining the Indian cricket team.
   A. for   B. of
   C. to   D. on

ANSWERS

1	2	3	4	5	6	7	8	9	10
B	A	D	B	B	D	D	D	B	D

11	12	13	14	15	16	17	18	19	20
B	D	B	D	B	D	B	B	A	B

SYNONYMS

A synonym is a word which conveys a meaning similar to the given word.

REMEMBER

Words	Synonyms
Add	Increase
Adequate	Enough
Adjust	Adapt
All	Aggregate
Allow	Permit
Abode	Dwelling
Apt	Proper
Assess	Appraise
Accuse	Calumniate
Abashed	Timid
Annoy	Displease
Ample	Enough, Sufficient
Amplify	Increase
Apathetic	Unenthusiastic
Accost	Address
Authentic	True

Words	Synonyms
Adjust	Fit
Approve	Assent, Allow, Accept
Adapt	Conform
Adversary	Opponent, Rival, Competitor
Beat	Whack
Benign	Kind
Breeze	Zephyr
Baffle	Puzzle
Booty	Spoil
Beauty	Charm
Beast	Animal
Bandit	Robber
Blaze	Shine
Bond	Tie
Bend	Twist
Bate	Diminish
Beg	Plead
Barbaric	Wild, Savage
Bashful	Shy, Reserved

Words	Synonyms
Begin	Start
Blend	Mix, Mingle
Bizarre	Funny
Below	Under
Bedevil	Confuse
Bemoan	Lament
Babble	Nonsense
Blame	Fault
Behaviour	Demeanour
Call	Accost
Copy	Imitate
Close	Shut
Caress	Love
Camp	Stay
Connect	Attach
Cut	Injure, Curtail
Cling	Stick
Conical	Funny
Convey	Carry
Conspicuous	Prominent
Cheerful	Happy, Pleasant
Curtail	Decrease
Cheerless	Sad, Dejected
Curious	Strange
Circumstance	Factor, Situation, Condition
Competent	Capable
Congruent	Overlapping
Cope	Deal, Endure
Confident	Sure
Complex	Intricate
Cajole	Coax, Flatter
Cunning	Crafty
Delectable	Joyful, Delightful
Devilish	Diabolical
Delicate	Soft
Devil	Fiend
Delay	Postpone
Dislike	Repugnance
Destroy	Ruin

Words	Synonyms
Dwell	Live, Dilate
Declare	Pronounce
Drunk	Flushed
Deficient	Lacking
Damn	Condemn, Curse
Decrease	Diminish
Destruction	Devastation
Efficient	Competent
Ethnic	Racial
Enthral	Enslave
Earnest	Serious
Envious	Jealous
Ending	Final
Egg	Incite
Extempore	At once
Extensive	Far-ranging
Extra	Surplus
Existence	Life
Exceed	Overstep
Enormous	Vast
Excessive	Superfluous
Free	Unhindered
Frigid	Cold
Feed	Cater
Fame	Reputation
Frame	Make
First	Initial
Frighten	Terrorise, Intimidate
Fervent	Fervid
Fall	Decline
Feeble	Frail
Fickle	Changeable
Finish	Conclude
Fraud	Deception
Forgiving	Placable
Grow	Develop
Greed	Avidity
Greet	Welcome
Grave	Serious
Group	Constellation

Words	Synonyms
Given	Bestowed
Gratitude	Thankfulness
Have	Possess
Hire	Rent
Hit	Strike
Handsome	Beautiful
Hinder	Prevent
Heap	Pile
Hope	Expect
Hard	Harsh
Help	Aid
Hymn	Song
Henpecked	Enslaved
Hoodwink	Mystify, Cheat
Humble	Polite, Urbane, Modest
Harass	Vex, Trouble
Impart	Instil
Intact	Untouched
Instal	Establish
Indict	Impeach
Imitate	Ape
Instigate	Incite
Initiate	Start, Introduce
Inimical	Unfriendly
Insufferable	Intolerable
Impartiality	Justice
Jolly	Merry
Joyful	Delectable
Join	Conjoin
Kind	Benign
Kill	Murder
Kindred	Similar
Kinship	Relationship
Keen	Sharp
Knowledge	Scholarship
Lazy	Slothful
Large	Substantial, Gargantuan
Listless	Careless, Lackadaisical
Lax	Loose
Little	Small
Lifelike	Realistic

Words	Synonyms
Lofty	High
Lenient	Soft, Gentle
Lacking	Deficient, Wanting
Lessen	Decrease
Middleclass	Bourgeois
Mitigate	Lessen, Abate
Modesty	Humility, Lowliness
Mix	Mingle, Blend
Mixture	Mingling
Mixed	Assorted
Modify	Decrease
Mean	Imply
Multifarious	Varied
Miscarry	Abort
Note	Notice
Noble	Stately
Native	Indigenous
Needful	Necessary
Notify	Declare
Nervous	Shaky, Tremulous, Timid
Natural	Spontaneous
Near	Close
Normal	Natural
Offend	Displease
Oppress	Persecute, Tyrannize
Opponent	Adversary
Obstruct	Hinder, Check
Offence	Fault
Offender	Villain
Overstep	Exceed
Overlapping	Congruent
Occult	Mystic
Profane	Unholy
Patience	Forbearance
Pornographic	Obscene
Plenitude	Abundance
Prominent	Important
Prodigal	Spender
Procrastinate	Postpone
Promote	Develop, Honour
Persecute	Tyrannise

Words	Synonyms
Profess	Claim
Pliant	Flexible
Plebian	Common
Polished	Sophisticated
Quake	Shake
Quit	Leave
Queer	Eccentric
Quell	Suppress
Quantify	Allot
Reply	Answer
Relinquish	Retire
Read	Peruse
Relation	Reference
Render	Do
Remainder	Residuals
Repeat	Reiterate
Repentant	Contrite
Retaliative	Retaliatory
Rumour	Hearsay
Reveal	Divulge
Ritualistic	Ceremonious
Soft	Delicate
Sort	Kind, Choose, Select
Selfish	Egoistic
Sensual	Earthly
Suppress	Quell, Check
Stimulate	Provoke
Tasteless	Insipid
Travel	Journey
True	Authentic, Faithful, Truthful
Turbulence	Turmoil
Tragedy	Calamity
Tasteful	Tasty, Delicious
Touching	Painful
Thankful	Grateful
Tremendous	Great, Huge
Tough	Strong
Terminate	Conclude, End
Theory	Doctrine
Tell	Relate
Tremble	Shake, Shiver
Urge	Spur

Words	Synonyms
Unbeaten	Unsubdued
Use	Utilize, Practise
Underhand	Unfair, Undue
Unfair	Unjust
Unravel	Reveal, Divulge
Unimportant	Common
Unconcerned	Apathetic
Unimitated	Inimitable
Unfortunate	Unlucky
Understand	Perceive, Comprehend
Vain	Proud, Haughty, Conceited, Shameless
Vale	Valley, Dale, Dell
Vice	Fault
Virtue	Quality
Veracity	Reality
Value	Price, Prize
Vex	Tease
Vibrate	Quiver, Shake
Violent	Excessive
Vivid	Clear, Lucid
Victory	Triumph
Vulgar	Indecent
Virtuous	Honest
Variegated	Varied, Multifarious
Well	Good
Yell	Cry, Shout
Yonder	There
Yearn	Wish, Desire
Yoke	Slavery
Zest	Earnestness, Enthusiasm
Zealous	Earnest

ANTONYMS

A antonym is a word which conveys a meaning opposite to the given word.

REMEMBER

Words	Antonyms
Abhor	Love
Abnormal	Normal
Able	Unable
Acceptable	Unacceptable
Adequate	Inadequate
Amusing	Boring

Words	Antonyms
Angry	Calm
Apex	Bottom
Attract	Repel
Bad	Good
Barren	Fertile
Beautiful	Ugly
Bitter	Sweet
Brave	Cowardly
Brief	Lengthy
Bright	Dull
Calm	Violent
Careful	Careless
Clear	Vague, Cloudy
Cold	Hot
Cruel	Kind
Dear	Cheap
Deep	Shallow
Difficult	Easy
Direct	Indirect
Dishonest	Honest
Disobey	Obey
Encourage	Discourage
Enormous	Tiny
Excellent	Bad
Expensive	Cheap
Eat	Fast
Fair	Unfair
Fake	Authentic
False	True
Famous	Notorious
Fool	Genius
Generous	Miserly
Genius	Fool
Genuine	Unauthentic
Gigantic	Tiny
Glad	Depressed
Good	Bad
Great	Little
Happy	Sad
Hard	Soft
Hate	Love
Honest	Dishonest
Idle	Busy
Immoral	Moral
Include	Exclude
Incorrect	Correct
Intelligent	Unintelligent
Kind	Cruel
Like	Dislike
Long	Short
Lucid	Vague
Major	Minor
Naive	Experienced
Nadir	Apex
Neat	Clumsy
Obedient	Disobedient
Obscure	Clear
Oppose	Support
Optimistic	Pessimistic
Out	In
Patience	Impatience
Peaceful	Belligerent
Pious	Impious
Polite	Impolite
Potent	Impotent
Prominent	Unimportant
Proper	Improper
Pure	Impure
Quick	Slow
Quiet	Disturbance
Real	False, Unreal
Reject	Select, Choose
Reliable	Unreliable
Respect	Disrespect
Right	Wrong
Robust	Feeble, Weak
Sad	Happy

Words	Antonyms	Words	Antonyms
Secret	Open	Strong	Weak
Sensible	Insensible	Big	Small
Severe	Mild	Easy	Difficult
Sharp	Blunt	Fast	Slow
Simple	Complex	High	Low
Sociable	Unsociable	Catchy	Unattractive
Tall	Short	Ugly	Handsome, Beautiful, Tidy
Tidy	Untidy		
Uncanny	Canny	Tasty	Insipid
Violent	Calm	Sonorous	Harsh
Vivid	Vague		

MULTIPLE CHOICE QUESTIONS

Directions (Qs. 1 to 20): *In the following questions choose the word which best expresses the meaning of the given word.*

1. ABSURD
   A. Foolish
   B. Simple
   C. Courageous
   D. Silly

2. ABANDON
   A. Lose
   B. Profit
   C. Vacate
   D. Foil

3. CAJOLE
   A. Pause
   B. Lenient
   C. Blast
   D. Lure

4. COMBAT
   A. Fight
   B. Conflict
   C. Shoot
   D. Quarrel

5. LAMENT
   A. Condone
   B. Console
   C. Complain
   D. Contribution

6. DEBACLE
   A. Disgrace
   B. Defeat
   C. Collapse
   D. Decline

7. SHIVER
   A. Fear
   B. Tremble
   C. Shake
   D. Ache

8. TORTURE
   A. Terror
   B. Harassment
   C. Torment
   D. Tranquility

9. LAUDABLE
   A. Lovable
   B. Commendable
   C. Profitable
   D. Oblivious

10. FIXED
    A. Sterile
    B. Static
    C. Stubborn
    D. Parennial

11. QUEER
    A. Unfamiliar
    B. Cute
    C. Curious
    D. Strange

12. SUFFICIENT
    A. Fit
    B. Proper
    C. Adequate
    D. Vast

13. GLOSS
    A. Brightness
    B. Soothing
    C. Rubbing
    D. Miracle

14. LONGING
    A. Prune
    B. Apathy
    C. Curtail
    D. Craving

15. JEER
    A. Applaud
    B. Magnanimity
    C. Avoid
    D. Scoff

16. ZENITH
    A. Minimum
    B. Nadir
    C. Plant
    D. Peak

17. GARB
    A. Distort
    B. Dress
    C. Trivial
    D. Rage

18. ABHOR
- A. Rude
- B. Reconcile
- C. Crave
- D. Detest

19. YIELD
- A. Shum
- B. Incisive
- C. Retain
- D. Surrender

20. YOKE
- A. Twist
- B. Release
- C. Link
- D. Extra

Directions (Qs. 21 to 38): *In the following questions choose the word which best expresses the opposite of the given word.*

21. TRAGIC
- A. Dramatic
- B. Strong
- C. Gentle
- D. Comic

22. ORAL
- A. Verbal
- B. Sane
- C. Minor
- D. Written

23. ADMIRE
- A. Hate
- B. Unlike
- C. Dislike
- D. Enough

24. VIOLENT
- A. Gentle
- B. Savage
- C. Haughty
- D. Decline

25. ADVERSITY
- A. Windfall
- B. Inprosperity
- C. Prosperity
- D. Slave

26. GENUINE
- A. Spurious
- B. Obscure
- C. Countless
- D. Apathetic

27. GRUDGE
- A. Essence
- B. Guile
- C. Goodwill
- D. Ill-will

28. STIFF
- A. Soft
- B. Courteous
- C. Lively
- D. Flexible

29. VANITY
- A. Conceit
- B. Pride
- C. Ostentious
- D. Humility

30. FRONT
- A. Upper
- B. Unusual
- C. Back
- D. Rear

31. ATTRACT
- A. Lured
- B. Longing
- C. Repel
- D. Disguise

32. COMFORT
- A. Discomfort
- B. Discontent
- C. Uncomfort
- D. Miscomfort

33. WELCOME
- A. Repel
- B. Accept
- C. Resist
- D. Fight

34. TACTFUL
- A. Naive
- B. Loose
- C. Strict
- D. Uncivilized

35. DUTIFUL
- A. Harmful
- B. Watchful
- C. Forgetful
- D. Remiss

36. RIGID
- A. Flux
- B. Adoptable
- C. Yielding
- D. Adaptable

37. RARE
- A. Petty
- B. Poor
- C. Small
- D. Common

38. ZEAL
- A. Despair
- B. Calmness
- C. Passiveness
- D. Indifference

ANSWERS

1	2	3	4	5	6	7	8	9	10
D	C	D	A	C	C	B	C	B	B

11	12	13	14	15	16	17	18	19	20
D	C	A	D	D	D	B	D	D	C

21	22	23	24	25	26	27	28	29	30
D	D	C	A	C	A	C	D	D	D

31	32	33	34	35	36	37	38
C	A	C	A	D	D	D	D

3. Sentence Completion

It is such an exercise which starts with the primary schools and continues in the highest level of competitive examinations. One must practise it regularly to score well.

Directions (Qs. 1 to 15): *Pick out the most effective word(s) from the given words to fill in the blanks to make the sentence meaningfully complete.*

1. The student ...... that book from the library to study at home.
   A. issued   B. borrowed
   C. hired   D. lent

2. I wish I ...... a king.
   A. was   B. am
   C. should be   D. were

3. He ...... to listen to my arguments and walked away.
   A. denied   B. disliked
   C. objected   D. refused

4. The flow of blood was so ...... that the patient died.
   A. intense   B. adequate
   C. profuse   D. extensive

5. When I met her yesterday, it was the first time I ...... her since Christmas.
   A. saw   B. have seen
   C. had seen   D. have been seing

6. Can you pay ...... all these articles?
   A. for   B. of
   C. off   D. out

7. I ...... you to be at the party this evening.
   A. expect   B. hope
   C. look forward to   D. desire

8. ...... being a handicapped person, he is very cooperative and self-reliant.
   A. Because   B. Although
   C. Since   D. Despite

9. The child broke ...... from his mother and ran towards the painting.
   A. away   B. after
   C. down   D. with

10. With his ...... income, he finds it difficult to live a comfortable life.
    A. brief   B. sufficient
    C. meagre   D. huge

11. He could ...... a lot of money in such a short time by using his intelligence and working hard.
    A. spend   B. spoil
    C. exchange   D. accumulate

12. Though the brothers are twins, they look ......
    A. alike   B. handsome
    C. indifferent D. different

13. Unfavourable weather conditions can ..... illness.
    A. cure   B. detect
    C. treat   D. enhance

14. No sooner did the bell ring, ... the actor started singing.
    A. when   B. than
    C. after   D. before

15. If I ...... realised it, I would not have acted on his advice.
    A. was   B. had
    C. were   D. have

Directions (Qs. 16 to 25): *In each question, an incomplete statement (Stem) followed by four fillers* *is given. Pick out the best one which can complete the incomplete stem correctly and meaningfully.*

16. Unless you work harder you will fail, means .....
A. if you fail you will work harder.
B. you must at least plan well than you will not fail.
C. hardly you will fail if you do not desire so.
D. if you do not put more efforts, then you will fail.

17. Even if it rains I shall come, means .....
A. if I come it will not rain.
B. if it rains I shall not come.
C. I will certainly come whether it rains or not.
D. whenever there is rain I shall come.

18. Dinesh is as stupid as he is lazy means .....
A. Dinesh is stupid because he is lazy.
B. Dinesh is lazy because he is stupid.
C. Dinesh is either stupid or lazy.
D. Dinesh is equally stupid and lazy.

19. He is so lazy that he .....
A. cannot depend on others for getting his work done.
B. cannot delay the schedule of completing the work.
C. can seldom complete his work on time.
D. dislike to postpone the work that he undertakes to do.

20. He always stammers in public meetings, but his today's speech .....
A. was fairly audible to everyone present in the hall.
B. was not received satisfactorily.
C. could not be understood properly.
D. was free from that defect.

21. In order to raise the company's profit, the employees .....
A. demanded two additional increments.
B. decided to go on paid holidays.
C. requested the management to implement new welfare schemes.
D. offered to work overtime without any compensation.

22. Although, he is reputed for making very candid statements, ...
A. his today's speech was not fairly audible.
B. his promises had always been realistic.
C. his speech was very interesting.
D. his today's statements were very ambiguous.

23. I felt somewhat more relaxed .....
A. but tense as compared to earlier.
B. and tense as compared to earlier.
C. as there was already no tension at all.
D. and tension-free as compared to earlier.

24. With great efforts his son succeeded in convincing him not to donate his entire wealth to an orphanage .....
A. and lead the life of a wealthy merchant.
B. but to a home for the forsaken children.
C. and make an orphan of himself.
D. as the orphanage needed a lot of donations.

25. Even though it is a very large house, ...
A. there is a lot of space available in it for children.
B. there is hardly any space available for children.
C. there is no dearth of space for children.
D. the servants take a long time to clean it.

ANSWERS

1	2	3	4	5	6	7	8	9	10
B	D	D	C	C	A	A	D	A	C

11	12	13	14	15	16	17	18	19	20
D	D	D	B	B	D	C	D	C	D

21	22	23	24	25
D	D	D	C	B

4. <u>Spotting Errors</u>

The most common errors in English are of spellings, grammar and usage of words. By regular practice, the errors can be easily spotted and minimised.

MULTIPLE CHOICE QUESTIONS

Directions: *In the following questions some of the sentences have errors and some are correct. Find out which part of a sentence has an error, the number of that part is your answer. If a sentence is free from errors, then your answer is D i.e., No error.*

1. (A) Either Ram or/(B) you is responsible/(C) for this action./(D) No error.

2. (A) The student flatly denied/(B) that he had copied/(C) in the examination hall./(D) No error.

3. (A) By the time you arrive tomorrow/(B) I have finished/(C) my work./(D) No error.

4. (A) The captain with the members of his team/(B) are returning/(C) after a fortnight./(D) No error.

5. (A) After returning from/(B) an all-India tour/(C) I had to describe about it./(D) No error.

6. (A) The teacher asked his students/(B) if they had gone through/(C) either of the three chapters included in the prescribed text./(D) No error.

7. (A) Do you know/(B) how old were you/(C) when you came here?/(D) No error.

8. (A) Beware of/(B) a fair-weather friend/(C) who is neither a friend in need nor a friend indeed./(D) No error.

9. (A) Copernicus proved/(B) that Earth/(C) moves round the Sun./(D) No error.

10. (A) The property/(B) was divided/(C) among the two brothers./(D) No error.

11. (A) I am quite certain/(B) that the lady is not only greedy/(C) but miserly./(D) No error.

12. (A) The brilliant success in the examination/(B) as well as his record in sports/(C) deserves high praise./(D) No error.

13. (A) I cannot find/(B) where has he gone/(C) though I have tried may best./(D) No error.

14. (A) If I was/(B) the Prime Minister of India/(C) I would work wonders/(D) No error.

15. (A) If it weren't/(B) for you,/(C) I wouldn't be alive today./(D) No error.

16. (A) He looked like a lion/(B) baulked from/(C) its prey./(D) No error.

17. (A) Widespread flooding/(B) is affecting/(C) large areas of the villages./(D) No error.

18. (A) If we really set to/(B) we can get the whole house/(C) cleaned in an afternoon./(D) No error.

19. (A) It's arrogant for you/(B) to assume you'll/(C)win every time./(D) No error.

20. (A) The two books are the same/(B) except for the fact that this/(C) has an answer in the back./(D) No error.

21. (A) Your husband doesn't/(B) believe that you are older/(C) than I./(D) No error.

22. (A) I could not/(B) answer to/(C) the question./(D) No error.

23. (A) Two years passed/(B) since/(C) my cousin died./(D) No error.

24. (A) I am learning English/(B) for ten years/(C) without much effect./(D) No error.

25. (A) Ramesh has agreed/(B) to marry with the girl/(C) of his parent's choice./ (D) No error.

26. (A) When he was arriving./(B) the party was/(C) in full swing./(D) No error.

27. (A) The most studious boy/(B) in the class/(C) was made as the captain./(D) No error.

28. (A) I am participating/(B) in the two-miles race/(C) tomorrow morning./(D) No error.

29. (A) When the boy committed a mistake/(B) the teacher made him to do/(C) the sum again./(D) No error.

30. (A) Whenever a person lost anything/(B) the poor folk around/(C) are suspected./(D) No error.

ANSWERS

1	2	3	4	5	6	7	8	9	10
B	D	B	B	C	C	D	D	B	C

11	12	13	14	15	16	17	18	19	20
C	D	B	A	C	C	C	A	A	C

21	22	23	24	25	26	27	28	29	30
C	B	A	A	B	A	C	B	B	A

EXPLANATORY ANSWERS

1. Replace 'is' by 'are'.

2. No error.

3. Replace 'have' by 'would have'.

4. Replace 'are' by 'is'.

5. Replace 'had to describe' by 'described'.

6. Replace 'either' by 'any'.

7. No error.

8. No error.

9. Omit 'that'.

10. Replace 'among' by 'between'.

11. Add 'also'.

12. No error.

13. Replace 'has he' by 'he has'.

14. Replace 'was' by 'were'.

15. Replace 'wouldn't be' by 'would not have been'.

16. Replace 'its' by 'his'.

17. Replace 'areas' by 'area'.

18. Replace 'set to' by 'set on'.

19. Replace 'for' by 'of'.

20. Replace 'in' by 'on'.

21. Replace 'I' by 'me'.

22. Omit 'to'.

23. Replace 'passed' by 'have passed'.

24. Replace 'am' by 'have been'.

25. Omit 'with'.

26. Replace 'was arriving' by 'arrived'.

27. Omit 'as'.

28. Replace 'in' by 'at'.

29. Omit 'to'.

30. Replace 'lost' by 'loses'.

5. One Word Substitution

There are many single words in English language which can be perfectly used for a number of words. These words help in expressing ideas in a short and correct manner for the right occasion. Such words not only increase the vocabulary but also enable you to economise in the use of words to a great extent.

Multiple Word Expression	*Substitution*
One who always looks towards the bright side of things	Optimist
One who always looks towards the dark side of things	Pessimist
The time when one develops from a child into an adult	Adolescence
The process of growing more plants in order to form a forest.	Afforestation
The science which deals with farming	Agriculture
From some other country or place etc.	Alien
A term, etc. giving more than one meaning	Ambiguous
A vehicle which is used to carry sick persons	Ambulance
An animal which can live both in water and on land	Amphibian
A lawless situation when there is no government	Anarchy
Belonging to the history of thousands of years old	Ancient
Once a year	Annual
A very old object but still valuable	Antique
Words of opposite meanings	Antonyms
Words of similar meanings	Synonyms
Signatures of a famous person	Autograph
A government led by one person with absolute authority	Autocracy
A written work of one's own life history	Autobiography
A person who has never been married	Bachelor
A person usually having no hair on his head	Bald
A place where one can deposit money and get interest	Bank
A person who cuts our hair	Barber
A building/group of buildings where soldiers live	Barracks
A person who makes buns and biscuits	Baker
A person who lives by asking people for food and money without doing any useful job	Beggar
The crime of having married to two persons at the same time	Bigamy
The branch of science which deals with the study of plants	Botany
Able to speak two languages	Bilingual

Multiple Word Expression	Substitution
Able to speak more than two languages	Polyglot
The branch of science which deals with the living organisms	Biology
A powerful snow storm	Blizzard
A great successful book or movie	Blockbuster
A short news on the radio or TV	Bulletin
A system in which the most important works are organised by the government officials	Bureaucracy
A person who has no vision in his eyes	Blind
A page or a series of pages on which the information of days, weeks, months, etc. is given	Calendar
A person who eats human flesh	Cannibal
A complete list of items often arranged alphabetically	Catalogue
A sudden disaster	Catastrophe
A period of 100 years	Century
A branch of science which deals with chemicals	Chemistry
A printed leaf usually issued by banks that we sign to carry certain financial deal	Cheque
A person who makes or mends shoes	Cobbler
A group of people who has been chosen by others to make decisions on their own	Committee
A building in which nuns live	Convent
An animal which feeds on other animals	Carnivorous
A person who does criticism	Critic
A person who cannot hear	Deaf
A condition in which one loses a lot of water from one's body because of vomiting, etc.	Dehydration
A system of government in which the people cast their votes to elect their leaders	Democracy
The study of skin problems	Dermatology
A long piece of land covered with sand	Desert
The art of managing relationships between countries	Diplomacy
A piece of information about the words in a book form	Dictionary
A piece of information about the telephone numbers of the people in a book from	Directory
A person in charge of a newspapers, magazine etc.	Editor
A person who thinks he is better than the others	Egoist
To leave your country and settle in some other country	Emigrate
A book or series of books giving almost all knowledge about an area or some persons etc.	Encyclopaedia
Study of insects	Entomology
Time when day and night are of the same duration	Equinox
To sell things out of the country	Export
To purchase things from some other country	Import
A plant or animal no longer in existence	Extinct
A situation when there is a shortage of food for a long period of time	Famine
An amount of money that we pay for some action or services	Fee
Related to women	Feminine
An animal strong and aggressive	Ferocious

Multiple Word Expression	*Substitution*
A piece of land where plants grow easily from the soil that is favourable to them	Fertile
A work of literature having some imaginary events	Fiction
A large amount of water covering certain area	Flood
A person who sells flowers	Florist
A religious ceremony for burying or cremating a dead person	Funeral
A substance which kills fungus	Fungicide
A person studying or having studied the diseases and the related things of female reproductive system	Gynaecologist
The murder of the person of the same group race or country	Genocide
A substance which kills germs	Germicide
A situation in which many people die because of fire during war	Holocaust
The act of killing a person deliberately	Homicide
A word having the pronunciation as the other one does but it differs in meaning	Homophone
A word having the same spelling as the other one does but it is pronounced in some other way	Homonym
A person who is attracted towards the person of the same sex	Homosexual
Go across and parallel to the ground	Horizontal
A substance which kills the insects	Insecticide
That cannot be corrected	Incorrigible
That cannot be defeated	Invincible
That cannot be eaten	Inedible
That cannot be seen	Invisible
A place in a school or college where books are kept for the benefit of students, teachers etc.	Library
A place in a school or college where scientific experiments are performed	Laboratory
An official who is a judge in the lowest court	Magistrate
A piece of music or a book before it is printed	Manuscript
Related to men	Masculine
One who believes in the existence of God	A theist
One who does not believe in the existence of good	An atheist
That can be believed	Credible
That cannot be believed	Incredible
That which dissolves in a solvent	Soluble
That which does not dissolves in a solvent	Insoluble
Hard writing that can be read	Legible
Hard writing that cannot be read	Illegible
A person who does jobs beneficial to mankind	Philanthropist
A person who goes on foot	Pedestrian
A person who fights for his own country	Patriot
An act of killing oneself	Suicide
A woman whose husband is dead	Widow
A man whose wife is dead	Widower
A person who eats vegetarian and non-vegetarian diets	Omnivorous

Multiple Word Expression	*Substitution*
Something which is everywhere at the same time	Omnipresent
One who knows everything	Omniscient
A child who does not have parents	Orphan
An award etc. given after the death of the person	Posthumous
The place where animals are kept for amusement and to increase the knowledge of the public	Zoo
The science which deals with the study of animals	Zoology

MULTIPLE CHOICE QUESTIONS

Directions: *In questions given below, out of the four alternatives, choose the one which can be substituted for the given words/sentences.*

1. Something that relates to everyone in the world
   A. General   B. Common
   C. Usual   D. Universal

2. An expression of mild disapproval
   A. Warning   B. Denigration
   C. Impertinence   D. Reproof

3. One who is not easily pleased by anything
   A. Maiden   B. Medieval
   C. Precarious   D. Fastidious

4. Murder of a king
   A. Infanticide   B. Matricide
   C. Genocide   D. Regicide

5. A remedy for all diseases
   A. Stoic   B. Marvel
   C. Panacea   D. Recompense

6. A dramatic performance
   A. Mask   B. Mosque
   C. Masque   D. Mascot

7. Study of birds
   A. Orology   B. Optology
   C. Ophthalmology   D. Ornithology

8. Ready to believe
   A. Credulous   B. Credible
   C. Creditable   D. Incredible

9. Incapable of being seen through
   A. Ductile   B. Opaque
   C. Obsolete   D. Potable

10. One who eats everything
    A. Omnivorous   B. Omniscient
    C. Irresistible   D. Insolvent

11. A place where bees are kept is called
    A. An apiary   B. A mole
    C. A hive   D. A sanctuary

12. One who cannot be corrected
    A. Incurable   B. Incorrigible
    C. Hardened   D. Invulnerable

13. One who is in charge of a museum
    A. Curator   B. Supervisor
    C. Caretaker   D. Warden

14. Continuing fight between parties, families, clans, etc.
    A. Enmity   B. Feud
    C. Quarrel   D. Skirmish

15. A voice loud enough to be heard
    A. Audible   B. Applaudable
    C. Laudable   D. Oral

16. A paper written by hand
    A. Handicraft   B. Manuscript
    C. Handiwork   D. Thesis

17. Habitually silent or talking little
    A. Serville   B. Unequivocal
    C. Taciturn   D. Synoptic

18. To slap with a flat object
    A. Chop   B. Hew
    C. Gnaw   D. Swat

19. A person who speaks many languages
    A. Linguist   B. Monolingual
    C. Polyglot   D. Bilingual

20. A light sailing-boat built specially for racing
    A. Canoe   B. Yacht
    C. Frigate   D. Dinghy

21. A fixed orbit in space in relation to earth
    A. Geological   B. Geo-synchronous
    C. Geo-centric   D. Geo-stationary

22. A style in which a writer makes a display of his knowledge
A. Pedantic   B. Verbose
C. Pompous   D. Ornate

23. A religious discourse
A. Preach   B. Stanza
C. Sanctorum   D. Sermon

24. A place that provides refuge
A. Asylum   B. Sanatorium
C. Shelter   D. Orphanage

25. Detailed plan of a journey
A. Travelogue   B. Travelkit
C. Schedule   D. Itinerary

26. A person who insists on something
A. Disciplinarian   B. Stickler
C. Instantaneous   D. Boaster

27. A drawing on transparent paper
A. Red print   B. Blue print
C. Negative   D. Transparency

28. One who believes that all things and events in life are predetermined is a
A. Fatalist   B. Puritan
C. Egoist   D. Tyrant

29. A school boy who cuts classes frequently is a
A. Defeatist   B. Sycophant
C. Truant   D. Martinet

30. The act of violating the sanctity of the church is
A. Blasphemy   B. Heresy
C. Sacrilege   D. Desecration

31. A place where monks live as a secluded community
A. Cathedral   B. Diocese
C. Convent   D. Monastery

32. One who is fond of fighting
A. Bellicose   B. Aggressive
C. Belligerent   D. Militant

33. Tending to move away from the centre or axis
A. Centrifugal   B. Centripetal
C. Axiomatic   D. Awry

34. Words inscribed on tomb
A. Epitome   B. Epistle
C. Epilogue   D. Epitaph

35. Leave or remove from a place considered dangerous
A. Evade   B. Evacuate
C. Avoid   D. Exterminate

36. Original inhabitants of a country
A. Abroge   B. Aborger
C. Aborgory   D. Aborigins

37. Government by the officials
A. Theocracy   B. Plutocracy
C. Bureaucracy   D. Democracy

38. Incapable of being exhausted
A. Inexhaustible   B. Inaexhaustible
C. Exhaustable   D. Non-tired

39. A person of good understanding, knowledge and reasoning power
A. Expert   B. Intellectual
C. Snob   D. Literate

40. One absorbed in his own thoughts and feelings rather than in things outside
A. Scholar   B. Recluse
C. Introvert   D. Intellectual

ANSWERS

1	2	3	4	5	6	7	8	9	10
D	D	D	D	C	C	D	A	B	A

11	12	13	14	15	16	17	18	19	20
A	B	A	B	A	B	C	D	A	B

21	22	23	24	25	26	27	28	29	30
D	A	D	A	D	B	D	A	C	C

31	32	33	34	35	36	37	38	39	40
D	A	A	D	B	B	C	A	B	C

6. Spelling Errors

There are thousands of words in English language. It is difficult to remember the spellings and meanings of all at once. Try to learn as many as you can. Use a dictionary regularly.

Directions: *Find the correctly spelt words.*

1. A. Damage   B. Dammage
   C. Damaige   D. Dammege

2. A. Efficiant   B. Effecient
   C. Efficient   D. Eficient

3. A. Schedule   B. Schdule
   C. Schedale   D. Schedeule

4. A. Occurad   B. Occurred
   C. Ocurred   D. Occured

5. A. Grieff   B. Grief
   C. Grieef   D. Grrief

6. A. Guarantee   B. Garuntee
   C. Guaruntee   D. Gaurantee

7. A. Meddicine   B. Medicine
   C. Medicene   D. Medicinne

8. A. Benefeted   B. Benefitted
   C. Benifited   D. Benefited

9. A. Acommodation   B. Acomodation
   C. Accomodation   D. Accommodation

10. A. Querrelsome   B. Quarrelsame
    C. Quarrelsome   D. Querralsome

11. A. Sympathetic   B. Smypathetic
    C. Sympothetic   D. Sympethetic

12. A. Prograssive   B. Progressive
    C. Progresive   D. Prograsive

13. A. Uncivilized   B. Uncevilized
    C. Uncivillized   D. Uncevelized

14. A. Extravagant   B. Extreragent
    C. Extreregant   D. Extravegent

15. A. Missunderstood   B. Miesunderstood
    C. Misunderstood   D. Misunderstod

16. A. Belligerent   B. Beligirent
    C. Belligarant   D. Belligerrent

17. A. Astonished   B. Astronished
    C. Astoneshed   D. Asstonished

18. A. Sincerely   B. Sencerely
    C. Sincerelly   D. Sincerrely

19. A. Rigourous   B. Rigerous
    C. Rigorous   D. Regerous

20. A. Satellite   B. Sattellite
    C. Satelite   D. Sattelite

21. A. Pesanger   B. Passenger
    C. Pessenger   D. Pasanger

22. A. Humurous   B. Humorous
    C. Humoreus   D. Humorrous

23. A. Exeggerate   B. Exaggerate
    C. Exadgerate   D. Exagerate

24. A. Fariegn   B. Forein
    C. Foriegn   D. Foreign

25. A. Excesive   B. Excessive
    C. Exccessive   D. Exccesive

26. A. Forcaust   B. Forcast
    C. Forecast   D. Forecaste

27. A. Paralleted   B. Paralelled
    C. Parralleled   D. Parallelled

48

28. A. Ocasion	B. Occassion	C. Occasion	D. Ocassion
29. A. Boquet	B. Bouquet	C. Bouquete	D. Bouquette
30. A. Chettering	B. Chaterring	C. Chattering	D. Chatering
31. A. Discourage	B. Disscourage	C. Discourege	D. Discaurage
32. A. Curageous	B. Courageous	C. Courrageous	D. Couregeous
33. A. Abandon	B. Abanddon	C. Abendon	D. Abbandon

34. A. Embarassment
B. Emberrassement
C. Embarrassment
D. Embbaresment

35. A. Eccintric	B. Eccentrie	C. Eccentric	D. Eccintrie
36. A. Occasional	B. Occassional	C. Occesional	D. Occessional
37. A. Querrel	B. Querral	C. Quarrel	D. Quarel
38. A. Contrebution	B. Contribution	C. Contributtion	D. Conterbution

39. A. Desgrace B. Disgrece C. Disgrice D. Disgrace
40. A. Harassment B. Herassment C. Harasment D. Harassmient
41. A. Imaginative B. Imeginative C. Imagenative D. Imaginetive
42. A. Suficient B. Suficiant C. Sufficient D. Sufficiant
43. A. Adequate B. Edequate C. Adaquete D. Edaquete
44. A. Exparienced B. Experianced C. Experienced D. Experrienced
45. A. Flatering B. Fletering C. Flattering D. Fletaring
46. A. Cuttiveted B. Culltrivated C. Cultivated D. Caltivated
47. A. Praiceworthy B. Peiseworthy C. Praiseworthy D. Praisaworthy
48. A. Profesional B. Professionel C. Professional D. Profissional
49. A. Ameteur B. Amateur C. Amataur D. Amateor
50. A. Unfevourable B. Unfevaurable C. Unfavourable D. Unfivourable

ANSWERS

1	2	3	4	5	6	7	8	9	10
A	C	A	B	B	A	B	B	D	C

11	12	13	14	15	16	17	18	19	20
A	B	A	A	C	A	A	A	C	A

21	22	23	24	25	26	27	28	29	30
B	B	B	D	B	C	A	C	B	C

31	32	33	34	35	36	37	38	39	40
A	B	A	C	C	A	C	B	D	A

41	42	43	44	45	46	47	48	49	50
A	C	A	C	A	C	C	C	B	C

1. India, in August 2019, signed 10 agreements in the field of space research, aviation, information technology, power and education with _____.
   A. Japan
   B. Russia
   C. Sri Lanka
   D. Bhutan

2. Edgar Chagwa was on a three-day state visit to India in August 2019. He is the president of _____.
   A. Zambia
   B. South Africa
   C. Romania
   D. Senegal

3. A Commission appointed to examine the sub-categorisation of Other Backward Classes was on July 31, 2019 given an extension of _____.
   A. Three Months
   B. Four Months
   C. Six Months
   D. Twelve Months

4. In August 2019, India has contributed _____ to the UN Special Purpose Trust Fund for the Resident Coordinator System.
   A. $ 5 million
   B. $ 1 million
   C. $ 2 million
   D. $ 4 million

5. President Ram Nath Kovind has signed into law a Bill that seeks to increase the sanctioned strength of Judges in the Supreme Court from 30 to _____.
   A. 33
   B. 35
   C. 38
   D. 40

6. As per the data compiled by the World Bank, India has been pushed to the _____ in the global GDP rankings in 2018.
   A. 5th place
   B. 6th place
   C. 7th place
   D. 8th place

7. Who among the following topped *Forbes* Magazine's list of the highest paid women in sports for the fourth straight year on August 6, 2019?
   A. Maria Sharapova
   B. Serena Williams
   C. Li Na
   D. P.V. Sindhu

8. Global e-commerce giant Amazon has entered into an equity deal to acquire 49% stake in _____.
   A. Refinitiv
   B. Fynd
   C. Aramco
   D. Future Coupons

9. The Modi government has launched the Pradhan Mantri Kisan Maan Dhan Yojana on _____ .
   A. August 9, 2019
   B. August 15, 2019
   C. August 1, 2019
   D. August 20, 2019

10. The Reserve Bank of India, on August 1, 2019, allowed _____ to offer regular banking services in the country.
    A. Bank of Spain
    B. Bank of Cylon
    C. Bank of China
    D. Bank of Bhutan

11. Who has been appointed the new CEO of Vodafone-Idea in August 2019?
    A. Ram Raghavan
    B. Ravinder Takkar
    C. Rishad Premji
    D. Mandar Vaidya

12. The State assembly that passed an Act to control the organised crime on August 6, 2019, is _____.
    A. Bihar
    B. Karnataka
    C. Rajasthan
    D. Haryana

13. Kosi-Mechi river linking project, which has been approved by the Centre, is associated with which State?
    A. Uttar Pradesh
    B. Sikkim
    C. Bihar
    D. West Bengal

14. Which State passed Bills against Lynching and Honour Killing on August 5, 2019?
    A. Madhya Pradesh
    B. Rajasthan
    C. Chhattisgarh
    D. Punjab

15. The State which has announced that it will implement the Centre's 'One Nation, One Ration Card' initiative in the State starting from September 1, 2019 is _____.
    A. Punjab
    B. Haryana
    C. Bihar
    D. Odisha

16. Who was awarded with the Vir Chakra, on the eve of 73rd Independence Day on August 14, 2019?
A. Harshpal Singh
B. Abhinandan Varthaman
C. Sapper Prakash Jadhav
D. Ajay Singh Kushwah

17. Which film was declared as the Best Feature Film at the 66th National Film Awards on August 9, 2019?
A. *Hellaro*
B. *Badhaai Ho*
C. *Andhadhun*
D. *Uri : The Surgical Strike*

18. Which one is not included in the list of Ramon Magsaysay Award 2019, announced on August 2 in Manila?
A. Kim Jong-ki
B. Ravish Kumar
C. Angkhana Neelapaijit
D. Alexandre Ziegler

19. Giuseppe Conte, who resigned on August 20, 2019 was the Prime Minister of which country?
A. Norway
B. Poland
C. Italy
D. Sweden

20. Who has been appointed as the new Cabinet Secretary on August 21, 2019 for a period of two year?
A. Ajay Kumar
B. Subhash Chandra
C. Ajay Kumar Bhalla
D. Rajiv Gauba

21. Which one is not selected for Institutions of Eminence (IoE) status, announced by UGC on August 2, 2019?
A. Ashoka University
B. Anna University
C. OP Jindal University
D. Shiv Nadar University

22. Which country on August 21, 2019 launched world's largest teacher training plan under which 42 lakh elementary-level government teachers to be trained?
A. Russia
B. India
C. China
D. Australia

23. As per MHA orders on August 19, 2019, all personnel of the Central Armed Police Forces (CAPFs) will now retire at a uniform age of _____ years.
A. 56
B. 58
C. 60
D. 62

24. World's highest lake—the Kajin Sara Lake—is recently discovered in which country?
A. Bhutan
B. China
C. India
D. Nepal

25. Who is world's highest paid woman musician, as per *Forbes'* list released on August 26, 2019?
A. Taylor Swift
B. Katy Perry
C. Beyonce
D. Rihana

26. Which country launched world's first floating nuclear reactor on August 23, 2019?
A. USA
B. Russia
C. China
D. Japan

27. The world's first human-monkey hybrid has been created by Spanish scientists in which of the following country?
A. Spain
B. Australia
C. Germany
D. China

28. Who have been bestowed with Rajiv Gandhi Khel Ratna award on August 29, 2019?
A. Bajrang Punia, Deepa Malik
B. Bajrang Punia, Poonam Yadav
C. Ajay Thakur, Sonia Lather
D. P.V. Sindhu, Deepa Malik

29. Who became the first Indian to win Badminton World Championships gold on August 25, 2019 in Basel, Switzerland?
A. Sai Praneeth
B. Chirag Shetty
C. P.V. Sindhu
D. Saina Nehwal

30. Who has been appointed as Team India (Cricket) head coach on August 26, 2019?
A. Tom Moody
B. Ravi Shastri
C. Mike Hesson
D. Robin Singh

31. Which among the following has got the World Heritage site tag in July 2019?
A. Pink City, Jaipur
B. Old Ahmedabad
C. New Delhi
D. New Raipur

32. The 19th Commonwealth Foreign Affairs Ministers' Meeting was held on July 10, 2019 in ....
    A. London   B. Paris
    C. New Delhi   D. Colombo

33. Sheikh Abdullah bin Zayed Al Nahyan visited India in July 2019. He is foreign minister of ....
    A. Saudi Arabia   B. Iraq
    C. UAE   D. Syria

34. Which rank did India possess in Global Innovation Index?
    A. 82nd   B. 52nd
    C. 75th   D. 105th

35. With which country India signed an agreement to upgrade Railway line in July 2019?
    A. Bhutan   B. Nepal
    C. Maldives   D. Sri Lanka

36. Which State has focussed largely on Welfare Schemes in its Budget presented in July 2019?
    A. Gujarat   B. Andhra Pradesh
    C. Rajasthan   D. Madhya Pradesh

37. The State assembly which passed the Cow Vigilantism Bill on July 17, 2019, is ....
    A. West Bengal   B. Karnataka
    C. Madhya Pradesh   D. Delhi

38. Haryana cabinet on July 16, 2019 approved the proposal to set up a sports university in ....
    A. Gurugram   B. Panipat
    C. Faridabad   D. Sonipat

39. President Ram Nath Kovind has given assent to a key Bill of .... that will pave the way for reintroduction of the provision of anticipatory bail.
    A. Uttar Pradesh   B. Gujarat
    C. Bihar   D. Haryana

40. On July 22, 2019 which State passed a Bill which reserves 75 per cent of private jobs across all categories in industrial units, factories, joint venture as well as projects that are in public private partnership mode?
    A. Haryana   B. Andhra Pradesh
    C. Karnataka   D. Tamil Nadu

41. Who has been appointed new chief secretary of Haryana?
    A. Keshni Anand Arora
    B. Uravashi Gulati
    C. Meenakshi Anand Chaudhary
    D. J.C. Anand

42. On July 20, 2019, which State notified ban on the manufacture and sale of any form of flavoured tobacco, including scented areca nut and flavoured pan masalas?
    A. Bihar   B. Rajasthan
    C. Maharashtra   D. West Bengal

43. The Asian Development Bank on July 18, 2019 lowered India's growth forecast from 7.2% to ....
    A. 6.8%   B. 6.5%
    C. 6.6%   D. 7.0%

44. The European Union on June 30, 2019 signed a long awaited free trade deal with ....
    A. Vietnam   B. Singapore
    C. Mozambique   D. None of these

45. Which country has decided to impose a tax of up to 18 euros on plane tickets for all flights from airports in the country to fund less polluting transportation projects?
    A. Italy   B. Germany
    C. France   D. UK

46. With which country India has inked a $50 million deal for MRSAM missiles in July 2019?
    A. USA   B. Israel
    C. France   D. South Korea

47. Who has been appointed the new Vice-Chief of the Army Staff in July 2019?
    A. M.M. Naravane
    B. K. Natarajan
    C. D. Anbu
    D. Rajendra Singh

48. Bollywood superstar Shah Rukh Khan is set to receive an honorary doctorate degree from La Trobe University in August 2019. The University is in ....
    A. Canada   B. China
    C. Australia   D. USA

49. Which institute is launching a first-of-its-kind programme, techMBA, for its undergraduate (UG) students from all the engineering streams?
A. IIT, Kanpur   B. IIT, Delhi
C. IIT, Kharagpur   D. IIT, Madras

50. The Central Board of Secondary Education (CBSE) will regulate admissions to classes .... in all its affiliated schools across the country from next year.
A. 7 and 8   B. 9 and 11
C. 7 and 9   D. 8 and 11

51. Wiebe Wakker, who completed the longest ever journey in an electric vehicle (1,01,000 km) on July 19, 2019 after a three-year drive that took him through more than 30 countries, belongs to which country?
A. Netherlands   B. New Zealand
C. Australia   D. Sweden

52. Kyriakos Mitsotakis was sworn in as Prime Minister of which country on July 8, 2019?
A. Italy   B. Latvia
C. Greece   D. Sweden

53. Who is set to become the first woman European Commission president after European parliamentary approval on July 16, 2019?
A. Christine Lagarde
B. Ursula von der Leyen
C. Anshula Kant
D. Margaret Atwood

54. Who is not included in the list of Governors, appointed in July, 2019?
A. Phagu Chauhan   B. Ramesh Bais
C. R.N. Ravi   D. N.S. Vishwanathan

55. Who has been chosen for the Sangita Kalanidhi award of the Music Academy this year?
A. M.S. Sheela   B. Aarti N. Rao
C. S. Sowmya   D. Seetha Narayanan

56. Which country launched its second lunar mission on July 22, 2019?
A. India   B. Israel
C. China   D. Australia

57. Which Indian State is going to set up country's first space park?
A. Andhra Pradesh   B. Karnataka
C. Maharashtra   D. Kerala

58. England on July 14, 2019 became the .... team to win the ICC Cricket World Cup.
A. Fourth   B. Fifth
C. Sixth   D. Seventh

59. Who won five International Golds in just 20 days in athletics in Europe in July 2019?
A. Dutee Chand   B. Hima Das
C. V.K. Vismaya   D. S. Gayakawad

60. Which country claimed all the seven gold medals at the 21st Commonwealth Table Tennis Championships held in Cuttack in July 2019?
A. India   B. Singapore
C. England   D. Malaysia

61. Which country conferred upon PM Modi the highest honour the Rule of Nishan Izzuddeen in June 2019?
A. Sri Lanka   B. Japan
C. Maldives   D. Bhutan

62. Which rank did India possess on Gender Index?
A. 85th   B. 95th
C. 75th   D. 105th

63. India's infant mortality rate has fallen from 42 in 2012 to .... in 2017.
A. 28   B. 35
C. 14   D. 33

64. The Election Commission of India on June 7, 2019 declared the .... as the national party.
A. National People's Party
B. YSR Congress Party
C. Telugu Desham Party
D. None of these

65. Who has been elected new Speaker of Lok Sabha on June 19, 2019?
A. Virendra Kumar
B. T.R. Balu
C. Sumitra Mahajan
D. Om Birla

66. The air strike by Indian Air Force on the terrorist training camp in Balakot, Pakistan was codenamed ....
A. Operation Bandar   B. Operation Thunder
C. Operation Rudra   D. Operation Pawan

67. Who has been named as the director of London's Nehru Centre?
A. Gopalkrishna Gandhi
B. Pavan Varma
C. Amish Tripathi
D. Vinay Sahasrabudhe

68. After Guwahati and Imphal, which airport is set to become the third international airport in the north eastern region?
A. Shilong   B. Agartala
C. Kohima   D. None of these

69. On June 14, 2019 which state launched a universal old age pension scheme?
A. Uttar Pradesh   B. Karnataka
C. West Bengal   D. Bihar

70. The state which has announced to build a museum to showcase the work of celebrated music composer R.D. Burman, is ....
A. Tripura   B. Maharashtra
C. Uttar Pradesh   D. Bihar

71. In which state the provision of anticipatory bail has been restored after 43 years in June 2019?
A. Delhi   B. Punjab
C. Uttar Pradesh   D. Karnataka

72. Where was a two-day Shanghai Cooperation Organisation Summit held in June 2019?
A. Bishkek   B. Shanghai
C. Bangkok   D. Kobe

73. The United States signed an agreement on June 7, 2019 with which country to curb migration from central America?
A. Canada   B. Mexico
C. Chile   D. France

74. On June 5, 2019 the US terminated preferential trade status for ....
A. North Korea   B. China
C. Iran   D. India

75. Spelling out his government's vision PM Narendra Modi set a goal to make India a $5 trillion economy by ....
A. 2030   B. 2022
C. 2024   D. 2028

76. Zuzana Caputova, who took the oath of office on June 15, 2019 is the first woman President of which country?
A. Slovakia   B. Turkmenistan
C. Austria   D. France

77. Who has been elected the External Auditor of the World Health Organisation (WHO) for four years (2020-23) at its 72nd Assembly at Geneva?
A. Sun Weidong   B. Brigitte Bierlein
C. Rajiv Mehrishi   D. Luo Zhaohui

78. With which country India has finalised the plan to acquire 30 weaponised Sea Guardian (or Predator-B) drones?
A. Israel   B. USA
C. France   D. Russia

79. The Indian Air Force on June 6, 2019 hammered out a ₹ 300-crore deal with which country for around 100 Spice 2000 bombs?
A. Israel   B. Russia
C. USA   D. France

80. The popular cartoon characters Motu and Patlu have found themselves a special corner at the Madame Tussauds in .... on June 4, 2019.
A. London
B. New York
C. Melbourne
D. New Delhi

81. British author J.K. Rowling has published two eBook shorts in Harry Potter series on June 27, 2019. The two eBooks are:
A. Potions and Herbology; Divination and Astronomy
B. Charms and Defence Against the Dark Arts; Potions and Herbology
C. Divination and Astronomy; Care of Magical Creatures
D. Charms and Defence Against the Dark Arts; Care of Magical Creatures

82. Who won the Zee TV's singing reality show Sa Re Ga Ma Pa Little Champs 2019 on June 9, 2019?
A. Pritam Acharya
B. Mohammed Faiz
C. Anushka Patra
D. Sugandha Date

83. Mohammed Shami on June 22 becomes the second Indian bowler to take a hat-trick in World Cup. The first Indian bowler to do so is ....
A. Ravi Shastri
B. Kapil Dev
C. Chetan Sharma
D. Anil Kumble

84. Who holds the record of smashing 17 sixes in an innings in the ongoing World Cup 2019?
A. Rohit Sharma
B. Eoin Morgan
C. David Warner
D. Jason Roy

85. Which Indian institute has not found a place among the top 200 in the prestigious 2020 QS World University Rankings released on June 19, 2019?
A. IIT-Bombay
B. IIT-Delhi
C. IISc-Bangalore
D. IIT-Madras

86. The all-India topper of the JEE Advanced-2019, Kartikey Gupta, belongs to which state?
A. Maharashtra
B. Rajasthan
C. Uttar Pradesh
D. Madhya Pradesh

87. Which movie was adjudged the Best Movie at the MTV Awards 2019 on June 17, 2019 in Los Angeles?
A. *A Star Is Born*
B. *Game of Thrones*
C. *Avengers : Endgame*
D. *Bird Box*

88. Who won Miss India World 2019 crown on June 15, 2019 in Mumbai?
A. Shivani Jadhav
B. Suman Rao
C. Shreya Shankar
D. Sanjana Vij

89. Nasa has renamed the street outside its Washington HQ to honour three black female mathematicians. Which one is not in that select group?
A. K. Johnson
B. D. Vaughan
C. ML Shetterly
D. M. Jackson

90. Which country on June 13, 2019 announced its plan to set up its own space station in next decade?
A. South Korea
B. Australia
C. Iran
D. India

91. How many seats has BJP won in April-May 2019 Lok Sabha elections?
A. 303
B. 315
C. 352
D. 282

92. A two-day SCO foreign ministers meet was held on May 21-22, 2019 in ______.
A. Beijing
B. Shanghai
C. Bishkek
D. Ahmedabad

93. With which country has India signed a pact on new oil refinery in May 2019?
A. UK
B. Mongolia
C. Nepal
D. Iran

94. The Ghaziabad-based mountaineer, who has scaled Mt. Everest, world's highest peak, on May 22, 2019, is ____ .
A. Mohit Bhatt
B. Rohit Sardana
C. Punit Sharma
D. Sagar Kasana

95. Javad Zarif visited India in May 2019. He is the foreign minister of ______ .
A. Kyrgystan
B. Mongolia
C. Iran
D. UK

96. Which country is the top oil supplier to India?
A. Iran
B. Iraq
C. Saudi Arabia
D. Kuwait

97. Sagar Cements in May 2019 completed the acquisition of 100 per cent stake in ______ .
A. Jajpur Cement
B. Oyo Hotels
C. Mindtree
D. TPG

98. Which among the following became the country's biggest company by revenue toppling state-owned Indian Oil Corporation?
A. Hindustan Petroleum
B. HDFC
C. Reliance Industries
D. None of these

99. President Ram Nath Kovind has given assent to which state's legislation under which chain snatchers in the state will face upto 10 year imprisonment?
A. Assam
B. Sikkim
C. Delhi
D. Gujarat

100. Which state offered incentive to Paddy Farmers to grow Maize and Pulses?
A. Karnataka
B. Haryana
C. Punjab
D. Himachal Pradesh

101. Governor of which state on May 20, 2019 signed an ordinance to provide 16 per cent reservation for Socially and Educationally Backward Classes in educational institutions from 2019-20?
A. Gujarat
B. Bihar
C. Goa
D. Maharashtra

102. The state, which is highly devasted by the cyclone Fani in May 2019, is _____.
A. Andhra Pradesh
B. Odisha
C. Kerala
D. Tamil Nadu

103. Who has sworn-in as the new chief minister of Sikkim in May 2019?
A. P.S. Golay
B. Sonam Lama
C. Pawan Kumar Chamling
D. Pema Khandu

104. US Prez. Donald Trump was on a four day state visit to _____ in May 2019.
A. Vietnam
B. South Korea
C. Japan
D. Singapore

105. Who has been appointed the new defence minister of India?
A. Rajnath Singh
B. Amit Shah
C. Gen. V.K. Singh
D. Nitin Gadkari

106. ISRO on May 22, 2019 successfully put into orbit an earth observation satellite _____ .
A. RISAT-1A
B. RISAT-1B
C. RISAT-2A
D. RISAT-2B

107. Which country has unveiled the world's first all-electric vertical takeoff and landing passenger jet after completing its first flight?
A. Germany
B. China
C. Japan
D. Australia

108. India and _____ commenced one of their biggest ever Naval exercise in early May in Goa.
A. Singapore
B. France
C. Japan
D. USA

109. Which country is hosting the fifth International Army Scout Masters Competition from July 24 to August 17, 2019?
A. India
B. Belarus
C. Armenia
D. Kazakhstan

110. Renowned author and illustrator of the best-selling The Tiger Who Came to Tea and other beloved children's books, died in London on May 22, 2019. Who is S/he?
A. B. Wainaina
B. Herman Wouk
C. Judith Kerr
D. Doris Day

111. UGC has decided to review the quality of PhD theses for which doctoral degrees were awarded in last _____ years by varsities across the country.
A. 5
B. 7
C. 8
D. 10

112. In which year the Pharm D course was started in India?
A. 2005
B. 2008
C. 2010
D. 2012

113. The popular TV game show Who wants to be a Millionaire that has finally come to end after 20 years of successful running, was one of the prime show of which country?
A. India
B. UK
C. USA
D. Canada

114. Who scaled Mount Everest for the 24th time on May 21, 2019 breaking his own record for the most Everest ascents within a week?
A. Kami Rita Sherpa
B. Madhusudan Negi
C. Shyamakant Manjul
D. Arpan Jadhav

115. Who was sworn in as Ukraine's youngest post-Soviet President on May 20, 2019?
A. Petro Poroshenko
B. Volodymyr Zelensky
C. Prabowo Subianto
D. Bill Shorten

116. Who was made CMD of ITC on May 13, 2019 two days after its long-serving chairman YC Deveshwar passed away?
A. DN Patel
B. Moin-ul-Haq
C. O.P. Chaudhary
D. Sanjiv Puri

117. Bong Joon-ho, who won the Cannes Palme d'Or top prize on May 25, 2019 for Parasite, belongs to which country?
A. China
B. South Korea
C. Japan
D. Great Britain

118. Who won the Man Booker International Prize on May 21, 2019 for Celestial Bodies—the first novel originally written in Arabic?
A. Annie Zaidi
B. Marilyn Booth
C. Aranzazu Ayala
D. Jokha Alharthi

119. Who emerged champions at the IPL-12 on May 12, 2019 in Hyderabad?
A. Chennai Super Kings
B. Mumbai Indians
C. Sunrisers Hyderabad
D. Delhi Capitals

120. Which team clinched the Premier League title with 98 points on May 12, 2019?
A. Manchester City
B. Chelsea
C. Arsenal
D. Liverpool

121. In April 2019 with which country India has renewed a memorandum of understanding on defence equipment cooperation?
A. USA
B. China
C. Australia
D. UK

122. Which rank did India possess on World Press Freedom Index 2019?
A. 153rd
B. 140th
C. 125th
D. 163rd

123. The Supreme court on April 23, 2019 constituted a three judge panel to inquire into the sexual harassment complaint by a former junior court assistant against CJI Ranjan Gogoi, is headed by ________.
A. Justice S.A. Bobde
B. Justice Indira Banerjee
C. Justice N.V. Ramana
D. Justice Abhilasha Kumari

124. Which among the following continues to be the top source country of migrants to Australia in 2017-18?
A. Pakistan
B. Philippines
C. China
D. India

125. In April 2019, India has evacuated its entire contingent of 15 CRPF personnel from ________.
A. Mozambique
B. Syria
C. Libya
D. Sudan

126. On April 18, 2019, which country has successfully launched its first satellite into space from the US to gather detailed geographical information?
A. UAE
B. Bhutan
C. Pakistan
D. Nepal

127. In April 2019, Volodymyr Zelensky has been elected president of ________.
A. Ukraine
B. France
C. Israel
D. None of these

128. Which European city rolled out strict vehicle emission charges in April 2019?
A. Paris
B. London
C. Bonn
D. Rome

129. The country, which became the first country in the world to commercially launch fifth generation (5G) services on April 5, 2019 is ________:
A. USA
B. Japan
C. South Korea
D. France

130. Omar al-Bashir, who ruled his country for 30 years was on April 11, 2019 overthrown by the armed forces. He was the president of ________ .
A. Mozambique
B. Sudan
C. Libya
D. Turkey

131. Which country designated Iran's Revolutionary guard as a terrorist group in April 2019?
A. UK
B. France
C. USA
D. Germany

132. Which country is the highest recipient of remittances in 2018?
A. India
B. China
C. USA
D. Mexico

133. The International Monetary Fund has projected that global growth in 2019 will be ________.
A. 3.7 per cent
B. 3.3 per cent
C. 4.2 per cent
D. 4.8 per cent

134. The country which emerged as the third largest solar photo voltaic market in the world in 2018, is ________.
A. USA
B. China
C. India
D. Brazil

135. Which state celebrated its 72nd State day on April 15, 2019?
A. Odisha
B. Andhra Pradesh
C. Karnataka
D. Himachal Pradesh

136. Mitsuhiro Iwamoto, a blind sailor, who became the first sightless person on record on April 20, 2019 to navigate a vessel across the Pacific Ocean, belongs to which country?
A. Japan
B. South Korea
C. North Korea
D. Taiwan

137. Who won the 14th edition of Afghan Star— The Afghan version of American Idol, in March 2019 in Kabul?
A. Shabnam Khan
B. Zahra Elham
C. Zahra Khan
D. Najma Akhtar

138. Who was selected as the 13th President of the World Bank on April 5, 2019?
A. A Bouteflika
B. Amal Clooney
C. Cyril Almeida
D. David Malpass

139. Who has been appointed as the first woman Vice-Chancellor of Jamia Millia Islamia University on April 11, 2019?
A. Jauhar Khan
B. Nadira Begum
C. Najma Akhtar
D. Rubia Khatun

140. Which institute ranked first in the National Institute Ranking Framework 2019?
A. IISc Bangalore
B. IIT Delhi
C. JNU
D. IIT Madras

141. Who has topped the Civil Services Examination 2018?
A. Akshat Jain
B. Kanishak Kataria
C. S. Jayant Deshmukh
D. Junaid Ahmad

142. Bilateral naval drill between India and ______ held from April 13 to 16, 2019 off Cam Ranh Bay?
A. Vietnam
B. Japan
C. Bangladesh
D. South Korea

143. The guided-missile destroyer, which was launched into water at the Mazagon Docks in Mumbai on April 20, 2019 is ______.
A. INS Mysore
B. INS Mormugao
C. INS Imphal
D. INS Mumbai

144. The Zayed Medal was conferred to PM Narendra Modi on April 4, 2019. It is the highest Civilian honour of which country?
A. Iran
B. Vietnam
C. Indonesia
D. The UAE

145. Who won the Prestigious Saraswati Samman 2018 for his collection of poems titled *Pakkaki Ottigilite?*
A. Hoda Barakat
B. Vikram Patel
C. K. Siva Reddy
D. Manjul Bhargava

146. Who won the World Press Freedom Hero award in April 2019?
A. Cyril Almeida
B. Yusuf Hamied
C. Hoda Barakat
D. Anant Parekh

147. What is EMISAT which is launched from Sriharikota, AP on April 1, 2019?
A. A Weather Satellite
B. A Military Satellite
C. A Communication Satellite
D. An Educational Satellite

148. Scientists in which country unveiled a 3D print of a heart with human tissue and vessels on April 15, 2019?
A. Israel
B. China
C. Germany
D. Australia

149. Which country earned ODI status in April 2019?
A. The USA
B. Papua New Guinea
C. Hong Kong
D. Both A and B

150. Who became the first woman to capture a championship at former all-male enclave Augusta National Golf Club on April 6, 2019?
A. Jennifer Kupcho
B. Maria Fassi
C. Yuka Yasuda
D. Yuka Saso

151. Which city has been adjudged India's cleanest city in the centre's cleanliness survey announced on March 6, 2019?
A. Surat
B. Ujjain
C. Indore
D. Ahmedabad

152. Who has been appointed new Chief Minister of Goa in March 2019?
A. Pramod Sawant
B. Vinay Budhiratne
C. Michael Lobo
D. None of these

153. Which among the following has received the Geographic Indication (GI) tag in March 2019?
A. Darjeeling Tea   B. Sirsi Supari
C. Nawara Rice   D. Kullu Shawl

154. The Assembly of which State unanimously passed a Bill on March 18, 2019 that seeks to detect foreigners illegally residing in the State?
A. West Bengal   B. Tripura
C. Mizoram   D. Assam

155. The state which has amended the Lokayukta Act in March 2019 to reduce the Lokayukta's tenure from eight years to five years, is _____.
A. Odisha   B. Andhra Pradesh
C. Haryana   D. Rajasthan

156. As per a report by Department of Industrial Policy and Promotion (DIPP) which among the following is the top destination for FDI equity in 2018-19?
A. Delhi NCR   B. Maharashtra
C. Gujarat   D. Karnataka

157. According to the latest Forbes list released in March 2019 who is the world's richest person?
A. Bill Gates   B. Jeff Bezos
C. Warren Buffet   D. Carlos Slim

158. Which rank did India possess in gold holding as per the latest report by the World Gold Council?
A. 8th   B. 5th
C. 9th   D. 11th

159. The world's most expensive city according to the Economist Intelligence Unit's Worldwide Cost of Living Survey, is _______.
A. Singapore   B. Zurich
C. Geneva   D. Caracas

160. According to an analysis of air quality which is the most polluted city in the world?
A. Faisalabad   B. Lahore
C. Hotan   D. Gurugram

161. The Election Commission on March 10, 2019 announced a ______ phase poll schedule for the 17th Lok Sabha.
A. Five   B. Four
C. Seven   D. Eight

162. The Five judge Bench, led by Chief justice of India Ranjan Gogoi, appointed a panel of mediators for Ayodhya dispute comprising ______.
A. F.M.I. Kalifulla
B. Sri Sri Ravi Shankar
C. Sriram Panchu
D. All of these

163. The United States and India on March 13, 2019 agreed to strengthen security and civil nuclear cooperation, including building _________ US nuclear power plants in India.
A. Five   B. Six
C. Three   D. Eight

164. Which nation did President Kovind visit from March 25-28, 2019?
A. Croatia   B. Bulgaria
C. Bolivia   D. Italy

165. Which rank did India possess in the World Happiness Index 2019?
A. 125th   B. 140th
C. 185th   D. 83rd

166. As per SIPRI report, published on March 11, 2019 India was the _____ largest arms importer in the world from 2014-18.
A. First   B. Second
C. Third   D. Fifth

167. Who has been designated as next Navy Chief on March 23, 2019?
A. Vice Adm Karambir Singh
B. Vice Adm Bimal Verma
C. Vice Adm Santokh Singh
D. None of these

168. The Union Cabinet on March 7, 2019 approved setting up of _____ new Kendriya Vidyalayas across the country.
A. 100   B. 75
C. 50   D. 40

169. ______ is launching a new M.Tech programme in 'Safe Mining' from the July semester this year.
A. IIT, Delhi   B. IIT, Bombay
C. IIT, Kanpur   D. IIT, Kharagpur

170. Karen Uhlenbeck, the first woman to win the Abel Prize in Mathematics on March 19, 2019 belongs to which country?
A. Norway   B. Brazil
C. France   D. USA

171. Who has been chosen for the 28th Vyas Samman 2018?
A. Liladhar Jaguri   B. Priyanka Dubey
C. Pragya Prasun   D. Seema Rao

172. Which country has chosen the chimpanzee as its new national symbol?
A. Burkina Faso   B. Gambia
C. Sierra Leone   D. Benin

173. In which country Europe's first underwater restaurant called 'Under' was opened on March 20, 2019?
A. Italy   B. Norway
C. France   D. Germany

174. The 13-year-old child prodigy, Lydian Nadhaswaram, who won the World's Best talent contest-2019 in March, belongs to ______.
A. India   B. USA
C. Canada   D. UK

175. Kummanam Rajasekharan, who resigned on March 7, 2019 was the governor of which State?
A. Arunachal Pradesh B. Tripura
C. Nagaland   D. Mizoram

176. Which country claimed its first ever victory in Test Cricket on March 18, 2019?
A. Nepal   B. Ireland
C. Afghanistan   D. Bangladesh

177. Who won the season's opening Australian Grand Prix on March 17, 2019 in Melbourne?
A. Lewis Hamilton   B. Valtteri Bottas
C. Max Verstappen   D. Sebastian Vettel

178. Which country on March 27, 2019 became the fourth country in the world having capability to shoot down satellites in the space?
A. India   B. Japan
C. France   D. Israel

179. Which country has set to complete artificial sun device this year, achieving an ion temperature of 100 million degrees Celsius?
A. USA   B. Japan
C. China   D. Russia

180. Who calculated the value of 'Pi' to a new record length of 31 trillion digits on March 14, 2019?
A. G. Satheesh Reddy B. Emma Haruka Iwao
C. Yoshua Bengio   D. Geoffrey Hinton

181. Mohammed bin Salman who visited India in February, 2019, is crown prince of ______.
A. Saudi Arabia   B. UAE
C. Jordan   D. Monaco

182. With which country India signed an agreement to strengthen cooperation in defence and civil nuclear energy in February, 2019?
A. South Korea   B. Argentina
C. Japan   D. USA

183. After Pulwama terror attack on February 14, 2019 what action did India take?
A. Revoked Pak's MFN Status
B. Duty on Pakistani goods hiked to 200%
C. Suspended cross-LOC bus services and trade
D. All of these

184. National War Memorial was inaugurated on February 25, 2019 in ______.
A. Ahmedabad   B. Hyderabad
C. New Delhi   D. Jaipur

185. On February 24, 2019 PM Modi launched the ambitious Pradhan Mantri Kisan Samman Nidhi Scheme that proposes transfer of ₹ ______ annually.
A. 2,000   B. 6,000
C. 10,000   D. 8,000

186. India's fastest train, which was flagged off by Prime Minister Narendra Modi at the New Delhi railway station on February 15, 2019, is ______.
A. Vande Bharat Express
B. Vande Mataram Express
C. Jai Bharat Express
D. Jai Jawan Express

187. The Ministry of Home Affairs has given powers to the Assam Rifles to arrest anyone and search a place without warrant in ______.
A. Assam
B. Nagaland
C. Manipur
D. All of these

188. On February 19, 2019 India launched a pan-India emergency number, that number is ______.
A. 911
B. 112
C. 211
D. 999

189. Which State presented a revenue surplus budget on February 12, 2019?
A. Telangana
B. Uttar Pradesh
C. Bihar
D. Odisha

190. The State which made it mandatory for all industries in the State to provide 70% employment to local youth on February 4, 2019, is ______.
A. Madhya Pradesh
B. West Bengal
C. Assam
D. Karnataka

191. Who has been appointed new DGP of Haryana?
A. Vineet Purohit
B. Manoj Yadava
C. Rakesh Sharma
D. Subodh Singh

192. On February 16, 2019 which State Assembly passed a Bill to make Sanskrit the second official language?
A. Haryana
B. Madhya Pradesh
C. Himachal Pradesh
D. Rajasthan

193. Who has been named the EY Entrepreneur of the year 2018?
A. Siddhartha Lal
B. Ritesh Agarwal
C. Bhaskar Bhat
D. None of these

194. In February 2019, the government has increased the minimum support price for raw jute by ______ per quintal.
A. ₹ 350
B. ₹ 310
C. ₹ 410
D. ₹ 250

195. North Korean leader Kim Jong-un and US President Donald Trump met second time on February 27-28, 2019 in ______.
A. Hanoi
B. Hawana
C. Berlin
D. Budapest

196. India's latest communication satellite—GSAT-31, launched on February 6, 2019 from French Guiana will replace ______.
A. INSAT 4A
B. INSAT 4CR
C. Both the above
D. None of these

197. Which country has launched world's first largely privately funded lunar flight on February 22, 2019?
A. Israel
B. Saudi Arabia
C. China
D. Australia

198. The magnetic North pole is wandering about ______ a year.
A. 20 miles
B. 25 miles
C. 32 miles
D. 34 miles

199. Who has been elected as Nigeria's President on February 27, 2019?
A. Atiku Abubaker
B. Muhammadu Buhari
C. Nayib Bukele
D. Juan Guaido

200. The government on February 2, 2019 appointed Rishi Kumar Shukla as:
A. CBDT Chairman
B. Election Commissioner
C. Air India CMD
D. CBI Chief

201. Indian Air Force's exercise—Vayu Shakti-2019, was held on February 16, 2019 in ______.
A. Jaisalmer
B. Ambala
C. Amritsar
D. Jodhpur

202. Who is Indian Air Force's first woman flight engineer?
A. Punita Arora
B. Hina Jaiswal
C. Madhuri Kanitkar
D. P. Bandopadhyay

203. Which film won the Best Picture Oscar award on February 24, 2019 in Los Angeles?
A. *Roma*
B. *Black Panther*
C. *Green Book*
D. *Bohemian Rhapsody*

204. Who won 'Album of the Year' award at the Grammy Awards 2019 held on February 10, 2019 in Los Angeles?
A. Childish Gambino (*This Is America*)
B. Cardi B (*Invasion of Privacy*)
C. Ariana Grande (*Sweetener*)
D. Kacey Musgraves (*Golden Hour*)

205. How many new Indian departments breached the top 200 club in the 'QS World University Rankings by Subject' released on February 27, 2019?
A. 22
B. 17
C. 26
D. 19

206. Who has been selected to set up India's first school board for Vedic education?
A. Rama Krishna Mission
B. Patanjali Yogpeeth
C. Modi Group of Education
D. Reliance Group of Education

207. _____ has included Hindi as the third official language used in its courts, alongside Arabic and English.
A. Iran
B. Qatar
C. Saudi Arabia
D. UAE

208. Which country has become the first Asian country to win a Test series in South Africa in February, 2019?
A. India
B. Sri Lanka
C. Pakistan
D. Bangladesh

209. Which pair won the 2019 Laureus World Sports Awards for Best Sportsperson and Best Sportswoman on February 18, 2019?
A. Novak Djokovic & Simone Biles
B. Novak Djokovic & Naomi Osaka
C. Tiger Woods & Naomi Osaka
D. Tiger Woods & Simone Biles

210. Which country won their first Asian Cup Football on February 1, 2019?
A. Japan
B. South Korea
C. Qatar
D. India

211. Who was the chief guest of the Republic Day celebrations 2019?
A. Cyril Ramaphosa
B. Vladimir Putin
C. Erna Solberg
D. None of these

212. A three-day Pravasi Bharatiya Divas event was held from January 21 to 23, 2019 in ....
A. New Delhi
B. Jaipur
C. Varanasi
D. Hyderabad

213. The Lok Sabha on January 8, 2019 passed the conten-tious citizenship (Amendment) Bill, 2019, that seeks to provide citizenship to non-Muslims from ....
A. Bangladesh
B. Pakistan
C. Afghanistan
D. All of these

214. The Union Cabinet on January 10, 2019 approved a proposal for a \$75 billion bilateral swap arrangement between ....
A. India and China
B. India and Nepal
C. India and Japan
D. India and Russia

215. Which of the following Andaman Islands has been renamed as Swaraj Dweep by PM Modi on December 30, 2018?
A. Ross Island
B. Neil Island
C. Havelock Island
D. Lotus Island

216. Government has proposed that the monthly pensions of the elderly poor, disabled and widows be increased from the current ₹ 200 to ....
A. ₹ 300
B. ₹ 500
C. ₹ 700
D. ₹ 800

217. On January 28, 2019 India has inked a pact for import of uranium from the central Asian country of ....
A. Uzbekistan
B. Kazakhstan
C. Tajikistan
D. Turkmenistan

218. As per a report by Global Consultancy firm PwC India is all set to beat the United Kingdom in 2019 to become the world's .... largest economy.
A. Third
B. Fourth
C. Fifth
D. Sixth

219. Among all the Gulf nations, the largest outflow of Indian workers in 2018 was to ....
A. Saudi Arabia
B. UAE
C. Kuwait
D. Qatar

220. Insurance behemoth LIC on January 21, 2019 completed the acquisition of 51 per cent controlling stake in ....
A. IDBI Bank
B. ICICI Bank
C. Vijaya Bank
D. Bank of Baroda

221. Which state posted highest rise in state GDP in 2017-18?
A. Telangana   B. Bihar
C. Gujarat   D. Karnataka

222. In January 2019, which state has decided to remove the condition of minimum qualification required to contest civic elections?
A. Gujarat   B. West Bengal
C. Rajasthan   D. Assam

223. The state, which has decided to form a state tiger protection force to save the big cat population in the state, is ....
A. Madhya Pradesh   B. Karnataka
C. Gujarat   D. Telangana

224. On January 12, 2019 which state launched the 'One family, one job' scheme that assures a job to one member of every family?
A. Jharkhand   B. Odisha
C. Sikkim   D. Kerala

225. Which country topped the Bloomberg Innovation Index 2019?
A. Finland   B. Sweden
C. South Korea   D. Singapore

226. The 106th Indian Science Congress was held in early January in ....
A. Jalandhar   B. Bengaluru
C. Hyderabad   D. Imphal

227. A lunar rover from which country successfully landed on the far side of the moon on January 3, 2019?
A. India   B. USA
C. Russia   D. China

228. ISRO on January 11, 2019 announced its plan to send Indian astronauts to space in ....
A. January, 2020   B. December, 2020
C. January, 2021   D. December, 2021

229. IMF's first woman chief economist is ..... .
A. Gita Kulkarni   B. Gita Gopinath
C. Gita Viswas   D. Madhuri Gabbard

230. India's newly appointed Chief Information Commissioner is:
A. V.K. Yadav   B. Ashwani Lohani
C. Sudhir Bhargava   D. Suresh Chandra

231. In which state the first pvt Howitzer gun-making unit was inaugurated by PM Narendra Modi on January 19, 2019?
A. Andhra Pradesh   B. Karnataka
C. Tamil Nadu   D. Gujarat

232. Defence minister Nirmala Sitharaman on January 20, 2019 inaugurated .... Defence Industrial Corridor.
A. Tamil Nadu   B. Karnataka
C. Uttar Pradesh   D. Maharashtra

233. Which one is not included in the list of Bharat Ratna awardees, announced on January 25, 2019?
A. Nanaji Deshmukh   B. Teejan Bai
C. Bhupen Hazarika   D. Pranab Mukherjee

234. Lance Naik Nazir Ahmad Wani, who has been posthumously awarded 'Ashok Chakra' on January 25, 2019 belongs to which state?
A. Arunachal Pradesh   B. Hyderabad
C. Jammu & Kashmir   D. West Bengal

235. Which movie won the Best Film (Drama) award at the 76th Golden Globe Awards on January 6, 2019?
A. *Bohemian Rhapsody*   B. *Black Panther*
C. *Green Book*   D. *Roma*

236. The first Asian country to win a Test series in Australia is ....
A. Pakistan   B. Sri Lanka
C. India   D. None of these

237. Which state finished as the top team with 228 medals at the Khelo India Youth Games, held in Pune in January, 2019?
A. Haryana   B. Maharashtra
C. Delhi   D. Karnataka

238. To cater to different kinds of learners, the CBSE will introduce two levels of examination in mathematics for class 10 students in ....
A. 2019   B. 2020
C. 2021   D. 2022

239. Who won Sa Re Ga Ma Pa 2018 grand finale held on January 27, 2019 in Mumbai?
A. Ishita Vishwakarma
B. Tanmay Chaturvedi
C. Sonu Gill
D. Nidhi Sharma

240. In which state India's biggest Ashoka Chakra having a diameter of 30 feet was unveiled on January 5, 2019?
A. Haryana
B. Uttar Pradesh
C. Gujarat
D. Kerala

241. Ibrahim Mohamed Solih arrived India on December 16, 2018 on a three-day state visit. He is president of ....
A. Sri Lanka
B. Myanmar
C. Maldives
D. Surinam

242. The Union Cabinet on December 6, 2018 approved the agriculture export policy which aims to boost agriculture exports and double them to $60 billion by ....
A. 2022
B. 2020
C. 2025
D. 2030

243. As per the Commercial Surrogacy Bill passed by the Lok Sabha on December 19, 2018 a married Indian woman with a child of her own can be a surrogate aged between ....
A. 25 to 30 years
B. 25 to 35 years
C. 30 to 40 years
D. 35 to 45 years

244. Who will be the chief guest at the Republic Day celebrations of 2019?
A. Vladimir Putin
B. Donald Trump
C. Aung San Suu Kyi
D. Cyril Ramaphosa

245. Government think tank NITI Aayog has prescribed reducing upper age limit to join civil services to .... years for general category candidates by 2022-23.
A. 25
B. 27
C. 28
D. 24

246. An anti-corruption court in Pakistan on December 24, 2018 sentenced ousted premier Nawaz Sharif to .... years in Jail.
A. 7
B. 5
C. 3
D. 10

247. On December 22, 2018 Gitega is declared new capital of ....
A. Somalia
B. Nauru
C. Burundi
D. Latvia

248. Bogibeel Bridge, India's longest rail-cum-road span was inaugurated on December 25, 2018 by PM Modi, is across the river ....
A. Ganga
B. Yamuna
C. Krishna
D. Brahmaputra

249. On the eve of former Prime Minister Atal Behari Vajpayee's 94th birth anniversary, PM Modi released a commemorative coin of ....
A. ₹ 20
B. ₹ 50
C. ₹ 100
D. ₹ 1000

250. In December 2018 which state started online licence for organ transplant?
A. Karnataka
B. Maharashtra
C. Tamil Nadu
D. Andhra Pradesh

ANSWERS

1	2	3	4	5	6	7	8	9	10
D	A	C	B	A	C	B	D	A	C

11	12	13	14	15	16	17	18	19	20
B	D	C	B	D	B	A	D	C	D

21	22	23	24	25	26	27	28	29	30
A	B	C	D	A	B	D	A	C	B

31	32	33	34	35	36	37	38	39	40
A	A	C	B	D	B	C	D	A	B

41	42	43	44	45	46	47	48	49	50
A	C	D	A	C	B	A	C	D	B

51	52	53	54	55	56	57	58	59	60
A	C	B	D	C	A	D	C	B	A

61	62	63	64	65	66	67	68	69	70
C	B	D	A	D	A	C	B	D	A

71	72	73	74	75	76	77	78	79	80
C	A	B	D	C	A	C	B	A	D

81	82	83	84	85	86	87	88	89	90
B	D	C	B	D	A	C	B	C	D

91	92	93	94	95	96	97	98	99	100
A	C	B	D	C	B	A	C	D	B

101	102	103	104	105	106	107	108	109	110
D	B	A	C	A	D	A	B	A	C

111	112	113	114	115	116	117	118	119	120
D	B	C	A	B	D	B	D	B	A

121	122	123	124	125	126	127	128	129	130
D	B	A	D	C	D	A	B	C	B

131	132	133	134	135	136	137	138	139	140
C	A	B	C	D	A	B	D	C	D

141	142	143	144	145	146	147	148	149	150
B	A	C	D	C	A	B	A	D	A

151	152	153	154	155	156	157	158	159	160
C	A	B	C	D	A	B	D	A	D

161	162	163	164	165	166	167	168	169	170
C	D	B	A	B	B	A	C	D	D

171	172	173	174	175	176	177	178	179	180
A	C	B	A	D	C	B	A	C	B

181	182	183	184	185	186	187	188	189	190
A	B	D	C	B	A	D	B	C	A

191	192	193	194	195	196	197	198	199	200
B	C	A	D	A	C	A	D	B	D

201	202	203	204	205	206	207	208	209	210
A	B	C	D	A	B	D	B	A	C

211	212	213	214	215	216	217	218	219	220
A	C	D	C	C	D	A	C	B	A

221	222	223	224	225	226	227	228	229	230
B	C	D	C	C	A	D	D	B	C

231	232	233	234	235	236	237	238	239	240
D	A	B	C	A	C	B	B	A	A

241	242	243	244	245	246	247	248	249	250
C	A	B	D	B	A	C	D	C	B

•••